Collaborative Consultation in Mental Health

MW00647062

Collaborative Consultation in Mental Health: Guidelines for the New Consultant offers a practical guide for professionals working 'indirectly' with clients through consultation with staff. As resources become more scarce in public services, and a greater number of people seek mental health interventions, professionals are increasingly called upon to consult with practitioners who conduct face-to-face work with clients. This book provides an essential guide for those who are interested in developing their consultation competence.

This book introduces the reader to the principles of a collaborative approach to consultation with practitioners, teams and agencies working in health, education, social care and mental health. The book takes the reader step-by-step through the collaborative consultation process, from preparing and setting up the context for consultation through to communicating effectively to build cooperative partnerships and evaluating consultation outcomes. *Collaborative Consultation in Mental Health* guides the consultant in how to apply and develop these principles and practices within group consultation and also addresses common dilemmas and challenges consultants encounter.

Collaborative Consultation in Mental Health will appeal to both new and experienced consultants working with adults, children, older people, people with intellectual disabilities and families across a range of contexts.

Glenda Fredman is a Clinical Psychologist, Systemic Psychotherapist, Consultant, Trainer and Supervisor. She contributes to a number of national public services and international organisations.

Andia Papadopoulou is a Clinical Psychologist, Manager, Supervisor, Consultant and Practice Tutor at the Islington Community Child and Adolescent Mental Health Service and the Anna Freud Centre.

Emma Worwood is a Clinical Psychologist, Manager, Supervisor and Consultant at the Islington Community Child and Adolescent Mental Health Service.

Collaborative Consultation in Mental Health

Guidelines for the New Consultant

Edited by Glenda Fredman,
Andia Papadopoulou and
Emma Worwood

 Routledge
Taylor & Francis Group

LONDON AND NEW YORK

First published 2018
by Routledge
2 Park Square, Milton Park, Abingdon, Oxon OX14 4RN

and by Routledge
711 Third Avenue, New York, NY 10017

Routledge is an imprint of the Taylor & Francis Group, an informa business

British Library Cataloguing in Publication Data
A catalogue record for this book is available from the British Library

Library of Congress Cataloging in Publication Data
A catalog record for this book has been requested

ISBN: 978-1-138-89908-7 (hbk)
ISBN: 978-1-138-89909-4 (pbk)
ISBN: 978-1-315-69665-2 (ebk)

Typeset in Times New Roman
by Deanta Global Publishing Services, Chennai, India

Contents

Figures

Tables

Boxes

Practice guides

Foreword

Rudi Dallos

I looked forward to reading this book by Glenda Fredman, Andia Papadopoulou and Emma Worwood with eager anticipation. Consultation and its importance are much discussed in mental health contexts often alongside a discussion of the importance of supervision, with the differences between these activities not always clearly differentiated. It is also becoming an expectation, for example on clinical psychology training programmes, that newly qualified clinical psychologists will rapidly, if not immediately, be able to offer consultation to other mental health colleagues. But where do we learn what consultation is, and how to do it? Glenda and her colleagues share their own journey, in the first chapter of the book, of how they were expected to be able to offer consultation early in their careers, as if it was an intuitive skill. But they go on to describe, as many of us can share, that starting to offer it can be an extremely daunting and confusing process. They found that there was 'no book to help us develop a practical competence in collaborative consultation'. That summarises nicely the essence of this excellent book.

The book is structured in two parts, the first setting out the guiding principles for collaborative consultation, and the second guiding us in how to apply and develop these in group consultation. The word 'collaborative' is essential to the book and it starts with a discussion of how, in consultation, we need to attend to the inevitable pull to take on the position of an expert as opposed to being able to share our expertise with colleagues. I really enjoyed the metaphor of the consultant as an anthropologist who tries to enter an organisation with sensitivity and takes care to understand its culture, values and competencies. Throughout the chapters, this metaphor serves to offer a sensitivity to language, how words are used and the varieties of expectations that members of a team may have about what consultation might mean. Though one chapter is dedicated specifically to the use of appreciative inquiry, the framework of building on competencies and promoting a sense of safety and trust runs throughout the book.

As I am writing this, I am becoming aware that it is becoming a book review in that I want to describe the specific content, techniques, richness of specific ideas, letters to consultees, ways of engaging organisations, ideas for evaluation, working with teams and specific populations, and so on. To add to this, as I was reading the chapter on evaluation of consultation, I found that I drew on the framework employed in this book and adapted it to use in my next consultation session tomorrow! So now there really is a book 'to help us develop a practical competence in collaborative consultation'.

Thank you for this gift Glenda, Andia and Emma.

Acknowledgements

The authors of this book contributed generously and creatively to this collaborative project. We have worked together for many years as clinical psychologists, colleagues and consultants, developing and fine-tuning our consultation practice. We have worked with each other in consultation teams and as co-consultants as well as offering each other consultation on our work with clients and on our own consultation practice. The guiding principles we have developed have given us, and the new consultants we supervise and train, confidence and energy to stay present and work creatively in organisational contexts challenged by resource pressures.

Our special thanks to members of the Islington Child and Adolescent Mental Health Service *consultation on consultation* group (Victoria Mattison, Nicola Webb, Jemma Rosen-Webb, Victoria Johnson, Anna Piciotto, Monica Lynch, Nina Stevens, Sonya Khan, Lorraine Walker, Teresa Sarmiento and Helen Aspland), whose enthusiasm for this project and generous sharing of consultation stories and dilemmas has sustained us through the writing and production of the book. Particular thanks to Victoria Mattison, Nicola Webb, Jemma Rosen-Webb and Victoria Johnson who contributed to early versions of many of the chapters. Yvonne Miller's vision for developing consultation laid the groundwork for embedding the practice within this service. Without her commitment and support, this work would never have started.

The *consultation on consultation* group within Services for Ageing and Mental Health in Camden and Islington made a considerable contribution to clarifying the principles and practices that inform this book, especially Eleanor Martin, Alison Milton, Mandy Clayton, Stefania Battistella and Marina Palomo, who gave useful and discerning feedback on many of the chapters in this book.

Our appreciation goes to our managers from all the services represented in this book for recognising the importance of and championing consultation work in our posts. They supported the developing of our skills by allowing us protected time for 'consultation on consultation' and by encouraging us enthusiastically to write about our practice.

We are indebted to Eleanor Anderson for her tireless editing of every draft chapter of this book; she brought the wisdom of an experienced consultant and therapist to the task, giving us valuable and often challenging feedback on the content as well as the form of our writing. We are very grateful to Philip Messent, who generously offered astute advice and suggestions on many chapter drafts, and to Matthew Coles for his time, care and patience to design and execute the figures in Chapter 8.

We are very grateful to Joanne Forshaw and Charlotte Taylor from Routledge for their helpful and responsive editorial assistance.

We acknowledge with deep gratitude the many consultees who have participated in consultations with us over the years, sharing their clients' stories, clinical dilemmas and creative practices with us; inspiring us with their knowledge, reflections and expertise; and enriching our practice as consultants and practitioners.

Contributors

Sarah Coles is a Clinical Psychologist, Supervisor and Systemic Psychotherapist. In this role, she has worked for eight years with adults with intellectual disabilities as a member of a multidisciplinary team in Oxfordshire. She provides teaching on a number of doctoral courses in clinical psychology on both systemic and intellectual disability modules as well as teaching on the Tavistock systemic psychotherapy course. Since 2017, Sarah has worked as a Family Therapist with children and adolescents in a CAMH service in Abingdon.

Rudi Dallos is a Professor and Research Director on the Doctorate in Clinical Psychology Training programme at the University of Plymouth. He has written several books, including *Formulation in Psychotherapy and Counselling*, *Reflective Practice in Psychotherapy and Counselling* and *Attachment Narrative Therapy*. He is currently involved in a research project (SAFE) exploring family therapy for autism where families co-consulting to each other is a significant component.

Glenda Fredman is a Clinical Psychologist, Systemic Psychotherapist, Trainer, Supervisor and Consultant. She is committed to enabling ethical practice within public services where she works at all levels of organisations with service users in therapy, with staff in training and with practitioners, teams and organisations in consultation. Glenda is author of *Death Talk: Conversations with Children and Families*; *Transforming Emotion: Conversations in Counselling and Psychotherapy*, co-editor of *Being with Older People: A Systemic Approach* and co-editor of *Working with Embodiment in Supervision: A Systemic Approach*.

Sheila McNamee is a Professor of Communication at the University of New Hampshire and co-founder and Vice President of the Taos Institute (taosinstitute.net). Her work is focused on dialogic transformation within a variety of social and institutional contexts including psychotherapy, organisations and communities. Among her most recent books are *Research and Social Change: A Relational Constructionist Approach*, with Dian Marie Hosking and *Education as Social Construction: Contributions to Theory, Research, and Practice*, co-edited with T. Dragonas, K. Gergen and E. Tseliou.

Eleanor Martin is a Clinical Psychologist, Systemic Psychotherapist, Trainer, Supervisor, Manager and Consultant. She is Joint Systemic Therapy Lead with Camden and Islington Mental Health Trust and Lead Psychologist in Camden Services for Ageing and Mental Health where she is committed to working with older people and their systems. Eleanor provides systemic training to trainee clinical psychologists on UCL, UEL and Royal Holloway clinical psychology training courses. She has presented nationally on systemic consultation and contributed to *Being with Older People: A Systemic Approach*.

Victoria Mattison is a Clinical Psychologist, Supervisor, Manager and Trainer. She is Professional Lead for Clinical Psychology at Islington Community CAMHS. Victoria has always enjoyed working with children and adults with learning disabilities and their families. She has completed a diploma in systemic psychotherapy at the Tavistock Clinic, and contributes regularly to the clinical psychology training courses at Royal Holloway and University College London. Victoria is co-author of *Saying Goodbye: Stories of Separation Between Care Staff and People With Learning Disabilities*.

Alison Milton is a Clinical Psychologist and Systemic Psychotherapist. She is Lead Psychologist for Services for Ageing and Mental Health in Camden and Islington NHS Foundation Trust and has over twenty years' experience working with older people, their families and networks. Alison contributes to the systemic psychotherapy training within Camden and Islington NHS Foundation Trust and is Joint Coordinator of the systemic teaching for the clinical psychology doctorate at University College London.

Andia Papadopoulou is a Clinical Psychologist with postgraduate training in systemic practice and in supervision. She practices as a Clinician, Supervisor, Trainer and Consultant in the NHS and in private practice. She works for Islington Child and Adolescent Mental Health Service as Joint Manager of the Under 5s service and lead of the Parent and Baby Psychology Service. She is a Practice Tutor at the Anna Freud Centre and contributes to the systemic consultation module for the clinical psychology doctorate at University College London.

Joel Parker is a Clinical Psychologist and Supervisor employed by Camden and Islington NHS Foundation Trust and an accredited Systemic Practitioner. He is particularly interested in using consultation and wider systemic approaches as a means of strengthening networks and communities involved in supporting people affected by intellectual disabilities. He is also interested in the use of mindfulness-based approaches, both in order to foster reflexive practice and as a complement to systemic and narrative approaches to therapy.

Selma Rikberg Smyly is a Clinical Psychologist and Systemic Practitioner at the Oxford Family Institute. Her career has included working in Zimbabwe, developing services for children with disabilities. More recently, she has worked in Oxford as a Consultant Psychologist with a specific remit to develop systemic practice within the adult intellectual disability service. Selma has taught and supervised on a number of clinical psychology training courses and presented her work at national and international conferences. She is currently working freelance as a Supervisor and Trainer.

Nicola Webb is a Clinical Psychologist, Trainer, Supervisor and Consultant. Formerly Joint Manager of Islington Child and Adolescent Mental Health Under 5s Service, Nicola now works with Sheffield's Paediatric Psychology Service. She has postgraduate training in systemic psychotherapy and in supervision. After twenty years working in inner-city areas with families and providing supervision and consultation to a range of public and voluntary sector professionals, Nicola remains passionate about services being respectful and appreciative of the knowledge of the diverse local communities they serve.

Emma Worwood is a Clinical Psychologist working in Islington Community CAMHS as Joint Manager of the Under 5s Service; Lead for CAMHS work into Children's Centres; and as a Clinician, Supervisor and Consultant. She has been Professional Lead for Clinical Psychology in this service, supporting the continued professional development of psychology colleagues, trainees and students. Emma has completed postgraduate studies in systemic practice and contributes to the systemic consultation module for the clinical psychology doctorate at University College London.

Chapter 1

Introduction

Collaborative consultation in mental health

Glenda Fredman, Andia Papadopoulou and Emma Worwood

We, the authors of this book, have been working for many years as clinical psychologists with people with health, mental health and social care problems. Our posts within public health and social care services have involved consultation with staff within different agency contexts such as schools, day centres and hospitals, which provide services to a range of client groups including children, adolescents, adults, older people and people with intellectual disabilities. Over the years, like many other professionals within public services, we have experienced increasing demands to 'share' our expertise, including ideas, theories, skills and experience, with those who are engaged in 'direct' face-to-face work. In the current climate of limited resources for and increasing demands on mental health interventions, this sort of 'indirect' consultation is receiving growing recognition for making a relevant and important contribution.

When we (Andia and Emma) and our clinical child psychology colleagues started to respond to requests for consultation several years ago, we all had completed rigorous training to doctorate level and acquired our professional skills and expertise under years of close supervision. At that time, like many of our colleagues, we held the view that practitioners who are adequately trained to provide a direct (clinical) service are also adequately prepared to support or develop the clinical practice of others; so we assumed that our consultation skills would come to us naturally or intuitively. When we started working with practitioner-consultees such as nurses, health visitors and teachers, however, we immediately recognised that consultation is different from many other areas of practice because of its indirect service delivery approach. We found that our mental health professional trainings had not equipped us to make the transition from practitioner to consultant and that consultation was definitely not as straightforward as it looked. Also, it soon became apparent to us that the staff and teams with whom we were consulting had considerable expertise in their specialist areas of practice. Being positioned as 'the expert' did not sit comfortably with us when the people with whom we were consulting often had more experience than we had, as newly qualified clinicians. Therefore, we wanted to learn how to work collaboratively with people in consultation, in ways that we could honour and make use of their wealth of skills, knowledge and experience.

How this book came about

Like many consultants of our time, we had to learn the practice of consultation on the job (Greiner and Ennsfellner, 2014), and so turned to the available literature to help us. We found texts on 'what is consultation?' (Casey et al., 1994; Dougherty, 2013), 'how it differs from supervision' (Lake et al., 2008) and 'why and where to use consultation' (Crothers et al., 2008), but no book to help us develop a practical competence in collaborative consultation. Over the following years, we met regularly with other 'novice consultants' to support each other on moving positions from clinical practitioner to consultant. We explored ethical and practical dilemmas involved in the process of consultation, such as the challenges of entering new organisations and systems and the 'meeting of worlds' between health, education, social care and the voluntary sector.

We have written this book because it is the book we authors were looking for when we started consultation, the book we had wished we had on our bookshelves and would have liked to recommend to new consultants. We invited our colleagues working in services for older adults (Eleanor Martin and Alison Milton, Chapter 10) and for adults with intellectual disabilities (Selma Rikberg Smyly and Sarah Coles, Chapter 8 and Joel Parker, Chapter 9) to join us in this writing project as they were developing approaches to collaborative consultation in their contexts of practice.

Consultation on consultation

I (Glenda) was invited by the manager of Andia and Emma's child mental health service to 'train' the clinical child psychologists in consultation. Since they were already offering consultation to schools, health visitors and children's centres, we all agreed that I would take the position of 'consultant' and offer 'consultation on consultation'. I created opportunities in this group for the new consultants to experience various consultation approaches by inviting them to bring their consultation work, including dilemmas and examples of interesting or inspiring practice, to the group for consultation. I positioned myself as the interviewing consultant and invited the group members to observe the process of the consultation, stopping the action from time to time so they were also able to 'reflect *on* the action' of the consultation while '*in* action' (Schon, 1987). Thus my practice as consultant mirrored the consultation approach and methods the group were experiencing and learning about.

With our colleagues, we (Andia and Emma) derived considerable support from our 'consultation on consultation' groups with Glenda. Like Preedy (2008), as new consultants, we found it extremely valuable to have protected time to consider our consultation practice, with opportunities to reflect on our developing competence and identity as consultants. We supported each other by sharing stories of our own consultation practice as well as experiencing, observing and practising consultation methods and skills. We connected our learning with collaborative, systemic, narrative and appreciative inquiry approaches, which over time became a common frame of reference that informed our ongoing consultation practice.

As the group gained confidence and skill through experiencing and observing consultations, group members began to take on the position of consultant to each other using 'practice guides' we had generated of key steps in the consultation process (p. x). When group members took the position of consultant, I (Glenda) moved position to 'live-supervise' their consultation practice *in* action and positioned some of the group as co-consultants to support the interviewing consultant, thereby using the group as a resource to the consultation process (Chapter 7).

I (Glenda) invited group members to document examples from their ongoing consultation practice and keep written records of their 'learning points' that emerged in each *consultation on consultation* session. We (Andia and Emma) chose to call these learning records 'minutes'; recording our learning enabled us to become observers to our consultation practice and thereby develop reflexivity. Our 'minutes' and learning records sparked the conception of this book and went on to inform our writing so that the questions and dilemmas presented in this book as well as the resolutions and possibilities are all grounded in practice.

What is consultation?

The word 'consultation' has many different meanings in different contexts. Most people will be familiar with the terms 'consultation' and 'consultant' used in a medical context to denote a meeting with an expert, usually a medical doctor, in order to seek advice or treatment, and the use of the title 'consultant' to denote a position of seniority within a profession, as in 'consultant clinical psychologist' or 'consultant psychiatrist'. Nowadays, the term *consultant* also appears in many other everyday areas of life such as 'financial consultant', 'wedding consultant' and 'travel consultant' (Gibson and Mitchell, 2008). Within mental health services, consultation has been viewed as offering thinking space to help practitioners use psychological frameworks to reflect on specific clients and develop their own skills (Preedy, 2008) and as an enquiring and reflexive approach to reviewing the work between a practitioner or team and a 'client' or 'service user' (Lake, 2008). Therefore, consultees with whom we meet might hold a range of different meanings for 'consultation'. For example, in Chapter 2, teacher-consultees anticipated judgement ('tell us what we do wrong') and criticism ('being disciplined'); in Chapter 3, health visitor-consultees expected expert advice, solutions and 'all the answers', and a child-care worker was looking for a five-minute 'chat'; in Chapter 4, child-care workers were 'looking forward' to 'time to stop and think', and possibly skills training.

Since the people commissioning consultation are not always clear about what they themselves want or expect from 'consultation', we try to engage commissioners and managers in a process of co-contracting to clarify together what the work involves (Chapter 2). With consultees, we take care with how we name and describe what we will be doing together by checking and coordinating our meanings of 'consultation'.

Going inside 'consultation'

If the work has already been ascribed the name 'consultation', we often begin with 'going inside the word' (Andersen, 1995; Fredman et al., 2010) 'consultation' to explore the meanings 'consultation' holds for the consultees. Sometimes we create a mind-map or linguagram (Lang and McAdam, 1996; Partridge, 2010) with consultees to explore what meaning *they* are giving to 'consultation'. Figure 1.1 shows an example of a linguagram we created at the start of our *consultation on consultation* groups in response to the question: 'what is consultation?'

> Starting with the word 'consultation' in the centre of the whiteboard, I (Glenda) invited the group to 'Look inside the word consultation … what do you see? … What do we mean by "consultation"? …. What sense do our consultees and commissioners make of the term "consultation"?' As the consultees generated words and phrases, I added them to the emerging mind-map, checking with the consultees each time whether their new ideas 'fit' with their previous ideas or were a departure. In this way, we grouped ideas, meanings and concepts into themes that connected with each other, thereby constructing a common language between us. By moving words and ideas around the board, we created opportunities for new meanings and perspectives to emerge and were able to elaborate the meanings we were giving to 'consultation'.

Mapping the meanings of 'consultation' in this way can create the opportunity for consultees to share previous experiences and expectations of consultation, giving us some understanding of their relationship to consultation. This process can open

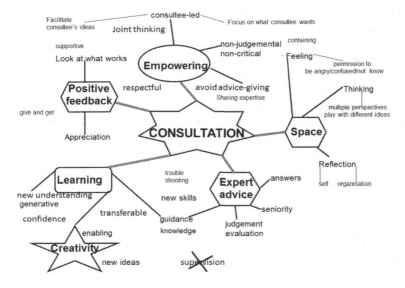

Figure 1.1   Linguagram of 'consultation'

space for consultants and consultees to negotiate how we can work collaboratively with each other, to clarify what consultees want from the consultation as well as the rights, duties, opportunities and constraints in the process. Sometimes we invite consultees to jointly co-create a name for the consultation work as a way of beginning our work together, simply asking 'What shall we call our work together?'

Distinguishing consultation from supervision

The word 'supervision' is derived from the Latin *super* (over) and *videre* (to see), implying both a 'seeing' from a 'higher' vantage point and an 'overview' or 'watching over' (Bownas and Fredman, 2016). Therefore implicit in the term 'supervision' is a monitoring function, accountability and the expectation that the supervisor is more experienced and trained in the work that the supervisee is undertaking. The word 'consultation' is derived from the Latin *com* (with) and *selere* (take, gather [the Senate] together), and also the Latin *consultare* 'consult, ask counsel of; reflect, consider maturely' and *consulere* 'to deliberate, consider' (Online Etymology Dictionary, 2017). The prefix 'co' within 'consultation' points to collaboration; there is an expectation that consultation is a joint activity.

We distinguish consultation from supervision in terms of differences in duties, responsibilities, accountability and differential power (Southall, 2005; Lake et al., 2008). The *supervisor* is accountable for the clinical services provided to the client via the supervisee, and the supervisee has the duty to document and follow the treatment plans agreed in the supervision. The *consultant*, on the other hand, does not hold responsibility for the consultees' actions following the consultation, and the consultee is free to accept or reject any or all of the consultant's offerings. Chapter 2 offers a framework for co-contracting with commissioners of consultation and with consultees to clarify 'who holds responsibility for what' in the work and addresses the negotiation of reporting and confidentiality in the contexts of risk and safeguarding.

Focus of consultation

Mental health consultation involves a consultant, consultee/s, a client and a work-related issue (Caplan, 1970; Lambert, 2004). 'The consultant indirectly provides services to the client via his or her consultative relationship with the consultee' (Crothers et al., 2008:5) to benefit the client, organisation or both.

In this book, we take a *consultee-centred* approach to consultation where the focus is on facilitating the consultee's work with the client rather than on solving the client's problem for the consultee (as in *client-centred* consultation). There is always a work-related problem or dilemma at the heart of the request for help from a consultee (Meyers et al., 1979; Kerr, 2001). One or several consultees may bring a shared problem for consultation, which may be about a specific piece of work with a client or a dilemma arising within a group setting, like a group of nursery children or a residential home for vulnerable adults. Whereas *consultee-centred* consultation foregrounds the consultee–client relationship and aims to improve consultees' competence and facilitate their development in order to benefit similar clients in the future, *client-centred* consultation focuses on the client and the services provided to them, and *system-centred* consultation focuses on staff-consultees' working relationships to promote the team, whole service or organisation's effectiveness and success.

In this book, we do not focus on organisational consultation (where we would work directly with the whole service, team or organisation); however, we are always mindful of the recursive relationship between client or consultee developments, the client-consultee relationship and the practices and relationships within the service or agency. Therefore, we evaluate the effects of the consultation on the agency or service and review how the organisational context is enabling or constraining the quality and outcome of consultation (Chapter 6). For example, Emma Worwood (Chapter 5) notes how wider political, social and organisational contexts in which we work inform the varied ways we picture our services and organisations, which in turn shape how we see working relationships and how we approach change. In Chapter 6, Victoria Mattison shows the effect of consultee-centred consultation on the whole school's practice of exclusion, and Chapter 10 shows how consultee-centred consultation opens space for staff to address their relationships with management.

Models of consultation

There is a growing literature on different models of consultation (Southall, 2005; Dougherty, 2013). For example, in *instructional consultation*, the consultant draws on evidence-based practices to convey knowledge and skills to consultees to promote client outcomes (Rosenfield, 1987; 1995; 2013), and in *behavioural consultation*, the consultant uses a structured and systematic problem-solving method that enables consultant and consultee to collectively identify, define and analyse the problem and evaluate the effectiveness of the intervention (Crothers et al., 2008). Both these models of consultation are client-centred and directive.

The authors of this book present a *collaborative* consultee-centred approach to consultation drawing on systemic (Boscolo et al., 1987; Fredman et al., 2010), collaborative (Anderson and Goolishian, 1992; Anderson, 1999; Madsen, 2007), narrative (Freedman and Combs, 2009; White, 2007) and appreciative (Cooperrider and Whitney, 2005; McAdam and Lang, 2009) approaches and they incorporate a range of research findings, theories and practices from the broader consultation literature to guide their consultation practice. We have tried to design this book to guide new consultants in the process and practices of a *collaborative* approach to consultee-centred consultation, making explicit the principles informing our approach.

Principles guiding our approach to collaborative consultation

Collaboration and partnership

To set the foundation for collaboration, we try to create a context for consultation that enables the best possible chance of working respectfully in partnership with consultees as co-participants. Chapter 2 offers guidelines for 'building a cooperative partnership' with consultees that include practices for co-contracting with people commissioning the work and with consultees. Chapter 6 offers a *Consultation Partnership Scale (CPS)* to monitor the ongoing progress of the partnership with consultees, enabling both consultant and consultees to become observers to the consultation process, thereby further opening space for collaborative dialogue and better coordination.

We hold that the consultant's expertise and responsibility lie in facilitating the process of exchange of ideas rather than providing advice or recommendations. Chapter 3 describes how the consultant can enable this dialogical process by jointly creating the focus for the consultation with consultees, clarifying what consultees *want* from the conversation rather than assuming what they *need*. As consultants, we place our own knowledges and expertise alongside those of consultees so that together we can make optimal use of the resources and competence that already exist among consultees and within the agency. Chapter 7 describes some of the ways we can actively involve the whole group in the process of collaborative consultation so that members can contribute to the well-being of each other's clients and to mutual learning.

Attention to power and difference

Mindful of the power differential inherent in all systems, we pay attention to the potential effects of power on the lives and work of consultees and the relationships we can construct with them. All the authors of this book pay attention to disparities in privilege and power between themselves, the consultees and the clients they serve in relation to their differences in gender, race, culture, class, age, sexuality, religion, education, physical and intellectual ability and status in the agency. Therefore, Chapter 2 points out the importance of co-creating a clear contract that includes clarifying how we work and addressing the power differential to create a context where consultees can feel comfortable and respected. Chapter 7 acknowledges that differences in status and power between group members will have an impact on how consultees engage with each other and the group. It offers practices to enable hearing and valuing all voices where each person can contribute their views, irrespective of their status or position in the organisation, in an atmosphere that fosters choice and takes care to invite accounts of competence and ability.

Appreciation

We have noticed that offering advice, correction or criticism that focus on problems and what people are *not* doing often brings the collaborative exchange of ideas to a standstill; consultees tend to take up positions of justification or self-protection and move away from curiosity (Chapter 3). All the authors of this book take an appreciative approach to their consultation practice that includes valuing the expertise of consultees, particularly in areas of their own work. We have found that an appreciative approach to consultation creates patterns of communication that are likely to carry over into consultees' own practice and relationships with their clients and colleagues. For example, by intentionally adopting an appreciative approach with child-care worker-consultees described by their manager as 'de-motivated and burnt out', Nicola Webb (Chapter 4) invited hope and increased creativity and openness to new ideas among the previously 'demoralised' staff team.

Recognising that preferred developments need witnessing to sustain consultees' competence and morale, as consultants we try to create opportunities for consultees to identify and draw attention to progress and to celebrate achievements. For example, Emma Worwood (Chapter 5) describes validating practices and affirming rituals to create opportunities for consultees to review, evaluate and take forward their progress.

The stance of appreciation and respect shown by the authors of this book made a significant contribution to the establishment of collaborative partnership in the consultations they describe. For example, Victoria Mattison (Chapter 2) notes how appreciating the considerable demands on the school secretary and the remarkable multitasking ability of the head teacher contributed to their offering valuable support to the staff consultation Victoria offered. Selma Rikberg Smyly and Sarah Coles' (Chapter 8) efforts to acknowledge and explicitly value the difficult work staff were doing with a client affected by intellectual disabilities, who was 'screaming' and 'kicking' them at the end of every shift, warmed the context for the staff to 'express their feelings with more confidence'.

Competence and abilities

The purpose of consultation is to enable consultees to resolve the particular issue they bring and also to develop competence and confidence to work with similar situations. Therefore we try to ensure that consultees leave seeing themselves as resourceful and competent in the work they do and in the way they support each other so that the new developments in their practice carry over to the quality of care they give their clients.

Aware that our training as clinical psychologists has oriented us to focus on problems, limitations and deficits with the risk of masking our perception of people's competence and resources, we try to tune our listening from the start to consultees' achievements and initiatives to acknowledge and enable the development of each person's abilities. Thus, when the consultants in Chapter 10 notice consultees 'feeling bad' about their work or blaming themselves for 'not doing [their] job properly', they try to encourage the consultees to talk from a position of competence and ability rather than from a position of 'not doing a good job', so that they can tell a different story about themselves that avoids undermining their professional identity.

Chapters 4 and 7 offer the practice of *ability spotting* to identify and draw attention to consultees' skills. By bringing their abilities into awareness, consultees can go on to use them with intention, purpose and confidence in other contexts. Chapter 10 draws on a solution-focused approach (de Shazer, 1985) that assumes that change is always happening; that whatever the problem, there are always exceptions; and that if something works, encourage or affirm it since using consultees' existing solutions is empowering as well as economical.

Not knowing too quickly

We begin with the assumption that practitioners and their agencies hold the competence to find solutions to their problems and dilemmas. Therefore, we try to avoid forging ahead as the 'expert' and to watch and wait for moments to connect and work *with* the consultees, valuing and respecting their expertise and the culture and practices of their organisation without imposing our specific models or ways of working (Chapter 2). However, we often find ourselves pulled to respond from an expert position, or as Andia Papadopoulou says in Chapter 3, we are 'somewhat seduced or pressured' by the 'expectation that we should know *all* the answers' when consultees seek advice or request direction from the consultant. The chapters of this book offer a repertoire of practices to help us restrain our own *knowing too quickly*. For example, all the authors of this book, informed by the systemic approach (Tomm, 1988), prefer using questions (to which there is no assumption of 'right' answers) to explore consultees' perspectives with curiosity, rather than statements, interpretations, instruction, direction or suggestions.

We do not, however, propose that we disregard our knowledge or ideas. Chapters 3 and 7 offer practices for consultants to contribute our professional or specialist theories and methods to the pool of ideas we have already been generating with consultees. When we offer our perspectives, we are transparent about the ways we have come to form our views and take care to introduce new ideas and specialist skills as tentative offerings (Chapters 8, 9 and 10).

Attending to multiple contexts

We pay careful attention to the social and cultural contexts that shape the actions, beliefs and relationships of consultees, their clients and ourselves as consultants. Chapter 2 recognises that the consultation partnership is informed by multiple contexts including consultants' and consultees' culture, ethnicity, race, religion, age, physical and intellectual ability, health, sexuality and gender, as well as the culture of the organisations in which they work. Chapter 5 describes how the picture or metaphor we hold of the organisation and our discourses create contexts that give meaning to relationships and therefore influence how practitioners go on to negotiate ending and change. Chapter 10 identifies different levels of context that inform requests for and expectations of consultation: interaction, relationship, meaning, professional identity and organisation, and notes the recursive relationship between these levels of context whereby change at one level will inform and influence change at another level.

Our intention is always to create a context for consultation that supports the development of mutually respectful working relationships. To help orient us to the opportunities for and challenges to creating collaborative contexts, Chapter 2 offers guidelines for getting to know the consultation context through attending to the organisation's environment, atmosphere, communication and culture of collaboration. Chapter 10 describes how responding first at the level of context at which we are invited to work can enable us to find a fit and coordinate with what consultees are wanting.

Mapping structure, relationships and meanings within the consultation context

We use relationship maps to orient us to the consultation context. Chapter 2 describes mapping when contracting with commissioners and managers to familiarise the consultant with the organisational structure, lines of management, responsibility, communication and reporting hierarchies within the consultation context, as well as to identify important relationships and connections with and between consultees. Mapping can throw light on what is clear to us and what may need clarification.

Attention to language and communication

Throughout this book, we approach the meanings of words as uniquely related to the people we are talking with. Therefore, we pay careful attention to how consultees use language to help us co-create and coordinate our meanings without assuming too quickly that we understand exactly what they are asking for. Chapters 3 and 7 offer practices for tuning in to consultees' language. Above (p. 4) and in Chapters 4 and 7, we show how using mind-maps or 'linguagrams' can make an important contribution to coordinating language and meanings with consultees, thereby establishing a common language of agreed shared goals and values in the process of collaborative contracting. Chapter 7 offers guidelines for this practice and notes its impact on building cohesiveness for group consultation to start well.

Our belief that how we talk about people influences what they and we become informs our approach to consultation and to our writing of this book. At all times, therefore, we try to talk (and write) respectfully about the people with whom we work, even when they are not with us, paying careful attention to the words or phrases we use. Chapter 2 shows how framing a request for consultation as a 'gracious invitation' enabled Victoria Mattison to 'hold in mind what a privilege it is for busy staff to prioritise some of their time for working with us' (p. 32), thereby positioning her respectfully with the commissioner and consultees to create a more appreciative atmosphere. Nicola Webb (Chapter 4) shows how she 'took care to choose language that could … generate hope' and 'put a lot of effort into using words that point to, enliven and inspire the best in people' (p. 59), since the language we use creates our reality.

Valuing multiple perspectives

Early on in the consultation process, we clarify with consultees that we will not be looking for 'only one correct' way forward, but rather exploring 'possible alternatives' with the intention of inviting them to entertain multiple and even contradictory ways of thinking about or responding to the issue. We ask questions to bring forth from consultees a repertoire of ideas and practices from multiple perspectives, rather than offer advice or interpretations informed by our own preferred theories[1]. Inviting alternatives or even contradictions can make it possible for consultees to make new connections and associations between these different perspectives, thereby creating opportunities for new ways to go on. By juxtaposing their different contributions, consultees can make more than the sum of the parts and see that different points of view can have relevance and use.

Recognising that consultees bring not only their own perspectives to the consultation, but also the perspectives of many other significant people with whom they and the clients are in relationship, we approach the views of all members of the clients' and consultees' wider system as a potential rich resource for the consultation process. We therefore encourage consultees to tap into their many and varied sources of ideas and practices and to 'play' with a variety of different perspectives from the point of view of not only the practitioners and agencies involved but, especially, the clients. We often use a map of the wider system to invite consultees to generate ideas from the perspectives of the *different people* in the system (Chapters 3 and 5). When support staff in a residential unit had different and opposing views that were pulling them into either-or positions on how to manage and respond to a client with intellectual disabilities, Joel Parker (Chapter 9) invited the consultees to generate ideas from *different contexts*, thereby opening space for them to 'play with multiple perspectives' rather than see their different ideas as contradicting each other. Thus the staff team was able to hold the complexity and tension inherent within the situation and share the rich range of ideas they had created together.

Reflecting conversations

Many of the authors of this book use versions of *reflecting conversations* (Andersen, 1987; Lax, 1995) to generate and value multiple perspectives. A key intention is to invite reflecting processes (Andersen, 1995) by separating talking and listening, whereby consultees can listen to the (outer) talks and also reflect on their own thoughts (inner talks). Thus different, even contradictory, beliefs and meanings can coexist so that new perspectives can emerge, creating new meanings and possibilities. In Chapters 8 and 10, two consultants work together as a team where one consultant (IC) interviews the consultee while the second, in the position of reflecting person (RP), listens to the interview. The consulting team (IC and RP) then talks tentatively and respectfully with each other about what has been said (not what is not said) while the consultees listen. The interview conversation with the consultees and the reflecting conversation between the interviewing and reflecting consultants create multiple understandings of the situation and hence a number of different ways to go on. In group consultation, we often position participants as co-consultants or reflecting persons to offer contributions after they have listened to the consultee discuss the issue they bring for consultation (Chapters 7 and 9). Chapter 8 offers guidelines for reflecting.

Including and reflecting on ourselves in the process

We are mindful that the issues consultees bring as well as the 'emotional temperature in the room' during consultation (Chapter 10) has an impact on ourselves, as consultants, and on how we engage with the consulting relationship. For example, the authors of this book describe the 'immediate energising effects of appreciative consultation on both our consultees and ourselves' (Chapter 4), note how the consultation approach 'nourishes and sustains' our own practice (Chapter 9), and also acknowledge a 'rising sense of panic that we would have nothing to offer' (Chapter 10). Therefore, Chapter 2 invites consultants to include ourselves in the relationship map of the system and to reflect on our own positions within the consultation process from the start.

We also tune into and make use of our personal and professional resonance with consultees' and their clients' experience. Wherever possible, we try to situate our ideas within our personal and professional contexts (Andersen, 1992). For example, in Chapter 8, Selma Rikberg Smyly situated her ideas about the loneliness of Jane, a woman with intellectual disabilities, in the contexts of her own gender, age and family, and Sarah Coles' resonance with the consultees' own feelings of professional incompetence and self-doubt opened space for the creative exploration of new understandings and more hopeful conversations around possibilities for change.

Positioning

Throughout this book, we identify different positions people can take during the consultation process. We refer to the people organising and authorising the consultation as 'commissioners'. 'Consultees' bring their 'client' work for consultation and we may further identify the consultee's position in their agency as in 'teacher-consultee' or 'health visitor-consultee'. 'Consultants' can take positions of *convenor* of the consultation, *conductor* of the session and *interviewer* of the consultee. In *group* consultation, we identify the positions of 'consultant' and 'group member' who can take the position of 'consultee', 'co-consultant', 'group participant' or 'observer'. Each position signals something about the practitioner's differential power, informing their respective rights, responsibilities and abilities to speak and to contribute.

As consultants, we pay attention to the positions we take up and the positions we are called into, and how we position ourselves and others in consultation.

Chapter 2 describes how we try to position ourselves in a 'cooperative partnership' with consultees, for example joining as a 'participant-observer' to learn the culture, logic and values of the system; Chapter 3 notes the tendency for consultees to position the consultant as 'the expert with all the answers' who will solve the problem or instruct the consultee, and Chapters 3 and 4 describe attempts to 'resist the pull towards an expert position' within a collaborative and appreciative consultation relationship. Chapter 7 describes how the consultant can take a 'decentred and influential' position, centring the knowledge, experience and expertise of consultees and group participants while remaining influential as consultants.

Different approaches to consultation offer the consultant and consultee different positions in relation to each other. For example, consultants who adopt a client-centred and directive approach, as in instructional or behavioural consultation, are more likely to position themselves to instruct, coach or direct the consultee and to be positioned with authority or expectation to evaluate or judge. The positions of 'internal' or 'external' consultant to the agency may also have different implications for the consultation partnership and process (Campbell and Huffington, 2008; Sears et al., 2006). For example, an internal consultant who belongs to the same agency may more likely be expected to have some familiarity with the organisation and its members; understand the culture, language, values and vision of the organisation; and be accessible and easy to confide in. However, an internal consultant to the organisation may also be seen to 'lack objectivity', be untrustworthy or even be part of the problem, especially if the problem is attributed to organisational issues. External consultants, new and unknown to the consultees, are often expected to offer an injection of fresh insights and impartial and unbiased perspectives; however, they are also more likely to be approached with suspicion by consultees if perceived as 'called in' by management to provide corrective instruction, monitoring or evaluation, as happened with Tom, the teacher-consultee in Chapter 2, who thought he was 'being disciplined' because he was 'not doing well'.

You, our reader, may choose to take different positions during your reading of this book. For example, you may elect to read from the position of external or internal consultant; you may also decide to move between the perspectives of commissioner of consultation, consultant offering consultation or consultee receiving consultation.

Reading and writing this book

This volume is written by consultants for consultants. Since we learn best when we can observe and participate in experiences, we authors have provided a window into our lived experience of the work with stories and transcripts that make visible our practices of collaborative consultation. In order to ensure that the people presented cannot be recognised by others, we have changed names and other potentially identifying characteristics. In some situations, we have merged examples or combined the experiences or reports of different people to construct one composite 'profile' to protect anonymity further.

We outline detailed steps in the collaborative consultation process, including how to start and set up work with services, commissioners and consultees (Chapter 2); key principles and practices to proceed with collaborative and appreciative consultation (Chapters 3 and 4); addressing and negotiating transitions and ending in consultation (Chapter 5); and evaluating consultation (chapter 6). The chapters link theory and practice, interweaving real life examples. We bring together our shared experiences and stories about dilemmas of consultation and some of the resolutions we explored. Since the issues presented here are ones that commonly occur for new consultants, we hope that they resonate with and are relevant to your practice.

Recognising that consultants are often working within constraints of time and resources and are therefore not always able to engage with all the steps in a consultation method, the chapters outline a range of consultation practices that the consultant can draw on. They offer examples of consultation with individual practitioners (Chapters 2 and 3) where the concern is not so complex, so that the essential elements of the process are more easily identified, and then show how to extend the key practices to groups (Chapters 8, 9 and 10) and how to use the group in the consultation process (Chapter 7). The chapters also address how consultants can sustain teams and work at different levels of context (Chapter 10).

The book is divided into two parts. Each chapter offers a 'map' that outlines key practices for the new consultant. **Part I**: *Guiding principles and practices for collaborative consultation* introduces you, our reader, to collaborative consultation. The chapters in this section address the essential domains of competence required for the consultation task, including understanding the context and culture in which the consultation takes place; attending to the working relationship between consultant, consultee and the wider system; communicating effectively to build working relationships with consultees; and systematically addressing the concerns the consultee brings to the consultation. **Chapter 2** offers principles and practices for getting started, outlining steps to prepare the ground for consultation, from receiving the request to conducting the first meeting. It explores how we join with agencies to build cooperative partnerships through getting to know the system, tuning in to the culture of the contexts we act into and reflecting on how we position ourselves. **Chapter 3** describes an approach to collaborative consultation where consultant and consultees explore dilemmas through a process of sharing expertise that opens space for new solutions and possibilities. It addresses challenges facing the collaborative consultant such as 'knowing too quickly' and resisting the pull of offering advice. **Chapter 4** describes an appreciative approach to consultation that has been particularly useful when consultees have come to consultation describing experiences of 'burnout', 'disillusion' and doubts about their abilities that hamper their work with clients. Informed by the Appreciative Inquiry approach, this chapter offers the consultant an approach to moving with the consultee from a problem focus to a possibility focus while witnessing and appreciating their struggles. **Chapter 5** offers an approach to consultation in the contexts of change and endings, particularly relevant in the current climate within public services where practitioners are frequently facing service restructuring or closure and hence required to negotiate transitions and endings with clients, colleagues and agencies. **Chapter 6** offers a range of approaches to reviewing and evaluating consultation.

Part II: *Extending consultation practices* guides the consultant in how to apply and develop, in group consultation, the principles and practices explored in Part 1. It also demonstrates the application of aspects of the approach across settings and with different client groups, people with intellectual disability (Chapters 8 and 9) and older adults (Chapter 10). **Chapter 7** describes how the consultant can actively involve the whole group with the process of collaborative consultation so that group members can be a resource to each other by contributing to the process of the consultation as well as offering a repertoire of new ways to go on. **Chapter 8** focuses on the use of reflecting processes in consultations with staff teams to introduce new ideas, shifts in thinking and different ways of seeing and understanding situations and clients from which alternative stories and actions may emerge. It offers useful guidelines for preparing and working with two consultants in the positions of 'interviewing consultant' and 'reflecting person'. **Chapter 9** addresses the importance for staff who offer direct care to clients to have opportunities to reflect discursively on their own experiences. It offers an innovative approach for inviting consultees to view problems and dilemmas from multiple perspectives. **Chapter 10** offers a framework to inform and guide work with staff teams at the different points in the consultation process identified in Part I. It identifies different levels of context that inform requests for and expectations of consultation as well as the practice or activity involved in consultation.

Guidelines for the new consultant

Professional training institutions are now recognising the need to equip their qualifying practitioners with skills in consultation. This book offers a repertoire of competencies for consultation to make the early experiences for the novice consultant less overwhelming by suggesting what to expect, what can be done to improve the quality of the experience for consultant and consultee, and what strategies can support productive reflection. The book invites new consultants to become reflexive practitioners through reflecting on their consultation practice and learning how to monitor their own developing consultation competence.

The guiding principles we present in this book have given us, and the new consultants we supervise and train, confidence and energy to stay present and work creatively in organisational contexts challenged by resource pressures. We have presented the consultation practices as if they follow a logical progression, so they might look like a sequence of steps. However, we commonly select practices to fit with the request for and context of consultation and often return to certain practices at different points in our work as we gradually make sense of what is being asked of us by others.

While we do provide 'maps' or 'practice guides', we ask you, our reader, to hold in mind, as we do, that 'the map is not the territory' (Bateson, 1979:30), and therefore to always prioritise consultees' feedback and agenda rather than assume that we should be working with a set method. We invite you, therefore, to treat the practice guides as guiding principles informing your approach to consultation rather than prescribed techniques, so that you ask yourself questions like

- How can I use this practice in *this* context with *these* consultees?
- What opportunities and constraints will working with this method have for the consultees, our consultation partnership, the clients, the organisation?
- Will this approach open or close space for reflection, creativity and hope?

Note

1 In this respect, we are influenced by the systemic approach described by Boscolo, Cecchin, Hoffman and Penn (1987).

References

Andersen, T. (1987) The reflecting team: Dialogue and meta-dialogue in clinical work. *Family Process, 26* (4), 415–428.

Andersen, T. (1992) Reflections on reflecting with families. In S. McNamee and K.J. Gergen (eds.) *Therapy as Social Construction.* Newbury Park, CA: Sage.

Andersen, T. (1995) Reflecting processes; acts of informing and forming: You can borrow my eyes, but you must not take them away from me! In S. Friedman (ed.) *The Reflecting Team in Action. Collaborative Practice in Family Therapy.* New York: Guilford.

Anderson, H. (1999) Collaborative learning communities. In S. McNamee and K.J. Gergen (eds.) *Relational Responsibility: Resources for Sustainable Dialogue.* London: Sage Publications.

Anderson, H. and Goolishian, H. (1992) The client is the expert: A not-knowing approach to therapy. In S. McNamee and K.J. Gergen (eds.) *Constructing Therapy: Social Construction and the Therapeutic Process.* London: Sage.

Bateson, G. (1979) *Mind and Nature.* London: Wildwood Press.

Boscolo, L., Cecchin, G., Hoffman, L. and Penn, P. (1987) *Milan Systemic Family Therapy: Conversations in Theory and Practice.* New York: Basic Books.

Bownas, J. and Fredman, G. (eds.) (2016) *Working with Embodiment in Supervision: A Systemic Approach.* Oxon and New York: Routledge.

Campbell, D. and Huffington, C. (2008) *Organizations Connected: A Handbook of Systemic Consultation.* London: Karnac.

Caplan, G. (1970) *The Theory and Practice of Mental Health Consultation.* New York: Basic Books.

Casey, M., Harris, R. and McDonald, K. (1994) Opportunities for consultation. *Clinical Psychology Forum, 76,* 36–38.

Cooperrider, D., and Whitney, D. (2005) *Appreciative Inquiry: A Positive Revolution in Change.* San Francisco, CA: Berrett-Koehler Publishers.

Crothers, L.M., Hughes, T. L. and Morine, K.A. (2008) *Theory and Cases in School-Based Consultation: A Resource for School Psychologists, School Counselors, Special Educators, and Other Mental Health Professionals.* New York: Routledge.

de Shazer, S. (1985) *Keys to Solution in Brief Therapy.* London: W.W. Norton.

Dougherty, A.M. (2013) *Prevention and Consultation.* Los Angeles, London, New Delhi, Singapore and Washington, DC: Sage.

Fredman, G., Anderson, E. and Stott, J. (eds.) (2010) *Being with Older People: A Systemic Approach.* London: Karnac.

Freedman, J. and Combs, G. (2009) Narrative ideas for consulting with communities and organizations: Ripples from the gatherings. *Family Process, 48* (3), 347–362.

Gibson, R.L. and Mitchell, M. (2008) *Introduction to Counseling and Guidance* (7th ed.) Upper Saddle River, NJ: Pearson.

Greiner, L. and Ennsfellner, I. (2014) Management consultants as professionals, or are they? *Organizational Dynamics, 39* (1), 72–83.

Kerr, M.M. (2001) High school consultation. *Child and Adolescent Psychiatric Clinics of North America, 10,* 105–115.

Lake, N. (2008) Developing skills in consultation 1: The current context. *Clinical Psychology Forum, 186,* 13–17.

Lake, N., Solts, B. and Preedy, K. (2008) Developing skills in consultation 4: Supporting the development of consultation skills – a trainer's and a manager's perspective. *Clinical Psychology Forum, 186,* 29–33.

Lambert, N.M. (2004) Consultee-centred consultation: An international perspective on goals, process and theory. In N.M. Lambert, I. Hylander and J. Sandoval (eds.) *Consultee-Centered Consultation: Improving the Quality of Professional Services in Schools and Community Organisations.* Hillsdale, NJ: Lawrence Erlbaum Associates.

Lang, P. and McAdam, E. (1996) *Beyond Risk and Above Suspicion.* Pre-publication manuscript.

Lax, W.D. (1995) Offering Reflections: Some theoretical and practical considerations. In S. Friedman (ed.) *The Reflecting Team in Action: Collaborative Practice in Family Therapy.* New York: Guilford Press.

McAdam, E. and Lang, P. (2009) *Appreciative Work in Schools: Generating Future Communities.* Chichester: Kingsham Press.

Madsen, W. (2007) *Collaborative Therapy with Multi-Stressed Families.* London: Guildford Press.

Meyers, J., Parsons, R.D. and Martin, R. (1979) *Mental Health Consultation in Schools: A Comprehensive Guide for Psychologists, Social Workers, Psychiatrists, Counselors, Educators and Other Human Service Professionals.* San Francisco, CA: Jossey Bass.

Online Etymology Dictionary www.etymonline.com/index.php?term=consultation. (Accessed 10th April 2017).

Partridge, K. (2010) Systemic supervision in agency contexts: An evolving conversation with clinical psychologists in a mental health trust. In C. Burck and G. Daniel (eds.) *Mirrors and Reflections: Processes of Systemic Supervision.* London: Karnac.

Preedy, K. (2008) Developing skills in consultation 3: Personal reflections on consultation as a newly qualified psychologist. *Clinical Psychology Forum, 186,* 25–28.

Rosenfield, S. (1987) *Instructional Consultation.* Hillsdale, NJ: Lawrence Erlbaum Associates.

Rosenfield, S.A. (1995) The practice of instructional consultation. *Journal of Educational and Psychological Consultation, 6,* 317–327.

Rosenfield, S. (2013) Consultation in schools – Are we there yet? *Consulting Psychology Journal: Practice and Research*, *65* (4), 303–308.

Sears, R.W., Rudisill, J. and Mason-Sears, C. (2006) *Consultation Skills for Mental Health Professionals*. Hobokon, NJ: John Wiley and Sons.

Schon, D.A. (1987) *Educating the reflective practitioner*. San Francisco, CA: Jossey Bass.

Southall, A. (ed.) (2005) *Consultation in Child and Adolescent Mental Health Services*. Oxford and Seattle, WA: Radcliffe Publishing.

Tomm, K. (1988) Interventive interviewing: Part III. Intending to ask lineal, circular, strategic, or reflexive questions? *Family Process*, *27* (1), 1–15.

White, M. (2007) *Maps of Narrative Practice*. New York: Norton.

Part I

Guiding principles and practices for collaborative consultation

Chapter 2

Principles and practices for getting started with consultation in mental health

Victoria Mattison and Glenda Fredman

This chapter describes the steps we take to prepare the ground for consultation, from receiving an initial request for consultation to conducting a first meeting. We address 'entering' new organisations, services and teams and beginning consultation with individuals or groups. We describe our approach to joining with agencies and practitioners to build cooperative partnerships through contracting with people commissioning this work, tuning in to the culture of the consultation contexts into which we act and understanding and mapping relationships within the consultation organisation. Our intention is to create a context for consultation that enables the best possible chance of working collaboratively and respectfully with others and makes optimal use of the resources and competence that already exist among consultees and within the agency. Therefore, in our meetings with consultees, we take time and care to engage respectfully with people from the beginning, to clarify the nature of the request for consultation and contract with attention to confidentiality, responsibility and power.

Beginning is a process

The process of consultation begins with the first request for our involvement, which often occurs long before our face-to-face contact with consultees starts. Guide 2.1 shows the steps we take. Although we present the steps in a sequence, they do not necessarily follow a linear pattern, and often we can return to certain practices at different points in our work as we gradually make sense of what is being asked of us by others.

Guide 2.1 Steps we take in the consultation process

Preparing the ground with the people commissioning the consultation

Mapping structure and relationships within the consultation context

Co-contracting with the people commissioning the consultation
  With whom the consultants work
  Who holds responsibility for what in the work
  Participation and attendance
  How we manage confidentiality
  Co-creating intended outcomes and goals for consultation
  Confirming practical arrangements
  Contracting letters

Getting to know the consultation context

Tuning in to consultees' culture, environment and communication
  Attending to environment, atmosphere and communication
  Reflecting on the culture of collaboration

Building a cooperative partnership with consultees

Introducing ourselves to consultees
Clarifying the nature of the request for consultation with consultees
Co-contracting to create contexts of safety and respect with consultees
  Acknowledging power and difference in the consultation relationship
Coordinating meanings of consultation

Entering systems and joining with consultees

Proceeding slowly
Using our map to guide us
Valuing and respecting consultees' expertise

Sorry – we've no idea why you are here

My manager and the head teacher of a local secondary school for children with learning disabilities had already met and agreed a plan for me (Victoria) to provide regular consultation to the teaching staff group. I was to be based one morning each week at the school for twelve months initially. I was new to this school. On my first morning, I met briefly with the head teacher who apologised that she had 'only ten minutes' and then, speaking very quickly, explained that the teachers were 'working very hard ... reacting to daily situations ... struggling with children who are most challenging in their behaviours' and 'need time to understand the children' and to 'debrief with each other at the end of the day'. As she escorted me to the staff room, explaining that she was 'rushing to another meeting', she added, 'I hope you can provide some consultancy to staff who are having difficulties in their relationships with each other'.

I sat down with a group of fifteen teachers and teaching assistants, introduced myself and explained that I was 'pleased to join for our first consultation meeting'. A washing machine was whizzing loudly, two teachers were making coffee and everyone was eating cake. They were laughing about how tough the day had been – one child had spat at the teacher and teaching assistant. When his mother was called in, she had sworn at the teacher as she was so distressed about her child's behaviour. I listened as they shared a couple of anecdotes, thinking they were using the time to 'debrief' and wondering how often they met as a staff group. I then introduced myself – asking them what they understood about my joining their meeting. One of the teachers looked at me quizzically and said, 'Sorry – we've got no idea why you're here'.

Since those early days of our consultation practice, we have learned the value of taking time to prepare the ground with people commissioning the consultation to support the development of our new working relationship.

Preparing the ground with the people commissioning the consultation

The teachers in this example show us that we cannot assume that commissioners and consultees always want the 'consultation' we are offering, that they are aware that it has been organised or what was agreed, or even that they know what we are talking about when we refer to 'consultation'. We therefore pay careful attention to the process of setting up and contracting, starting, where possible, with the people who have commissioned the work.

Meeting with the commissioners of the work, and especially the people who hold the budgets, provides us, as consultants, with the opportunity to establish from the start what context we are invited into – including clarifying how decisions are made in the organisation, what lines of communication we should follow and how funds and resources are distributed (Caplan and Caplan, 1993). To explore these questions, we try to start as early as possible with mapping the consultation context.

Mapping structure and relationships within the consultation context

We have found that the mapping process can be useful at different stages of setting up and beginning the work, as part of contracting with commissioners and managers, and in early meetings with consultees. Creating relationship maps can help familiarise the consultant with the organisational structure, lines of management, responsibility, communication and reporting hierarchies within the consultation context, as well as identify important relationships and connections with and between consultees. It throws light on what is clear to us about the consultation context and what may need clarification.

To map the consultation context, we consider 'who' questions: who is requesting and commissioning the consultation; who are the stakeholders; who will be involved and participating, and who supports, can offer resources or might challenge the consultation. Once we have included significant people on the map, we can explore relationships, including how consultees are connected with each other and with commissioners, lines of hierarchy and accountability and responsibility. We also include ourselves on the map, thereby making explicit how we are already connected to the situation. This enables us to consider what position we are being invited into, what is hoped for from our involvement, whether or how what we have to offer might fit with the resources of others in the system and who else can enable or support the consultation.

Box 2.1 offers examples of questions we use to guide us in the mapping process. Sometimes we ask those commissioning the consultation to help us 'draw a map to give us a picture of who will be involved in this work' and show us 'how you are connected'. If I (Victoria) had mapped the system of relationships with the service manager and the head teacher, I might have made a smoother start with this staff group of teachers.

Box 2.1 Guiding questions for mapping the consultation context

Who is requesting and commissioning the consultation?

Whose idea was this consultation?
Who is asking for what for whom?
Who has requested/commissioned this consultation?
Do consultees know who is commissioning the work for whom? (Who told whom what?)

Who are the stakeholders?

Who wants to know/has an opinion on the process and outcome of the consultation?
(Who wants feedback? Who wants to know what?)
Who else knows about this consultation?

What previous conversations have people had already? (Who has spoken to whom about what? Who has agreed what with whom?)
Who supports and offers resources (material and relational) to the consultation?

What are the expectations/hopes for our contact?

Who understands what about the consultation? Who wants what for whom? (Who is asking for what at an organisation and management level; how has this been set up?)

Who will be participating?

Who will join the consultation?
Who should/could be included in the work?
Who should not be included?
(How has this been decided, and what are the possible effects of not including someone?)

How are consultees/commissioners connected?

Who will be affected?
Who else is connected/involved? How are they/we connected?
Who is accountable to whom (duties/responsibilities)?

Who supports/offers resources/challenges this consultation?

Including ourselves

What position are we being invited into?
How does what we have to offer fit with the resources/expectations of others in the system?

I (Victoria) requested a second meeting with the head teacher, at a time that suited her, assuming she was commissioning this consultation for the teachers. Acknowledging that she had already discussed the contract for the consultation with my manager, I asked her to 'help me make sure the consultation I am offering your staff team fits with what you want and ensures we get the best outcome for the teachers and the pupils in your school'. We now call these meetings 'set-up meetings', which we arrange routinely at the start with people commissioning the consultation.

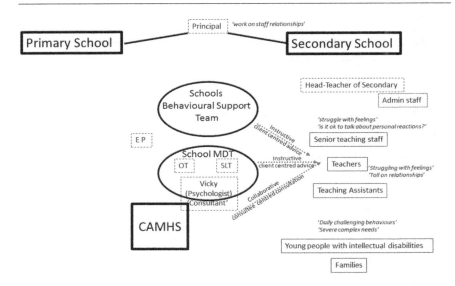

Figure 2.1   Mapping the structure and relationships of secondary school

At a subsequent meeting, the head teacher gave me more of a picture of 'who was asking for what for whom'. As we talked, I drew a map. The head teacher explained that the 'original idea' for the consultation had come from the principal of both the primary and secondary schools for 'work on the relationships between teaching staff'. Referring to the map we were developing together (see Figure 2.1), I asked what the different staff in her secondary school might say about this 'idea'. I learned that many of the teaching staff were 'struggling with some very upsetting and angry feelings about challenging behaviours' they were facing daily in class; the head teacher thought they were 'unsure whether it's acceptable to talk about their own reactions to the work'. She thought that the significant challenges facing the teachers who were supporting children and young people with 'severe and complex needs' were 'bound to take its toll on their relationships'.

When I explored 'who else is involved', I learned that the 'in-house behavioural support team' offered 'advice … guidance … support' to individual teachers on their 'work with individual children'. Speech and language therapy (SLT), occupational therapy (OT) and educational psychology (EP) also offered dedicated sessions to both primary and secondary schools and the schools could refer specific children and families to the Child and Adolescent Mental Health Services (CAMHS).

Mapping the structure and relationships of the consultation context in this way can enable us, as consultants, to anticipate the impact of our entering the organisation, thus giving us a sense of where and how to enter and join, how we position ourselves, with whom we should talk first and how we respond. Thus the map enabled me to take account of my own position in the school. Making it clear that I did not want to 'step on anyone's toes', by looking at the map together, the head teacher and I were able to reflect on what, whether and how consultation might fit with what was already being provided in the school. As well as enabling consultants to learn about the organisation we are invited into, 'mapping' also encourages consultees to become observers of their own systems and practices.

Co-contracting with people commissioning the consultation

The people commissioning the consultation are not always clear about what they themselves want or expect from 'consultation', what the work involves, what it can offer or how it can be used by staff-consultees. Therefore, we have found it helpful to engage commissioners and managers in a process of co-contracting to clarify together:

- How and with whom we work in consultation;
- Who holds responsibility for what in the work;
- Participation and attendance;
- How we manage confidentiality;
- Goals for consultation;
- Practical arrangements.

With whom the consultant works

Since the traditional role of mental health practitioners and clinicians like psychiatrists, psychologists and therapists has been to work directly with patients and clients on problems located within the client (patient, child or family), we often find at the start of our consultation work that consultees hold an expectation or preference that the consultant will provide direct services to the client constructed as 'having' the problem. Therefore, I (Victoria) clarified with the head teacher that I would be offering 'indirect' consultation so that, as the consultant, I would meet with the consultees and not with the pupils or families (clients).

Who holds responsibility for what in the work

I went on to clarify that, as the consultant, I would take responsibility for 'guiding the process of the consultation' while the consultees 'provide the content and problems for consultation', including relevant contextual information. We agreed that the teacher-consultees would be responsible for the pupil/family (client) outcomes of the work and not I, as the consultant. Thus, in consultee-centred consultation, the consultant's focus is on facilitating the consultee's work with the client rather than on solving the client's problem for the consultee (as in the client-centred consultation that the behavioural support team was offering) or addressing working with the whole service, team or organisation (as in system-centred consultation).

When the head-teacher remarked, 'I can see that you will be helping the teachers to be confident to use what they already know, but we also see you as a specialist in mental health', I (Victoria) explained that we take a 'collaborative approach' to consultation which assumes a non-hierarchical relationship between consultant and consultees; I would not be monitoring or evaluating the consultees' competence. I clarified that I would be assuming and drawing on the teacher-consultees' wealth of knowledge and experience of working with children with learning disabilities and with their families. I would contribute my specialist knowledge and ideas if asked for; the consultees would then be free to take what was useful and leave what was not. (In Chapter 3, Andia Papadopoulou and Glenda Fredman describe the process of sharing specialist knowledge with consultees in collaborative consultation.)

Clarifying the consultant and consultees' rights, duties and responsibilities usually opens space for clarification of *accounting and reporting relationships* in the consultation process, for example, whether attendance would be monitored, who wants what feedback on the consultation from whom and with whom the consultant and consultees might need to negotiate time and support for attendance when it conflicts with other duties.

Participation and attendance

We always try to address *participation* and *membership* of the consultation group, including who can attend, whether the consultation group could be open or closed and what commitment is required for membership. We also discuss whether and how managers participate and the possible opportunities and constraints of their being part of group consultation.

Therefore I (Victoria) went on to check expectations about consultees' *attendance*, how often consultees can or should attend and whether participation could be voluntary for the teaching staff, explaining that mandatory participation can pose a challenge to creating a collaborative partnership with consultees. The head teacher noted that teachers' participation in consultation was 'not forced' but that they 'all know they are expected to attend', opening space for us to clarify how we record attendance and whether and to whom this is reported.

How we manage confidentiality

We do not automatically assume that conversations between consultants and consultees will remain confidential before clarifying the organisation's policies, procedures and requirements for sharing relevant information, for example in relation to safeguarding or risk. Therefore, before we meet with consultees, we negotiate explicitly with commissioners and managers how we will manage confidentiality and the limits of confidentiality. We usually ask for help to clarify 'what you expect us to share with whom and in what circumstances' (Stott and Martin, 2010:93).

Over the years of consulting with a range of services, we have learned that different organisations and professions interpret and relate to 'confidentiality' in quite different ways. For example, sharing stories about pupils and parents between teachers in the staff room in the presence of other staff members who may not be working with those children or families is quite common in school contexts. However, the British Psychological Society code of ethics states that psychologists are obligated to protect confidential information and make a more formal agreement with people with whom they consult that they will not disclose any details of their conversations or meetings without permission, unless they are concerned about 'risk of harm'. Therefore, where possible, we make explicit the ethical standards of privacy and confidentiality of our respective professions. This sort of discussion usually opens space for us, as consultants, to clarify with the people commissioning the work what they would like us to agree with the consultees about reporting or feeding back from the consultation and what they have informed consultees about who needs/wants to know what about the work.

We introduce these clarifications early on in the process of setting up a consultation with commissioners and managers, not as requirements or provisos, but to open space for transparent discussion about the consultation we and they are respectively providing and receiving, thereby coordinating and negotiating the groundwork for a collaborative consultation relationship.

Co-creating goals for consultation

We go on to clarify the intended outcomes of the consultation by asking questions such as: 'Let's imagine it is six months' time and the consultation from our service has been very useful: what do you notice that lets you know this has been effective? What is happening? What is different for the staff (consultees)/ children and families (clients)/yourself (commissioner/manager)?' We therefore try to clarify what people *want* rather than what they *need*, to co-create the focus and formulate meaningful goals with them using *their* words (see Chapter 3). We document the goals as a baseline to refer back to when evaluating progress over time (see Chapter 6). We try to establish baselines as early as possible when we contract with the people commissioning the consultation and when we first meet with consultees. The head teacher of the school for young people with learning disabilities wanted the teachers to 'feel more confident' and 'competent' working with children with 'complex needs'. She also hoped they could use the consultation to 'support each other' with the 'stressful demands of the job'.

Confirming practical arrangements

We usually conclude our conversation with an agreement about the *frequency and length of consultation sessions* and the *dates, times and venues*. Agreements made with commissioners (including budget holders and managers) at an organisational level are generally formal; they define explicit duties and responsibilities and often there is some form of written contract.

Contracting letters

We conclude the *set-up* process by drawing up a written 'contract' in a letter that is circulated to all present after the meeting and includes suggestions for how the work may go ahead between the consultant and consultees. Some of the key components we use in *contracting letters* include:

- **Thanking people for attending** the *set-up meeting* 'to help us prepare for the consultation with …'.
- **An appreciative statement** of the consultation context acknowledging the abilities, values of and also challenges for the consultees and the organisation; for example 'we appreciate the time you have made for this meeting with all the competing demands on your time. We were struck by the importance of … to your team and, your commitment to …'.
- **Acknowledging significant achievements,** for example, 'Congratulations to you all for your recent outstanding Schools Inspection report. We look forward to hearing more about how you achieved this despite the cuts in resources to your service'.
- **An outline of the goals, focus and expectations** for future consultation work discussed in the meeting.
- **A summary of what we agreed about confidentiality, accounting and reporting.**
- **A summary of key action points agreed including** when, how and by whom the consultant will be introduced to the consultees; times, dates, attendance and so on.
- **Plans for a review** with the consultant and the commissioner/manager to consider how the consultation work has met the expectations from that initial meeting.

Getting to know the consultation context

From our earliest contact with commissioners, managers and consultees, we notice and are affected by the environment, atmosphere and styles of communication within the organisation or services with whom we are consulting. 'Systems introduce themselves to outsiders from the first moment of contact: all "visitors" have to do is keep their eyes and ears open' (Reder and Duncan, 1990:153). Therefore, the process of interaction and communication will reveal immediately information about the rules, relationships and culture of the organisation as well as how consultees hope to make use of the consultant.

Tuning in to consultees' culture

Each organisation, agency or team we work with will have its own culture, structures and logic. We try, therefore, to understand as much as we can about the logic of that system and the values, beliefs and philosophy of the organisation that might support, inform, constrain or offer resources to the consultation work.

When Emma Worwood started offering consultation to a new staff team at a children's centre, she discovered that cooking, bringing in food to share and eating together were precious to the largely Bengali, all-female staff team and was a significant part of the culture of the centre. By accepting the women's kind offer to eat with them, Emma was able to learn that shared mealtimes were opportunities for staff to talk about their work and the activities of the centre.

By stepping back and positioning ourselves as anthropologists or as 'guests' in the consultees' culture (Ricoeur, 2007), we are able to 'be with' and observe the day-to-day living and working of our consultees, thereby learning a lot about the culture of their agency, their routines and rituals, the demands on them including pressure or stressors, what is important and precious to them and their language and beliefs about clients. Emma took the time to ask questions about the 'day-to-day' work of the children's centre staff. By inviting staff to share their stories, she got a flavour of their invaluable work, relationships and some of their struggles, thereby enabling her to find a suitable fit for consultation with the values and practice of the consultees.

Attending to environment, atmosphere and communication

The atmosphere of the organisation usually strikes us immediately; for example, whether it is ordered or chaotic, friendly and welcoming or discomfiting.

I (Victoria) recall the first time I walked into a primary school where I had been invited to offer regular staff team consultation. I was moved by the aesthetic merging of so many cultures, ethnicities and religions within one community. There was a sign in reception with 'welcome' translated into about twenty different languages. It was December, and I noticed a table by the school office with 'festivals of light' displays for Chanukah, Diwali and Christmas, all illustrated with beautiful photographs of the children celebrating and remembering different stories associated with these times. I also noticed the diverse groups of children from so many different cultures walking through the corridors – boys wearing turbans; girls with hijabs; Black, White and Asian faces; a male teacher wearing a kippah; and a sign on the office door about a coffee morning for Somali-speaking parents the following day. I thought about how often we take for granted the rich tapestries of culture that exist in our local schools, and how much more we could appreciate the conscious intention of staff to celebrate and value the culture and rituals of each child and adult in the fabric of the school.

The first person I encountered was the school secretary, who appeared flustered and overwhelmed by a number of children and parents who were waiting to speak to her. Doing my very best to smile warmly and appreciatively, I commented that 'this beautiful display is such a lovely way to welcome new people to your school'. The secretary returned my smile, relaxed and generously offered to lead the way to the head teacher's room, despite the demands on her time.

Like Lang and McAdam (1990), we try to approach a request for consultation as a 'gracious invitation'. Holding in mind what a privilege it is for busy staff to prioritise some of their time for working with us is usually a good place to start. It creates a more appreciative atmosphere, where there is respect for the consultee. This is the 'posture' (Fredman, 2007) I tried to hold in my brief meeting with the head teacher, Mrs Jamieson.

> Mrs Jamieson's office was tiny and dark, along a narrow corridor with blue walls and worn carpets. There were piles of papers and books everywhere, and three children were waiting outside to speak to her. I looked at her apologetically, appreciating the time she could give me, intending to set the scene for a conversation about the school's hopes for this new 'link' with our service. Before we even got going, Mrs Jamieson explained that she would need to keep her office door open so that she could see the children sitting in the corridor, as she was sharing playground duty. Suddenly her mobile phone went off; she answered it quickly and began to have a complicated and urgent conversation, putting her hand over the phone to whisper, 'I am so sorry, I am always on duty – I won't be a minute …'.

Being sensitive to spontaneous communications when we first meet another system can help us, as consultants, to make the most of the encounter. Thus I was able to acknowledge respectfully the huge number of demands on Mrs Jamieson's time and note, 'It is important that the way we work with your school does not feel like an added demand on what you and your staff are already holding …'.

Paying attention to an organisation's relationship to time and space can help orient us, as consultants, to the opportunities and challenges to creating collaborative contexts for consultation as well as give us clues for engaging the consultees in consultation. Witnessing first-hand the considerable demands on the school secretary and the remarkable multitasking ability of the head teacher enabled me to respond appreciatively and respectfully to them both; they each went on to contribute considerable support to the staff consultation I offered. Reder and Duncan (1990) identify a familiar tension facing hard-pressed frontline practitioners who work with children: they need to be available to respond to crises, which take precedence over planned work; however, working ethically and safely with children also demands reliable, protected and planned contacts. By mapping the tension between responsibility for cases and taking time to reflect in consultation in a time-pressured service, Sylvia Duncan describes how she enabled a busy social work team to clarify their need for overt permission and support from their middle managers for planned and protected time for their attendance at consultation.

Reflecting on the culture of collaboration

Understanding the consultation context also includes noticing how the organisation or agency engages in collaboration, team work, leadership and working relationships. We have worked with agencies that fall on a broad continuum from 'collaborative working', which encourages joint and cooperative working to services organised into 'separate units', or 'silos' with segregated management systems that work in parallel or competitively with each other.

A map of the service's layout including the architecture of the building and how rooms are allocated (Sherry, 2012) can shine a light on the opportunities for, and obstacles to, collaboration and communication within the organisation. The leadership style of the head or manager can also give us ideas about the quality of collaboration in the service, often mirroring what motivates the staff; for example, whether they are driven by rules and directives from above, moved by their personal principles or inspired by a commitment to their team. Where heads of service support or encourage a collaborative environment, consultee-centred collaborative consultation has more potential to develop. If, on the other hand, collaboration is lacking or absent in the service culture, consultees, like Tom, the teacher below (p. 34), might experience a consultant as critical or feel negatively evaluated or defensive (Newman, 2009).

Working with managers and leaders to create collaborative environments involves working at the level of the organisation and is beyond the scope of this book (see McAdam and Lang [2009] and Campbell [2000] for examples). However, exploring how much collaboration is valued and what types of collaboration are supported can help us find ways of working with consultees that fit with their culture. Therefore, it is not that a consultant cannot or should not engage in consultee-centred, collaborative consultation in organisations that privilege individualistic or competitive working cultures; developing collaborative cultures can begin with a single or small group of consultees if the consultant is able to engage the consultees in a cooperative partnership.

Building a cooperative partnership with consultees

The relationship with the consultee is the most important element in the mental health consultation process (Crothers et al., 2008). Hence, building a working relationship with consultees is 'one of the most important components of effective consultation' (Rosenfield, 2012:9). Mindful that strong working relationships create the foundation for collaborative teamwork (Sanborn, 2004), therefore, we take care how we introduce ourselves to consultees to ensure they feel safe enough to reflect on their practice so they can entertain multiple different and sometimes contradictory perspectives with us and each other.

Introducing ourselves to consultees

We often begin with an appreciative welcome comment like, 'Thank you for joining' or 'Welcome. I am pleased to meet with you'. We provide our name and locate ourselves in the context of our work (who we are; what we do) as in, 'My name is Victoria Mattison. I am a clinical psychologist working with Islington Community Child and Adolescent Mental Health Service. As well as my clinical practice with

children and families, I meet with staff, like yourselves, in schools to offer consultation on their work with children and families'. We go on to spell out and clarify the
relationships that brought us to the meeting. For example, 'I have been invited by
Mrs Jamieson, the head teacher of your school, to work with you all in consultation'.
And we check, 'What have you been told? ... What do you think of that idea?'

> I (Victoria) had been offering individual consultation to staff in a local
> primary school for over a year at the request of the school's head
> teacher and the Special Education Needs Coordinator[1] (Senco). The
> Senco informed me that there was a new teacher, Tom, who the head
> teacher had suggested 'may benefit' from meeting with me, because he
> 'seemed to be struggling in his class with a handful of children with quite
> complex needs'. As was our usual practice with the teachers in this
> school, I offered the Senco a time for the teacher, Tom, to meet with me.
>
> When Tom arrived, I welcomed him and introduced myself by name.
> He nodded and I noticed that he looked very nervous and uncertain.
> Therefore, I checked, 'Has Elspeth (Senco) explained who I am? What
> did she tell you about our meeting?' Tom replied, 'Elspeth told me I had a
> consultation at three with the psychologist – that's all'.

Both the Senco and I had overlooked that Tom was a new teacher who was unfamiliar with the way the teachers in this school had been using and valuing consultation
with me over the past year. Recognising that I had assumed, without checking, that
the Senco had explained my role in the school to Tom, and acknowledging that I had
not taken sufficient care to prepare the ground for this first meeting, I took time with
Tom to locate myself in the context of my work with the school.

Clarifying the nature of the request for consultation with consultees

Asking for help involves a move from a private to a public arena, whereby our
work becomes open to scrutiny (Lang and McAdam, 1990). Since it is common for people who ask for help to believe that the helper will perceive them as
incompetent (Rosenfield, 1987; Fredman and Rapaport, 2010), asking for 'help'
from another professional can feel exposing. When requests for consultation
come from a third party within the same service, especially if this person is a
supervisor or manager, feeling exposed or incompetent may be magnified, as
happened with Tom and the staff group of teachers above who were 'referred' for
consultation by the Senco and head teacher. Therefore we have learned to clarify
understandings with consultees about why we might have been invited to work
with them, what has been agreed and who has spoken to whom about what, with
questions like

- Whose idea was it for us to meet?
- What did [they] tell you/explain about this consultation/meeting?
- What do you think [they] wanted from our consultation/meeting? What are
  your views on this?

These questions opened space for Tom to explain that he was not at all clear why we were meeting. He 'guessed' the head teacher had suggested he 'needed consultation' because he was 'not doing well'; he was concerned that he was 'being disciplined' and wondered whether the head teacher was aware of 'just how stressed' he was feeling. I was able to clarify that our conversations were not connected to monitoring his performance or evaluating his competence and therefore I would not be feeding back details of our conversations to the head teacher. Hence Tom and I could go on to contract how we would work together and negotiate 'confidentiality'.

We often explore whether consultees have engaged in any similar types of work or outside agency support in the past, how that has been received and what has worked well or less well for them and their service. Answers to these questions can guide us as consultants to find a good enough fit with consultees' preferred ways of working so that we do not repeat what they disliked or found unhelpful or uncomfortable in previous consultation. Tom, the teacher above, told me he had had a difficult experience with a previous 'mentor' while he was in teacher training who took opportunities to 'have a chat' to let him know how badly he was doing. He had recently arrived from a school with a predominantly individualistic culture in which the teachers worked in isolation from each other. He described the head teacher from his former school as 'hierarchical' and 'quite suspicious of outside services coming in'. Not yet inducted into the collaborative and mutually appreciative environment of this new school, Tom was drawing on his previous experience. Hence he was ascribing evaluative meanings to the term 'consultation' and bracing himself for instruction and criticism from the consultant.

Co-contracting to create contexts of safety and respect with consultees

When contracting with consultees, as in any other phase of the consultation process, we try to invite collaborative dialogue to enable the consultee to understand and offer their perspective on the process of consultation, learn enough about the process to feel comfortable with it and make an informed decision about whether or not to engage in the process.

Setting forth the contract

We often begin: 'I will start by explaining how we work in consultation ... you are welcome to ask any questions'; and we check: 'How does this fit for you?' Thus we begin by *setting forth* those details of the consultation process that are already established or are not negotiable, for example, that we will follow the ethical guidelines[2] of our profession to ensure the protection of clients' safety, respect and dignity.

We explain confidentiality and its limits at the outset of the consultation relationship to clarify what information shared between the consultant and consultee remains confidential and to ensure that the consultee is aware that confidentiality may be waived under certain circumstances, such as if the client is in imminent danger.[3] We also *set forth* what we have agreed with managers/commissioners of the consultation, for example, suggested timeframes, times the consultant will be available and how to request a consultation. We might discuss the purpose of consultation, including our intentions for sharing ownership of each step of the process, and our expectation that ideas generated in our conversations could be relevant or useful with other clients in the consultees' practice. We always check for agreement with the consultees so we are clear we have 'informed consent' for these pre-set aspects of the consultation contract.

Bringing forth to co-create contexts of safety, comfort and respect

We go on to *bring forth* from consultees what they want, or we should agree for them to feel comfortable and respected in the process of consultation, with questions like: 'What would you like us to agree for you to feel comfortable and respected by me?', thereby generating ideas from the consultees to help us learn how they prefer us to 'be with' them in consultation.

> Tom was a young, newly qualified, Black teacher who was 'told' by the Senco to meet with me for consultation. He was working in a school with a very senior and experienced older female White management team. Here was I (Victoria), another White woman in my forties, offering Tom a space for 'consultation'. Aware that our age, race and class difference would be contributing to a power imbalance between us, I checked with Tom: 'For this sort of consultation to be useful, it is important that you feel comfortable and respected by me. So can you help me – as another White woman – to know how to work with you here, so you feel comfortable and respected by me?' Tom smiled and sat back in his chair. The atmosphere between us felt lighter and opened space for us to engage in a more collaborative conversation.

Coordinating meanings of consultation

> As soon as I (Victoria) uttered the phrase, 'I offer consultation to schools' to the teachers in the staff team (p. 23), one teacher exclaimed, 'Oh you're the consultant!' and another retorted, 'She's here to tell us what we do wrong …'.

The word 'consultation' has many different meanings in different contexts (see Chapter 1). Therefore, consultees with whom we meet might hold a range of different meanings for 'consultation', including meeting with an expert; receiving advice or support, or as the teachers in this chapter assumed, 'being disciplined'; or 'to tell us what we do wrong …'. Since we approach consultation as a 'cooperative partnership' (Zins and Echul, 2002:627) in which consultant and consultee work together collaboratively in a non-hierarchical relationship, we take care with how we name and describe what we will be doing together by checking and coordinating our meanings of 'consultation' with consultees, using questions like

• What is your understanding of 'consultation'?

- What are your previous experiences of consultation?
- Do you prefer to use a different word (to consultation)?

Sometimes we invite consultees to jointly co-create a name for the (consultation) work as a way of beginning our work together, simply asking 'What shall we call our work together?'

If this work has already been ascribed the name 'consultation', we might begin with 'going inside the word' (Andersen, 1995) 'consultation' to see what is there, creating a 'linguagram' (McAdam and Lang, 2000), or word map, as we describe in Chapter 1. The 'linguagram' can give us some understanding of consultees' relationship to consultation: what meaning they are giving to consultation, their previous experience of consultation and their expectations, opening space for us to negotiate how we can work collaboratively with each other and what *they* want from the consultation.

Entering systems and joining with consultees

Collaborative consultation involves coordinating and creating contexts to connect with consultees. Therefore we set out to join with agencies and consultees to learn more about the contexts within which we will be working. We have learned the importance of *proceeding slowly*, entering into the system with care and getting to know how things work. *Using our map* of the structure and relationships of the consultation context to guide us enables us to reflect on possible ways we might position ourselves to enter the organisation and join with consultees to enhance opportunities for collaborative partnerships.

We take different positions when starting consultations: joining as a participant-observer to learn the culture, logic and values of the system, as Emma does (p. 31), and asking questions with curiosity to explore the beliefs and logic of the consultees and the consultation system. Rather than immediately assuming that consultees 'need' our help or support, like Emma, we try to avoid forging ahead as the 'expert' and instead express interest and curiosity in *their* work 'to help me learn more how you work and the issues you are working with'. Therefore we watch and wait for moments to connect and work with the consultees in a non-intrusive way, *valuing and respecting* the culture and practices of the organisation and expertise of the consultees without imposing specific models or ways of working or 'wading in' by trying to set up new structures.

Making our competencies apparent while not appearing too presumptuous about them involves a delicate balance between acknowledging and drawing on the skills and abilities of the consultees and demonstrating competencies that the consultees can recognise as potentially useful to their work. Held (1982) spells out some steps we can take to achieve this balance, including

- Appreciating the expertise of the staff-consultees, particularly in areas of their own work;

- Acknowledging that as a consultant new to this system we have much to learn about the way the system operates before being able to make a useful contribution, therefore seeking the help and advice of the staff-consultees;
- Asking relevant questions that permit the consultees to show their own skills and abilities, thereby validating their sense of competence;
- Noticing, highlighting, communicating and validating the resources and strengths in the consultee system;
- Giving meaning to problems consultees present as their attempts to improve the situation, and as their caring and commitment to the well-being of their clients and/or agency.

In this chapter, we reflect on some of the principles and practices that guide our beginning consultation with individuals or teams. Although the focus is largely on 'entering' new teams and organisations and 'joining' with consultees, reviewing the process of beginning work may also be of interest to consultants who would like to revisit or review their position within a team or organisation or re-contract their work with consultees.

We are aware that we invest a lot of time in the process of beginning consultation, which might feel like an added strain for those of us working in and with 'time-pressured' services. We have found that careful attention to how we begin has generally created time and space for ourselves as consultants, for the consultees and for the services within which we work, reflecting the adage frequently quoted by Peter Lang (Lang and McAdam, 1990): 'well begun, half done'.

Notes

1 In the United Kingdom, Special Education Needs Coordinators (Sencos) are qualified teachers who have responsibility for managing well-being, learning and education and coordinating the provision of support for all pupils with special education needs in a school.
2 Although there may not be specific professional ethical guidelines for consultation, our professional codes of ethics will provide a set of principles and standards for appropriate ethical behaviour that can be generalised to the practice of consultation. You, the reader, might like to look at your professional code of ethics and ask yourself: how does it inform how I am with consultees; what do we need to agree/clarify?
3 Meyers et al. (2004) also caution practitioners to be cognisant of the risks to confidentiality in the consultative process as a result of using email and the storage of electronic files, and to use procedures to increase protection of confidential information, including file encryption and firewalls.

References

Andersen, T. (1995) Reflecting processes; acts of informing and forming: You can borrow my eyes, but you must not take them away from me! In S. Friedman (ed.) *The Reflecting Team in Action. Collaborative Practice in Family Therapy*. New York: Guilford.

Campbell, D. (2000) *The Socially Constructed Organization*. London and New York: Karnac.

Caplan, G. and Caplan, R.B. (1993) *Mental Health Consultation and Collaboration*. San Francisco: Jossey-Bass.

Crothers, L.M., Hughes, T.L. and Morine. K.A. (2008) *Theory and Cases in School-Based Consultation: A Resource for School Psychologists, School Counsellors, Special Educators and Other Mental Health Professionals.* New York: Routledge.

Fredman, G. (2007) Preparing our selves for the therapeutic relationship. Revisiting 'hypothesizing revisited'. *Human Systems: The Journal of Systemic Consultation and Management, 18,* 44–59.

Fredman, G. and Rapaport, P. (2010) How do we begin? Working with older people and their significant systems. In G. Fredman, E. Anderson and J. Stott (eds.) *Being With Older People: A Systemic Approach.* London: Karnac.

Held, B. (1982) Entering a mental health system: A strategic-systemic approach. *Journal of Strategic and Systemic Therapies, 1,* 40–50.

Lang, P. and McAdam, E. (1990) Referrals, referrers and systems of concern. A chapter about good beginnings designed to lead to quicker endings! Available from: http://www.taosinstitute.net/Websites/taos/files/Content/5694552/McAdam-lang-_Referrals,_Referrers_and_the_System.pdf. Retrieved 10 December 2016.

McAdam, E. and Lang, P. (2000) Voices of reconciliation. IFTA world family therapy congress, Oslo, 17 June. Available from: www.taosinstitute.net/Websites/taos/files/Content/5694552/McAdam-Lang_-_Voices_of_Reconciliation.pdf. Retrieved 10 December 2016.

McAdam, E. and Lang, P. (2009) *Appreciative Work in Schools: Generating Future Communities.* Chichester: Kingsham Press.

Meyers, J., Meyers, A.B. and Grogg, K. (2004) Prevention through consultation: A model to guide future developments in the field of school psychology. *Journal of Educational Psychological Consultation, 15,* 257–276.

Newman, D.J. (2009) A grounded theory of supervision in pre-service level consultation training. (Doctoral Dissertation). University of Maryland, College Park, MD. Available from: http://www.drum.lib.umd.edu/bitstream/handle/1903/9607/Newman_umd_0117E_10650.pdf;jsessionid=2DC40EF60B462ED043FCFCD7D5F4DD80?sequence=1. Retrieved 2 December 2016.

Reder, P. and Duncan, S. (1990) On meeting systems. *Human Systems: The Journal of Systemic Consultation and Management, 1,* 153–162.

Ricœur, P. (2007) *Reflections on Just.* Translated by David Pellauer. Chicago: University of Chicago Press.

Rosenfield, S. (1987) *Instructional Consultation.* Hillsdale, NJ: Lawrence Erlbaum Associates.

Rosenfield, S. (ed.) (2012) *Becoming a School Consultant: Lessons Learned.* New York: Routledge.

Sanborn, M. (2004) *The Fred Factor.* Colorado Springs, CO: Waterbrook Press.

Sherry, E. (2012) Making the case for consultee-centered consultation: a novice consultant's perception of culture and relationships. In Rosenfield, S. (ed.) *Becoming a School Consultant: Lessons Learned.* New York: Routledge.

Stott, J. and Martin, E. (2010) Creating contexts for talking and listening where older people feel comfortable and respected. In G. Fredman, E. Anderson and J. Stott (eds.) *Being With Older People: A Systemic Approach.* London: Karnac.

Zins, J. E. and Erchul, W.P. (2002) Best practices in school consultation. In A. Thomas and J. Grimes (eds.) *Best Practices in School Psychology, 1,* 625–643. Bethesda, MD: National Association of School Psychologists.

Chapter 3

Collaborative consultation

Moving with consultees towards new possibilities

Andia Papadopoulou and Glenda Fredman

This chapter describes an approach to collaborative consultation where consultant and consultee join their expertise to explore dilemmas and challenges towards developing new possibilities. With examples from practice, we illustrate how we take a collaborative consultation approach to bring forth multiple perspectives and share specialist knowledge so that consultees can find new ways to go on.

> 'So, what do I do? How can I help this family?' asked Annie, at our weekly lunchtime health visitors' consultation meeting, as she concluded her brief, animated and passionate presentation of her work with a Somali mother and her children. As the words of her request echoed in my head, I (Andia) suddenly became aware that all eyes in the room, including those of Miranda, my newly appointed colleague joining me that day, had settled on me in anticipation. I felt an urge to blurt out my evolving ideas and respond to Annie's request with a clinical formulation. This was, after all, a complex and challenging case.
>
> As I prepared to articulate my response, I glanced around the room, scanning the faces present. I was reminded of how pleased I was to welcome seven members of this staff team to our consultation group that day. We had worked together for many years, connecting through the families to whom we offered services. Their faces reminded me of all the skilful ways they had dealt with similar challenges in their work with families over the years. Reconnecting with their skills and abilities further reminded me of the team's impressive resourcefulness and commitment to helping families and sparked my curiosity to find out more about what others in the group could offer. My urge to share my thoughts on the case began to fade and instead I asked, 'Annie, can you help us understand what you mean by "do" here?' And then, 'How would you know you have helped the family?' 'What would they be doing?' 'What would you notice?' I went on to explore further, first with Annie, 'What ideas have you had already?' And then, with the group, 'What ideas do you all have that may be useful to Annie?'

The pull towards an expert position

Annie looked to me, as the consultant facilitating the group, for solutions to the difficulties she was experiencing with her client-family. She invited me to give her advice on what to do and how to help. Requests for consultation often come out of beliefs like Annie's, that consultants have the solutions that will make the difference. This may come from an assumption that consultants have expert knowledge or skills that they bring from their specialised training and work experience with specific client groups.

Annie's request for advice and solutions positioned me as the expert within the group. She assumed that as a clinical psychologist, I would have a clearer understanding of the situation than she had and better ideas about what to do to engage the family with the services she was offering. Annie was acting out of a professional worldview that assigned responsibility to the consultant to share their specialised expertise, a worldview that Madsen has described as the 'discourse of professional expertise' (Madsen, 2006). At first, perhaps out of a sense of professional obligation to be helpful, I found myself pulled to respond from that expert position and give the advice asked for. Perhaps I was also somewhat seduced or pressured by the expectation that I should know *all* the answers. By the time Annie had concluded telling us about the family, I had already formed many ideas and even a 'formulation' to share with her, and could have happily gone on to talk about the ways that she could move things forward for this family. At that point I was enthusiastically engaging with my own preferred ideas, so much so that I was probably 'falling in love' with them (Boscolo et al., 1987) and was ready to privilege them over Annie's and her team's.

Connecting and collaborating

Recognising that pull to take an expert position, I was reminded of the risks of rushing in with an offering and 'knowing too quickly' (Anderson and Goolishian, 1992). The assumption that there are experts who automatically know more about the consultees' dilemma than they know themselves can obscure consultees' knowledge and limit the collective wisdom (Madsen, 2007). Mindful that I might interrupt the opportunity to tap into the rich resources of these experienced practitioners or, worse, risk deskilling the group by imposing my view, I took care to reconnect with the team's skills and abilities and explore with curiosity what Annie wanted from our conversation as well as what the group could offer. Thus I was acting out of a worldview or 'discourse of collaboration' (Madsen, 2007) which honours consultees' wisdom and experience.

Intending to take a collaborative position and *work with* rather than *consult to* the group enabled me to suspend my own views and connect with curiosity to find out what Annie and the group had to offer. By looking around the room, I took time to slow down, step back for a moment and connect with the resources of Annie and her colleagues. Rather than directly advise, *talk to* or *tell her* what to do, I intended to *talk with* her and all the participants in the group. Thus, informed by a discourse of collaboration and using a consultee-centred model of consultation,

I wanted to create space for the expertise of all in the group to come forth; space where we could all generate ideas, offer suggestions and feel supported to contribute solutions to the inquiry (Anderson and Goolishian, 1992). Like Anderson and Burney (1997), we hold that the consultant's expertise and responsibility lie in facilitating the process of dialogical exchange of ideas rather than providing advice or recommendations. To enable this dialogical process, the consultant starts with jointly creating the focus for the consultation with the consultees.

Co-creating a focus for the consultation

> Karen, a family support worker in a children's centre where I (Emma) work, took the opportunity to approach me in the outreach office while the mother with whom she was meeting took a phone call. Explaining she had 'only five minutes to chat' and 'needed a moment to think', Karen asked if she could 'pick [my] brain' about a young child's 'sudden clinginess'. The mother had expressed concerns about whether her daughter's sudden protest at separation from her could be a sign of her being abused by another adult. Karen told me that she had begun to check out the safety of the child and there were no indications the child was at risk; Karen felt 'stuck' with how to continue.
>
> Eager to be helpful, I asked 'Karen, what do you want to take from our brief chat? What do you want to be able to do?' Karen thought about my questions for a moment and said, 'I would like to be able to talk with this mother about other possible reasons for this sudden clinginess'. I went on, 'Can you help me understand what you mean when you say "sudden clinginess"? Is that the mother's word, "clinginess"?' Karen replied that the mother had used the word 'clinginess' when discussing that the child's father was out of the country unexpectedly. I asked, 'Do you have any ideas about the "clinginess"? Have you talked to anybody else about this little girl's "clinginess"?'
>
> I learned that Karen had wondered with another colleague, who knew the family, if the father's sudden absence could be significant. We talked about the ideas of Karen and her colleague, including how a two-year-old may need to both be close to and show independence from a parent and how unsettling separations may be at this age, especially when unexpected. Looking at her watch, Karen said that she had to rejoin the mother and, with a smile, made her way to her meeting, looking more relaxed than when we started.

Despite having limited time, Karen takes advantage of her brief encounter with Emma to ask for ideas to help the mother she is meeting. Emma invites Karen to pause and ponder what she would like to take from their 'brief chat'. Even with the time pressure, Emma takes a collaborative position in the consultation to first clarify what Karen *wants* from their conversation rather assume what Karen *needs*.

We always try to create the focus for our conversation jointly with consultees rather than think that we know what they *need* to talk about. When pressed for time or invited to give snippets of advice on the hop, as Emma was with Karen, we have commonly found ourselves thinking, 'I know what they need' or 'I know what this is all about'. Taking up this sort of *expert position* too quickly, however, has often left us *talking to* or *educating* consultees about issues related more to our own agendas than to theirs, offering ideas that do not fit with their contexts or concerns, giving unsolicited or unwanted advice or deskilling the consultees. By checking what Karen would 'want to take' from their conversation and what she would 'want to be able to do', Emma resisted connecting too quickly with her own preoccupations and the wealth of theories, knowledge and skills related to 'clinginess' that she has developed throughout her professional career. Thus she was able to learn that Karen was looking for 'other possible reasons for this clinginess' that she might share with the mother.

We try to ensure that we use the time to talk about what is relevant and useful to consultees in relation to the request they bring for consultation. Therefore, having agreed on a focus for the conversations with the consultees, the consultants (Emma and Andia) asked questions like, 'What do you want to do?' and 'How will you know you have helped the family? What will they be doing?'

Looking back from the future

To help us identify what consultees want from the consultation, we invite them to anticipate solutions (de Shazer, 1985) right from the beginning of a consultation. We ask them to consider the outcome of the consultation from a time in the future where the 'problem' is not around (Lang and McAdam, 1997), with questions like 'Imagine we are now at the end of this conversation and you say to yourself, "That was very useful. Now I know how to go on". What have we discussed here today? What have we sorted out? What are you able to do? What have we made clearer?' or 'What have we worked out together?' Or, 'Let's say it is a month from now and the dilemma that has brought you here is resolved. What is happening? What are you pleased with?'

These questions invite consultees to project themselves to the end of the session, the future (Penn, 1985), to a time when they have made effective use of the consultation, and to look back on what they have achieved and how they accomplished that. Therefore it is important that we use the present or past tense (rather than the future, hypothetical or subjunctive) to frame the questions ('What *are* you pleased with?' 'What *have* we sorted out?'), implying that the consultation was useful and the preferred change has already happened.

Consultees have often told us that taking time to work out what they want from the consultation and what they want to be different has contributed considerably towards their finding ways to go on. Emma's questions enabled Karen to reflect for a moment, focus on what was important for her to get from the five-minute 'chat' and clearly articulate what she wanted from the conversation with Emma, to help her go on with her client. Our experience is consistent with research that has shown that taking time to define the consultee's problem or dilemma is the most important stage in the consultation process and most predictive of useful outcomes (Bergan and Tombari, 1976).

Not assuming too quickly

In her work as a child psychologist, Emma often hears parents talk about children's 'clinginess', and in our consultation practice with staff, we frequently encounter requests for what to 'do' and how to 'help' people. It is easy to assume what people mean when they utter those seemingly, to us, simple to understand words. Since making meaning is a social process whereby the meaning of our words is constructed through our lived experiences, people may have different experience-formed meanings for the words they use. By asking Karen, 'Is this the mother's word?' when tuning in to 'clinginess', Emma widens the context to explore not only how Karen uses the word but also to check how the mother might describe the problem. By exploring the different experience-formed meanings of the word in this way, she opens space for new meanings to emerge.

Therefore we pay careful attention to the words consultees use and how they make meaning with language to help us clarify the focus of our consultations without assuming too quickly that we understand exactly what they are asking for. In this way, we are also able to resist using professional jargon or personal forms of slang, which can become barriers to effective consultation (Crothers et al., 2008) or interfere with the collaborative problem-solving ability of consultees (Knotek, 2003).

Tuning in to language

Attending to the language that Karen uses to describe her dilemma, Emma tunes in to 'clinginess', a key word Karen has used repeatedly. Using Karen's language, Emma engages with her in a conversation about 'clinginess', asking her to tell her a bit more about it so she can understand the meaning of the word for Karen and for the mother before she moves on to ask Karen if she has 'any ideas about what the "clinginess" is about'. In a similar way, when Annie asked what to 'do' with her client-family, I (Andia) tuned in and picked up 'do' and 'help' as key words for Annie and asked her to help us understand her meanings of these words.

Tuning in to Karen's and Annie's key words helped the consultants join and use the consultees' language, thus listening out for what was important for them and staying with their focus rather than imposing the consultants' own agenda. Key words, which carry important meanings for the person, are often associated with non-verbal expressions like pauses, change of voice tone or pitch, intonation and change in body posture. They seem to call for a response and they touch or move the speaker and/or the listener (Fredman, 2007). I (Andia) noticed Annie's brief pause and then increase in volume and exhalation of breath as she uttered 'do'.

We find we can only begin to understand the meaning of the words of the consultee when we know how to use the words in the particular context of the consultee with whom we are talking (Wittgenstein, 1953). Summarising our understanding of consultees' requests using their key words helps us check whether we are co-creating meanings with the consultees or imposing our own constructions. Thus I went on to summarise what Annie talked about as a way of checking that I had understood her meaning and use of 'do' and 'help' in this context, by asking, 'So Annie, let me see if I have understood what you mean by "do" here. You are looking for ideas to **support the family to attend** appointments with a psychologist? And you want to **support their engagement** with the child mental health service?'

Many consultees have told us that hearing their words fed back or summarised to them has helped them take a different perspective on their situation. Thus our summarising does more than checking out if we have understood; it also places consultees in a position where they can step back and review what they have said as it is repeated back to them. In this way, they can take an observer perspective to themselves and are able to reflect on and evaluate their own, perhaps previously taken-for-granted, talk.

Co-creating meanings with consultees in this way does not mean agreeing or coming up with a common, single meaning. It involves appreciating, including and co-ordinating the meanings with all involved rather than excluding or simplifying meanings. As I used Annie's key words (in bold), I became aware of what I understood and what was less clear to me. I was aware that I was not sure whether I was using the word '**support**' in the way Annie was intending. So I clarified, 'Can you say a bit more about what you mean by "**support**"– to help me understand?' Annie took a while to consider my question and then explained that she wished she could find a 'good way to talk' with the family about engaging with the psychologist that did 'not put pressure' on the family to do what she wanted.

Inviting Annie to 'go inside the word' (Andersen, 1995) 'support' to look at what else was there not only helped me to further coordinate meanings with Annie, but also opened space for new ideas that enabled Annie to go on with the family. Therefore, right from the beginning of our conversations with consultees, we aim to tune into and join their language, summarise what we hear and then check and clarify our understandings with them (Stott and Martin, 2010).

Bringing forth consultees' resources

In collaborative consultation, we set out to build a foundation of competence, connection and hope with consultees from which they can resolve current difficulties. We begin by recognising and consolidating the strengths, abilities and expertise of all people involved as potential resources to the situation.

> Initially, Annie focused on her and the clients' difficulties to help me understand her struggles engaging the family with child mental health services. As I listened I heard that, despite the struggles, she had built a strong and trusting relationship with both the parents and the children in this family; over the past year they had looked forward to seeing her and appreciated her advocating for their housing and nursery placement.

By 'double listening' (White, 2000) to Annie's descriptions of both the problem as well as the progress, I connected with not only the difficulties she was facing, what 'isn't and should be', but also the resources and opportunities to go on, 'what is and could be' (Madsen, 2007:28). We can further bring forth resources to the problem situation by exploring what consultees have done to make progress possible, how they have stopped the situation getting worse and other ideas they have to address the dilemma with questions like 'What have you already tried?' 'What effect has this had?' 'What has been most/least useful?' 'What sense do you make of this?' 'What other ideas do you have?' 'What ideas do you draw from working with similar situations?' We also invite consultees to share examples of what has been going well, which usually opens space for the development of more positive stories about the client and throws light on the competency of the consultees (Martin and Milton, 2005).

> Tuning in to how Annie had made progress with the family enabled me to witness her warm, engaging skills, compassion and problem-solving abilities, thereby connecting the group and me with hope for the family who had the fortune to have Annie in their lives. Aware of Annie's expertise as an experienced health visitor, I invited her to share with the group how she had managed to maintain such an engaging relationship with the family, how she had overcome similar challenges in her work with other families and what ideas she had already in relation to engaging this family with child mental health services. Annie explained that she had been able to accompany the family to initial appointments successfully, but the family missed follow-up meetings once left to attend on their own. She began to wonder if the family felt more comfortable when she was with them and considered asking the family whether and how her presence made a difference.

Generating a repertoire of ideas and practices from multiple perspectives

The problems practitioners bring for consultation affect not only their clients or patients but many other people connected or involved. Therefore consultees bring not only their own perspectives to the consultation, but also the perspectives of many other significant people with whom they and the clients are in a relationship. We approach the views of all members of the wider system as a potential rich resource to the consultation process. Therefore, from the start, we listen out for and note who else in the system might offer a valuable perspective. For example, Emma noted Karen's reference to several people in the system whose views might offer a significant resource, including the mother, the father, the child and Karen's colleague.

We also invite consultees to 'widen the system' by asking 'Who else knows/ is involved/concerned/affected/has or would have a view about this dilemma?' 'What would they say?' It was with this intention that Emma asked Karen, 'Have you talked to anyone else?' and I asked Annie, 'Who else (in addition to the large network of practitioners and family members) would have an opinion on supporting the family's engagement with child mental health services?' We often use a map of the wider system to invite consultees to generate ideas from the perspectives of the different people in the system (see Chapters 2 and 5 for examples of creating and using systemic maps). Annie added her colleagues, her manager and the child mental health clinician to the family map, opening space for me to explore, 'What ideas might your colleagues have for you about how to support the family's engagement with child mental health services?' and 'What would your manager/the child mental health clinician recommend?' 'What would the mother suggest you do?' and 'What would the children say?' In this way, we try to generate a repertoire of ideas and practices that the consultee might use as a resource for the issue or question brought for consultation.

Early on in the consultation process, we clarify with consultees that we will not be looking for 'only one correct' way forward, but rather exploring 'possible alternatives'. For example, we sometimes suggest that we 'start off collecting a selection of ideas to see what options we have, before looking in more detail at what fits the situation you are describing here'. Thus we invite consultees to entertain multiple and even contradictory ways of thinking about or responding to the issue. Annie's colleagues present on that day were also invited to offer their ideas.

As we generate multiple perspectives, we try to avoid an evaluative stance that might suggest that views can be right or wrong, good or bad, by avoiding using dichotomies such as 'agree-disagree'. Instead, we ask questions like, 'Is that the way you think about it?' or 'Who else could offer a different idea?' 'What would others say, like the client's family/community/your team?' Sometimes we invite consultees to extend their repertoire of ideas by looking at an issue through a different lens, such as 'culture' or 'gender', with questions like 'If you look at this from the perspective of your/the client's culture, what different ideas do you have?' We therefore encourage consultees to tap into their many and varied sources of ideas and practices and to 'play' with a variety of different perspectives from the point of view of not only the professionals and agencies involved, but especially the clients, including children, parents and their community. (In Chapter 9, Joel Parker offers further creative ways to invite consultees to entertain and 'play with perspectives' in group consultation.)

> Inviting Annie to contemplate different viewpoints in this way generated a rich resource of ideas. Annie thought her colleague might suggest the family would be more receptive to a home-based intervention; she thought her manager, concerned about the long waiting list for their service, might say that Annie had 'done enough' for this family when there were others waiting 'with greater needs'. Annie's male colleague, Avi, wondered if the father might be concerned about 'being judged' by mental health services and whether the mother was unsure what the child mental health practitioner could offer that was different from Annie's input. My colleague, Miranda, thought the children might 'see this as a day out' with their parents and enjoy the lovely new toys in the child mental health service therapy rooms. Rahana, one of the team's senior health visitors, thought the child mental health service might question whether the parents were 'committed enough' to offer them further appointments. When Annie looked at the situation through the lens of the client's culture, she said that 'the mental health service looks very white suddenly'.

We try to receive the different ideas generated by the consultee in a way that communicates that there are no 'right' or 'wrong' ideas or perspectives that should be privileged over others. Our intention is to explore with consultees which of the ideas shared could be more or less useful to them and the situation at the time. Inviting consultees to juxtapose different perspectives makes it possible for the consultee to make new connections between these different perspectives, thereby creating opportunities for new stories to emerge. As Annie generated a collection of ideas, she began to look at the original issue she presented (how to support the family to attend and how to engage the family with mental health services) in new ways. She began to wonder whether the family wanted further help from services at that moment, what sense the parents were making of 'psychology and mental health' and how the workers at the children's nursery might contribute to support the family's situation.

We welcome the opportunity to have more than one person participate in the consultation, since each group member offers a potentially rich repertoire of ideas to the process. Juxtaposing their different contributions can make more than the sum of the parts possible. In Chapter 7, we address further how we approach and work with the group as a resource to the consultation process.

Capturing, naming and giving back

Above we describe how we ask questions to bring forth the ideas and practices consultees have already considered and undertaken in relation to the issue they bring to consultation. Our intention is to tap into and generate a repertoire of skills, abilities and ideas already familiar to the consultees, close to their experience. Therefore we try to avoid too unusual questions that might distract consultees from their train of thought and we do not introduce theories or concepts that are too complex to make sense of (Anderson and Burney, 1997). Through this process we have witnessed many consultees giving accounts of competencies they have developed in the course of their professional and personal experience which they seem to be performing on a sort of 'autopilot', so that their knowledge and skills have become invisible to their immediate awareness, as a sort of 'unconscious competence' (Bradley, 1997). Often, from years of experience, these abilities have become embedded into their professional identity, as in 'this is what all health visitors do … everyone knows this'.

> As I (Andia) listened to Annie describing what had made it possible for her to engage with the family, I was noting the way she skilfully built the family's trust by her frequent visits, telephone calls, genuine interest and commitment to work with them on goals they had identified, such as securing a nursery place and applying for housing. I also recognised Annie's abilities to calm this mother in her distress, listen attentively as she disclosed the many adversities she and her family had faced and enable her in a validating and non-judgemental way to express painful feelings. Recognising Annie's efforts to comfort and connect this mother with hope for the future, I could see why this family had engaged so well with Annie: they had felt heard and understood; they had found an ally in Annie.

It seemed that Annie was not aware of the skills of listening and being with this mother that she was employing, such as attending to her distress with empathy, genuine interest and a calm and containing manner, thereby enabling her to put very difficult feelings into words so she could slowly work out ways to address her family's problems. Annie was using these skills without conscious intention. Naming consultees' abilities connects them with their competencies, bringing their skills into awareness so they can go on to use them with intention and purpose. Therefore we try to *capture, name and give back* to the consultees the abilities and ideas they have been using. Thus I named the abilities I noticed Annie using: 'You have already been doing so much to enable this mother to engage with you, Annie, like making yourself available for her to talk about difficult experiences; your reliable presence; taking the mother's perspective and validating her distress; working with her on what she wants rather than "putting pressure" (Annie's words) on her by imposing what you think she needs'. A wide smile appeared on Annie's face as she reflected on my 're-presenting' her abilities: 'I hadn't realised I was doing all this before now!' By capturing, naming and 're-presenting' the practices the consultee has described, we invite the consultee to become reflexive to their own practice.

Scaffolding ability from the known and familiar to new possibilities

When I asked Annie for her ideas on how she had managed to maintain such an engaging relationship with the family, I invited her to connect with her established knowledge and well-practised experience. Naming all the skills that she confidently demonstrated through her account of her work with the family, I was tapping into Annie's 'known and familiar' ideas and practices (White, 2007).

> As Annie gave an account of her work with this young mother, I noticed that she was using most of the practices that constitute the 'Listening Visits' approach, a non-directive counselling approach that health visitors routinely employ in their work with postnatally depressed mothers (Holden et al., 1989). I knew that Annie and her colleagues had been trained in the 'Listening Visits' approach. Therefore, I went on, 'Annie, I noticed that you have found some "good ways to talk" (Annie's words) with this mother. For example, you mentioned that you visit this mother at home, you ensure you have some uninterrupted time together, you encourage her to talk about her feelings and you gently encourage her to consider different options rather than give her direct advice'.
>
> As I 're-presented' what Annie had been doing, I noticed she was writing notes of what I was saying. I added, 'I see you are noting down these skills; I have just given back to you what you told me you are already doing. You have done an amazing job here using Listening Visits practices to help this mother and her family feel heard and emotionally contained'.

Once again, I have *captured, named and given back* to Annie the skills she has been using with this mother. This time, I went a step further to connect her practice to an established therapeutic approach (Listening Visits) with which Annie is familiar. Often consultees show surprise and pleasure when we give a name to what they are doing or when we point out that their practice is in line with an established clinical or theoretical approach. Annie remarked, 'I didn't realise that was what I was doing. But, of course, I *am* doing Listening Visits – even if [this mother] doesn't have postnatal depression she is still suffering extreme distress; listening in this way is really helping her. Now I know what I'm doing … I will carry on doing it!'

The purpose of consultation is to enable consultees not only to resolve the particular issue they bring for consultation, but also to work better with similar cases and benefit many other clients in the future (Caplan, 1970). This is particularly relevant in the current climate of limited resources and increasing demands for mental health services. Hence we intend consultation to support the development of consultees' expertise by enabling consultees to use with other clients in their service what they have learned in the consultation. Connecting what Annie was doing with a concept or theory familiar to her (Listening Visits) and with skills she knows how to practice (listening skills) provided her with a useful scaffold to reconceptualise what she was doing in terms of the Listening Approach so that she could go on to use this (Listening) approach and perform these practices *with intention* when she meets similar circumstances in the future.

Contributing our specialist knowledge and experience

Sometimes consultees ask us directly for our 'professional opinion'. For example, in Chapter 2, a head teacher commissioning Victoria Mattison's consultation remarked, 'I can see that you will be helping the teachers to be confident to use what they already know, but we also see you as a specialist in mental health … we also want your specialist knowledge and professional opinion'. In the course of our consultation work over the years, we have noticed that our reticence to offer theories or provide practical suggestions has seemed to constrain our relationships with consultees so that we have sensed some consultees viewing us as 'withholding information' and have wondered if we were frustrating their development (Fredman, 1997:120).

Therefore we accept the invitation to contribute our professional or specialist theories and methods to the pool of ideas and practices we have already been generating with the consultees. One way we contribute our specialist expertise is by connecting consultees' known and familiar knowledge and skills that we have generated together with theories and concepts new to them that we draw from our own specialist trainings or professional expertise.

As I (Andia) listened attentively to Annie and the group sharing their thoughts and enthusiastically bouncing ideas off each other, I noticed that many of their ideas related to the family's experience of connecting with mental health services. Annie had wondered if her presence helped the family 'feel more comfortable with services', while her colleague Avi had offered the suggestion that the father might 'feel worried about being judged' by services. To bring forth more examples of the consultees' knowledge and skills, I wondered aloud, 'I heard some of you talk about the family's feelings towards mental health services. Can you say a bit more about where your ideas come from?' Annie suggested, 'Maybe they had difficult experiences with professionals in the past … perhaps they find it difficult to accept help from others' and Avi added, 'or they may have trust issues'.

The group's ideas connected well with the theory and practice of 'relationship to help' (Reder and Fredman, 1996; Fredman and Rapaport, 2010). I have drawn immense inspiration from this approach to address my own challenges with engaging clients over the years. I could have mentioned 'relationship to help' ideas the first time I heard Annie wondering about 'how to help this family … engage with child mental health services'. However, I would have missed hearing the consultees' own thoughtful and creative ideas and I would have interfered with placing their expert experiences at the heart of the conversation. Instead, I curbed my enthusiasm, asked more questions to bring forth their knowledge and skills and listened with curiosity. When I noted that many of their ideas shared a thread with the 'relationship to help' approach, I saw the opportunity to *capture and name* their knowledge and skills and to connect them with a theory from my specialist knowledge, which might move them to a new level of conceptualisation.

I went on, 'Your ideas about how to help the family feel comfortable and your thoughts about their feelings towards mental health services – how they feel about accepting help, their trust, their worries about being judged, whether they have had difficult experiences with professionals in the past – connect with a concept I find really useful, which we refer to as the clients' "relationship to help". The theory says that, as clients and practitioners, we hold beliefs about giving help and receiving help which we bring to our relationship with each other and which can significantly influence how we connect with each other – and so have an impact on the outcome of referral and treatment. Our beliefs about help are shaped by our previous experiences with taking and giving help from services within our own families, and also our cultural stories about this. According to this approach, we can explore clients' relationship to help by clarifying who proposed this sort of help and whether the clients want this help. We could also ask about previous help and whether this had been useful or not, and why. Exploring relationship to help in this way can help us appreciate how we need to "be with" clients so they feel comfortable and respected by us; it also gives us some ideas about what approach will most engage or fit for the client'.

In this way, as consultants, we are transparent about the ways we have come to form our views. We share relevant aspects of the theories we are using, offering them to open curiosity rather than presenting them as the right way to think or act. We propose new ideas and specialist skills as tentative offerings, creating the opportunity for consultees to challenge or refuse our offerings if they do not seem to fit. Thus we put forward our specialist knowledges 'not as truths but as more or less useful ideas that might contribute' to the repertoire of ideas of the consultees (Fredman, 1997:67).

Exploring fit

Therefore, we invite consultees to evaluate the various contributions according to their own personal and professional contexts and those of the clients with whom they are working. So we may pause with consultees to consider the possible uses of a particular set of knowledges and the opportunities or constraints that might present when working with different clients and in different contexts, with questions like 'What do you think about these ideas?' 'Are they relevant or useful with Ms J?' 'How might you use them?'

> Annie reflected on the racial and class differences between herself and the mother and wondered what sense this mother was making of her 'White professional's' encouragement to attend mental health services. She said she would like to talk with both parents about their views of child mental health services: 'I had an idea about this. Now I have the questions to help me ask about this'.
>
> I went on to explore with Annie and her colleagues, 'Are these ideas useful with other families you work with?' Avi said he had been thinking about two families he was working with where 'I can use this – it is like we have a "framework"'. The group talked about taking time to talk with clients about their experiences of receiving help, what they had found helpful in the past and what not so helpful.

The consultee has the last word

We intend that consultees will leave the consultation session seeing themselves as resourceful and competent in the work they do and in the way they support each other, and that this, in turn, will have an impact on the quality of the care their clients receive. Therefore we try to end consultation sessions by ensuring consultees have the last word and that this connects them with their own skills and abilities. Therefore, towards the end of the consultation, I invited Annie to evaluate the different ideas we had shared and identify those she preferred: 'Annie, what struck you from today's conversation? What were you drawn to?' 'Which ideas do you want to take with you?' 'Do you have other ideas that you would like to add?' Annie said she was surprised at how much she had already done to engage this family. She added, 'Talking about the family's race and culture makes me think we need to pay more attention to this with other families'.

Reflection

We have come to view collaborative consultations as fascinating 'wonderlands' where, from the beginning of our time with consultees, we work to create spaces for mutual exchange and 'wonderment'; where the magic of 'key words' draws us in with curiosity, touches us and moves us to open space for new possibilities to go on. This is a journey that we embark on together; consultants and consultees bring along their personal and professional resources as contributions to the journey, to share with each other as offerings for the taking.

There are often struggles and pulls towards positions of expertise that can challenge the ethos of collaboration. We see it as the responsibility of the consultant to recognise and navigate such pulls, taking time to tune in, not only to the consultees' requests, but also to their skills and abilities, exploring different perspectives and bringing forth consultees' resources. As the Greek poet Cafavy reflects at the end of his legendary poem 'Ithaka', it is the journey and not the destination that makes us 'wealthy with all you have gained on the way' (Savidis, 1992). The journey cannot be rushed.

Guide 3.1 Collaborative consultation: A practice guide

Co-creating a focus with consultees: Clarifying what consultees want

Future focused questions
Invite consultees to project themselves into the future, to a time when they have made effective use of the consultation:

- *Imagine we are now at the end of this conversation and you say to yourself, 'That was really useful. I got something useful from that ... Now I know how to go on ...'.*
- *Or 'Let's say it is a month from now and the dilemma that has brought you here is resolved'.*

Then invite consultees to look back from this future using present or past tense questions, implying that the consultation has been effective:

- *What have we discussed here today ... sorted out ... made clearer ... worked out together?*
- *What are you able to do ... understand now?*
- *How do you know you have helped [the client]? What are they doing now?*

Listening for meaning, intentions, hopes and dreams – not facts

Tune in to language
- Note key words consultees use which may carry important meanings.
- Listen for resources in the system rather than plan solutions.
- Listen for achievements and abilities rather than for problems.
- Listen for new connections the consultant is making/learning.

Summarising to clarify and check meanings/ understandings

- Use consultees' key words and weave them through the conversation.
- Fill in gaps tentatively to check whether we are co-creating meanings with the consultees rather than imposing our own constructions.

Bringing forth consultees' solutions, ideas and abilities as potential resources

- *What have you tried?*
- *What has worked well?*
- *What ideas do you draw from working in similar situations?*

Generating a repertoire of ideas and practices from multiple perspectives

Invite consultees to entertain multiple and even contradictory ways of thinking about or responding to the issue:

- *We are collecting a selection of ideas to see what options we have, before looking in more detail at what fits the situation you are describing here.*

Invite consultees to widen the system:

- *Who else is involved/concerned/significant/has a view on this?*
- *What ideas might they have for you about …? What would they suggest?*

Receive the different ideas generated by the consultee in a way that communicates that there are no 'right' or 'wrong' ideas or perspectives that should be privileged over others:

- *Is that the way you think about it?*
- *Who else could offer a different idea?*
- *What would others say, such as the client's family/community/your team?*

Extend the repertoire of ideas by looking at an issue through a different lens such as 'culture' or 'gender':

- *If you look at this from the perspective of your/the client's culture, what different ideas do you have?*

Capturing, naming and giving back

Notice and name the abilities and ideas consultees have been using:

- *You have already been doing so much to … like ….*

Connect the consultees' named competent practice with concepts/practices with which the consultees are familiar.

Contributing specialist knowledge and experience

Connect consultees' known and familiar knowledge and skills we have generated together with theories and concepts we draw from our specialist knowledge to move them to a new level of conceptualisation:

- *Your ideas about ... connect with a concept I find really useful which we refer to as ... The theory says that ....*

Exploring fit

Explore with consultees which of the ideas generated in the consultation could be more or less useful to them, clients and the situation they bring for consultation:

- *What do you think about these ideas?*
- *Are they relevant or useful with Ms J?*
- *How might you use them?*

Support the development of consultees' expertise

Invite consultees to connect what they have taken from the consultation to their practice with other clients in their service:

- *What struck you from today's conversation? What were you drawn to?*
- *Which ideas do you want to take with you?*
- *Do you have other ideas that you would like to add?*
- *(How) are these ideas useful for other clients you work with?*

References

Andersen, T. (1995) Reflecting processes; acts of informing and forming: You can borrow my eyes, but you must not take them away from me! In S. Friedman (ed.) *The Reflecting Team in Action. Collaborative Practice in Family Therapy.* New York: Guilford.

Anderson, H. and Burney, J.P. (1997) Collaborative inquiry: A postmodern approach to organizational consultation. *Human Systems: The Journal of Systemic Consultation and Management,* 7, 177–188.

Anderson, H. and Goolishian, H. (1992) The client is the expert: A not-knowing approach to therapy. In S. McNamee and K.J. Gergen (eds.) *Constructing Therapy: Social Construction and the Therapeutic Process.* London: Sage.

Bergan, J.R. and Tombari, M.L. (1976) Consultant skill and efficiency and the implementation and outcomes of consultation. *Journal of School Psychology,* 14, 3–14.

Boscolo, L., Cecchin, G., Hoffman, L. and Penn, P. (1987) *Milan Systemic Family Therapy: Conversations in Theory and Practice.* New York: Basic Books.

Bradley, F. (1997) From unconscious incompetence to unconscious competence. *Adults Learn*, *9* (2), 20–21.

Caplan, G. (1970) *Theory and Practice of Mental Health Consultation*. New York: Basic Books.

Cavafy, C.P. (1992) Ithaka (trans. from Greek by E. Keeley and P. Sherrard). In G. Savidis (ed.) *Collected Poems*. Revised Edition. Princeton: Princeton University Press.

Crothers, L.M., Hughes, T.L. and Morine, K.L. (2008) *Theory and Cases in School-Based Consultation*. New York: Routledge.

de Shazer, S. (1985) *Keys to Solution in Brief Therapy*. London: W. W. Norton and Company.

Fredman, G. (1997) *Death Talk: Conversations With Children and Families*. London: Karnac.

Fredman, G. (2007) Preparing our selves for the therapeutic relationship: Revisiting 'hypothesizing revisited'. *Human Systems: The Journal of Systemic Consultation and Management*, *18*, 44–59.

Fredman, G. and Rapaport, P. (2010) How do we begin? Working with older people and their significant systems. In G. Fredman, E. Anderson and J. Stott (eds.) *Being With Older People: A Systemic Approach*. London: Karnac.

Holden, J.M., Sagovsky, R. and Cox, J.L. (1989) Counselling in a general practice setting: Controlled study of health visitor intervention in treatment of postnatal depression. *British Medical Journal*, *298*, 223–226.

Knotek, S.E. (2003) Making sense of jargon during consultation: Understanding consultees' social language to effect change in student study teams. *Journal of Educational and Psychological Consultation*, *14* (2), 181–207.

Lang, P. and McAdam, E. (1997) Narrative-ating: Future dreams in present living. *Human Systems: The Journal of Systemic Consultation and Management*, *8* (1), 3–13.

Madsen, W.C. (2006) Teaching across discourses to sustain collaborative clinical practice. *Journal of Systemic Therapies*, *25* (4), 44–58.

Madsen, W.C. (2007) *Collaborative Therapy with Multi-Stressed Families*, London: Guildford Press.

Martin, E. and Milton, A. (2005) Working systemically with staff working in residential homes. *Context: The Magazine for Family Therapy and Systemic Practice: Grey Matters: Ageing in the Family*, *77*, 37–39.

Penn, P. (1985) Feed-forward: Future questions, future maps. *Family Process*, *24*, 299–310.

Reder, P. and Fredman, G. (1996) The relationship to help: Interacting beliefs about the treatment process. *Clinical Child Psychology and Psychiatry*, *1*, 457–467.

Stott, J. and Martin, E. (2010) Creating contexts for talking and listening where older people feel comfortable and respected. In G. Fredman, E. Anderson, and J. Stott (eds.) *Being with Older People: A Systemic Approach*. London: Karnac.

White, M. (2000) Re-engaging with history: The absent but implicit. *Reflections on Narrative Practice: Essays and Interviews*. Adelaide, Australia: Dulwich Centre Publications.

White, M. (2007) *Maps of Narrative Practice*. New York: Norton.

Wittgenstein, L. (1953) *Philosophical Investigations*. Oxford: Blackwell.

Chapter 4

An appreciative approach to consultation

Bringing forth the best in people

Nicola Webb and Glenda Fredman

The Oxford English dictionary's first definition of 'appreciate' is 'recognise the full worth of', and synonyms include 'value, respect, prize, cherish, treasure, admire' (Oxford English Dictionary, 2016). Appreciation, that includes valuing, respecting and cherishing what people bring to their work, is integral to the collaborative approach to consultation we describe in this book, which is informed by collaborative systemic therapy approaches like Anderson (1997) and Madsen (2007). Our approach to appreciative consultation that we describe in this chapter is further guided by the principles and practices of Appreciative Inquiry (Cooperrider and Whitney, 2005), where 'appreciative brings forth a sense of respect, actively valuing what people-in-relationship do to create a "good life". It brings forth a sense of curiosity and fascination' (McAdam and Lang, 2009:1).

Appreciative Inquiry (AI)

In the late 1980s, David Cooperrider and Suresh Srivastva (1987) developed Appreciative Inquiry (AI), a strengths-based approach to positive change that has been used successfully in communities and organisations all around the world. Central to their approach is asking questions and inviting people to envision the future in ways that build on the existing strengths of people or the situation and that foster positive relationships. AI is seen as an alternative to 'problem solving', aiming to develop or build on what works rather than trying to fix what does not work. It involves appreciating, valuing and inquiring into 'the best of what is' in order to imagine and envision 'what might be', followed by collaborative conversations to design desired futures, 'what should be', that are grounded in what people are already doing well (Bushe, 2013).

In our consultation practice we draw on the following AI principles:

- What we focus on becomes our reality.
- People and organisations move in the direction of the questions they ask.
- The language we use creates our reality: 'words create worlds' (Whitney and Trosten-Bloom, 2010:50).
- There is always something that works (well) – that 'gives life'.

- People learn faster from looking at what they do well, as the skills needed are already there.
- What we do today is guided by our image of the future: our images of the future become our future.
- Positive affect (such as hope, excitement, inspiration and joy) and collaborative relationships increase creativity and openness to new ideas.

Therefore, as consultants, we try to tune in with appreciative ears and eyes, intentionally 'seeking to discover people's ... unique gifts, strengths, and qualities, actively searching and recognising people for their contributions and achievements' (Cooperrider, 2001:12) and selectively highlighting 'life-giving forces' to people and the organisation, which may be abilities, ideas, beliefs or values.

> Eileen, the head of the children's centre where I (Nicola) work half a day a week, asked me to meet with the centre's three child-care workers for a series of consultations. She was worried about 'recent concerns expressed by parents' that the centre's child-care staff were 'lacking skills to help their children to settle in crèche'. She was also concerned that staff were 'rather de-motivated and burnt out'. Eileen wanted to 'sort this problem out quickly'.

I (Nicola) found myself reflecting on what I knew of these workers and wondering about the effect on their morale of the context in which they worked. They were three women of Bangladeshi, Somali and Polish origin, working with children from birth to five years and their families in a children's centre in a socially and economically deprived part of the borough. The families using the centre came from a range of backgrounds; many faced poverty and overcrowded accommodation, had little social support and accessed few services (especially statutory services). I was aware that, in general, child-care staff are low-paid and usually have minimal time to reflect on their practice, and that little attention is given to what supports and sustains them in their work. With demands on services to become more 'efficient', staff are often expected to do more work in less time and have fewer opportunities to feel valued, respected and cherished. Feeling undervalued in this way leaves many of the staff doubting their own competence to do their work.

When consultees are feeling devalued or demoralised in this way, we find that intentionally taking an appreciative approach to consultation, which focuses on what works well and engages everyone in collaborative conversation, can invite hope and increase creativity and openness to new ideas. However, I (Nicola) was mindful that Eileen was inviting me to 'sort [a] problem out'. Wanting to honour her request and connect with her meanings, therefore, I asked Eileen to 'help me understand what you mean by "demotivated" and "burnt out". Can you give me an example?' Eileen responded, 'I think they feel undervalued ... they seem lacking in energy and creativity'.

What we focus on becomes our reality

'Tuning in to [Eileen's] language' (Papadopoulou and Fredman, Chapter 3), I (Nicola) was struck by her words 'parents' concern', 'lacking skills', 'feel under-valued' and 'lacking energy and creativity'. Our intention, as consultants, is to draw attention to what 'gives life' to people's work and to their organisation and to diminish problems. Focusing on problems, on the other hand, 'orients our looking' (Shotter, 2010) towards what is wrong or missing so that we tend to see everything through this problem frame and risk emphasising and amplifying the unwanted problem (Hammond, 1998). Therefore I (Nicola) took care to adopt an appreciative attitude, exploring with curiosity what was 'giving life' ('energy and creativity' in Eileen's words) to the children's centre and to the work of these child-care workers.

People and organisations move in the direction of the questions they ask

The moment we inquire into something, our question orients the looking of the person or group. Therefore, we aim to ask questions that draw attention to consultees' abilities and the values which underpin these, and that invite sto-ries of the best of what is, and ask consultees to contemplate positive futures. Acknowledging that inquiring is an intervention (Whitney and Trosten-Bloom, 2010) and that questions are never neutral, they are 'fateful' (Bushe, 2007:4), we therefore ask ourselves 'What effect is my question having? Is it helping to gener-ate conversations about the good, the better, and the possible?' rather than 'Is my question leading to right or wrong answers?'

The language we use creates our reality

Mindful that inviting Eileen to go into detail regarding the 'concerns' about the workers, what they are 'lacking' and the 'burn out' could make these problems the only reality, I (Nicola) took care to choose language that could bring forth her preferred realities and generate hope. Aware that 'there are multiple realities' and 'we can create reality in the moment' (Hammond, 1998), I went on to clarify with Eileen what topic she wanted us to focus on in the consultation. 'The words and topics chosen for inquiry have an impact far beyond just the words themselves. They invoke sentiments, understandings and worlds of meaning' (Bushe, 2013:2). Therefore, we put a lot of effort into using words that point to, enliven and inspire the best in people.

Defining and clarifying the topic for consultation

The first step in the AI process is selecting topics that will become the focus of the consultation. We therefore invite the people commissioning the consultation and the consultees to choose affirmative topics that represent what people really want to develop or learn more about and that will likely evoke conversations about their desired future and create enthusiasm and inspiration (Whitney and Trosten-Bloom, 2010). Since people tend to grow in the directions about which they inquire, affirmative topic choices should encourage consultees to identify outcomes they want to see grow and flourish in their practice and services.

> Therefore I (Nicola) asked the manager, Eileen, who was commissioning this consultation, 'What topic can we focus on in these consultations so this group of staff can take steps in the direction you want to see your centre go?' She responded immediately, 'Working excellently with parents' and went on to tell me about a 'current drive' by the commissioners of services to evaluate children's centres on 'how well we work with parents'. When I asked, 'What does "working excellently with parents" look like?', Eileen explained, 'I would really like to hear parents expressing satisfaction with [the child-care workers'] settling skills', which opened space for Eileen and me to elaborate on a large sheet of paper a positive focus for this consultation, so that I could go on to share in our first meeting with the child-care workers this topic for consultation ('Working excellently with parents: settling children').

The positive, future oriented question, *'What can we focus on so staff can take steps in the direction you want to see your centre go?'* invited the manager to imagine her preferred future for her service. Using *her* 'life giving' language, I further explored: 'Would you also like to see their *"energy and creativity"* grow? You mentioned this as a sort of antidote to the *"burn out"* you described?' Eileen chose to place 'energy' and 'creativity' at the base of her topic map 'as they are the bedrock of all we do here'.

Planning for appreciative consultation

Having the support of consultees' managers and leaders is essential to the efficacy of an appreciative approach. Therefore I (Nicola) took time to prepare the ground for this consultation with Eileen, the service manager, paying careful attention to the process of setting up, contracting for consultation and explaining how we would work. (See Chapter 2 for guidelines.)

> I clarified that I would start by sharing with the child-care workers Eileen's topic for the consultation ('working excellently with parents: settling children') and then invite them to add their own focus. I added, 'I am sure there are already areas of excellence in your service ... So as a way of getting to know the child-care workers I will begin with looking at what works well, gathering examples so we can build on what they are already doing'. Eileen breathed out as if expressing relief, saying, 'I really like this ... that is a great way to bolster their morale ... they do some really good work ... I know they are dedicated'. We agreed that Eileen would tell the

child-care workers that she had asked for the consultation to 'support their work' and 'develop excellent work with children' so the 'parents are very satisfied' with the centre. We also agreed that I would invite the child-care worker-consultees to evaluate the consultation after each session. (See Chapter 6 for guidelines on evaluating consultation.)

Following my conversation with Eileen, I developed a plan for my first meeting with the three child-care workers, which included sharing Eileen's intentions and hopes for the consultation; contracting how we would work together; negotiating that I would meet with the three of them for the first session, where we would agree on what to feed back to Eileen and would keep reviewing how we keep her involved; clarifying what the consultees wanted to get from our consultations; and then co-creating a positive focus that included their manager's and their own hopes for the work.

Co-creating a positive focus for consultation with consultees

I (Nicola) arrived at the children's centre at nine o'clock on a bright spring morning and was greeted by Shahara, Lena and Amaal, who had put the kettle on and assembled four comfortable chairs in a circle ready for us to begin. 'We have so been looking forward to this time', said Lena. 'What have you been most looking forward to?' I asked curiously. 'Having some time to stop and think about what we do. Our job is tough ... sometimes it feels too much', said Shahara. The other two nodded in agreement. 'Parents have been complaining that we don't know how to settle their children in our crèche', added Amaal. 'Maybe they think we're not up to it and are not very professional', followed Lena. I reflected, 'So you're looking forward to stopping and thinking about what you do ... when your jobs are so tough?'

Amaal and Lena had immediately alerted me to 'problems' in their practice: 'it feels too much', 'parents complaining', 'we're not up to it', perhaps believing that their manager had wanted me to help them analyse and fix these problems. I also noted these women were 'looking forward' to using our time together to enable something different to happen. Therefore, guided by the principle that 'an optimistic consultant creates possibilities; a pessimistic consultant creates chronic difficulties and intractable problems for the people with whom he is working' (Lang, 2003), I resisted the pull to connect with the problem discussion and stayed with my intention to co-create a positive, future focus for our work together. Intending to connect the consultees with their manager's positive image of the future, therefore, I went on, 'Eileen has a vision of the future in which you all feel "*energised*" and you are "*working excellently with parents*". She has proposed one topic for us to work with: "*settling children*" in this centre. How does this fit with how you want to use our time together?' Lena responded quickly, 'That sounds good – we can do with more energy'. When I asked, 'What do you want to add to Eileen's suggestion? Anything else you would like to focus on to boost this energy or to develop the excellence of your children's centre?' Amaal suggested

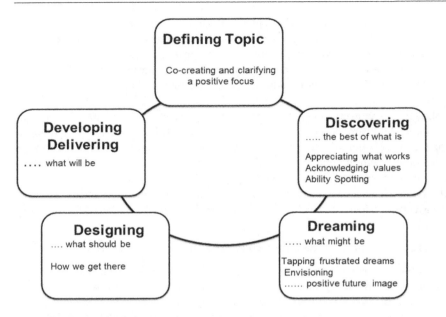

Figure 4.1   Appreciative Consultation Cycle

tentatively, 'We need more skills for settling the children' and Lena and Shahara nodded. (See Chapter 3 for detailed discussion on co-creating a focus for consultation with consultees.)

Identifying, naming and *defining* the topic for consultation in terms of what people want to see happen sets the stage for the consultant to take the consultees through the next steps of the appreciative consultation process that involves *discovering* the best in their practice; inviting them to *dream* and envision their preferred future; *designing* a plan of how to get to where they want to be; and inviting them to prepare for how they will *develop*, *deliver* and sustain their preferred practice (Cooperrider and Whitney, 2005) (Figure 4.1).[1]

Discovering the best of what is

Having co-created a positive focus for the consultation, we go on to identify and appreciate 'the best of what is' already happening by interviewing consultees on their own 'best of' experience, peak times or moments of excellence, where they have experienced their work or their service as most alive and effective.

Appreciation 'draws our eyes towards life-giving elements ... excites our curiosity, generates passion and provides inspiration to the envisioning mind' (McAdam and Mirza, 2009:183). Therefore, in the *Discovery* phase of appreciative consultation, we aim to generate stories, images and maps of the best of consultees' existing practice by inquiring into 'what gives life' (what inspires) and the important values connected (what is precious) as well as what works well, including the strengths and abilities involved. Our intention is to draw out rich descriptions of what works, exceptions, successes and the most vital or alive moments, as well as what consultees value and really care about. Inviting consultees to reflect on what has made the high points possible draws their attention away from analysing deficits towards focusing on developments and achievements. Highlighting what works can connect the positive qualities in people and their organisation in ways that heighten energy and vision for change; hope grows and abilities are enriched. Thus inquiring into 'the best of what is' opens space for people to imagine 'what might be' in order to create new, generative ideas or images that point to and provoke change. Creative possibilities frequently emerge from stories that are grounded in performance at its best.

Valuing everyday practice

Since traditional approaches to consultation tend to examine the problem in detail, arrive at a formulation and then prescribe a solution, consultees have often found invitations to describe the *best* of their practice or to *appreciate* their qualities as too unusual. We commonly encounter a reticence to congratulate oneself (for fear of 'boasting') or even to be 'too positive' towards the other; one consultee expressed concerns that appreciative talk would be 'white-washing all that is wrong and not dealing with it'. To warm the context for AI, therefore, we often begin consultation with a more open and curious question like 'what do you do in your daily practice?'

> Thus I (Nicola) went on, 'I know you work with parents and children in so many different ways. To help me understand and learn more about your work, can we capture all you do with parents here on this paper? What are the contexts in which you come into contact with parents and children in your work?' With no further prompting, the group called out, 'Parents popping into the centre asking for information or help with something ... cook and eat sessions... stay and plays ... crèches for parenting groups ... toy libraries ... crèches for English language classes'. As they were calling out, I repeated their phrases, at the same time capturing their words on the paper (Figure 4.2). An atmosphere of excitement enveloped the room. Amaal and Shahara nodded and smiled as Lena laughed, 'We never realised we do so much!'
>
> I continued, 'What do the parents most appreciate of what you offer?' Lena responded first with 'giving their children time and space to do things they can't do at home' and the others added more offerings such as 'noticing their child's individual strengths and interests ... giving ideas to help their child develop ... sharing news from the day in crèche ... giving examples of how we have helped their child'. As they called out enthusiastically, I added their contributions to the 'Working with Parents and Children' map we had started to generate.

As we filled the paper, it seemed that the workers were growing taller in their seats. Bringing forth appreciative perspectives from others, exploring 'who appreciates what' with questions like, 'What do the parents appreciate most about what you

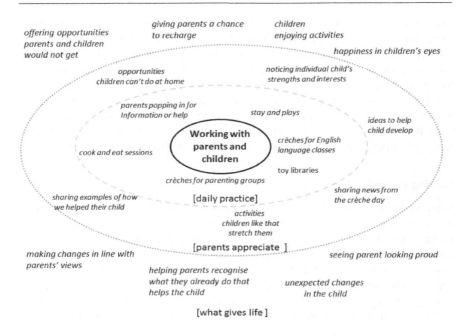

giving parents a chance to recharge

children enjoying activities

offering opportunities parents and children would not get

happiness in children's eyes

opportunities children can't do at home

noticing individual child's strengths and interests

parents popping in for information or help

stay and plays

ideas to help child develop

Working with parents and children

crèches for English language classes

cook and eat sessions

toy libraries

crèches for parenting groups

[daily practice]

sharing examples of how we helped their child

sharing news from the crèche day

activities children like that stretch them

[parents appreciate]

making changes in line with parents' views

seeing parent looking proud

helping parents recognise what they already do that helps the child

unexpected changes in the child

[what gives life]

Figure 4.2   Mapping the best of what is

offer?' invites consultees to further value themselves through the eyes of others. We have found that inviting consultees to begin with appreciating their usual daily practice creates an opportunity for grounding themselves in what they know and what is familiar, their everyday activity, before we go on to explore new possibilities. Consultees have frequently told us how 'affirmed' and 'validated' they have felt by 'having someone interested in what we do'. Focusing on the 'small and the ordinary' (Weingarten, 1998) in this way enables us to draw attention to previously unnoticed skills and abilities, thereby offering entry points to stories of possibility and hope.

Bringing forth what gives life

Guided by the AI principle that 'positive affect increases creativity and openness to new ideas', we try to bring forth what inspires, energises and gives hope to consultees. Questions like 'What do you appreciate in your work?' 'What inspires you?' and 'What is precious – that you would not want to give up or lose?' can bring forth accounts of what gives life to people's work and their service as well as giving us, as consultants, a sense of some of the values important to the culture of their organisation.

> When I (Nicola) asked the child-care workers, 'What aspects of your work with parents get you looking forward to the day at work?', Lena was the first to respond with, 'Giving parents a chance to recharge' and 'Seeing the happiness in the children's eyes when they are enjoying the activities we prepare'. The question 'What keeps you going in this work

when things are really tough?' provided another entry point to what was giving life to the child-care workers' work, including 'seeing a parent looking proud when we point out what they do to help their child' and 'seeing unexpected changes in the children – that's a gift'. I added their rich examples of what gave life to their work onto the map we were creating of 'the best of' their practice (Figure 4.2).

Exploring the values and commitments that connect with what consultees appreciate about their work can give us, as consultants, a deeper appreciation of what sustains the consultees when their work is difficult. Therefore I invited the consultees each to select from the map two statements of 'what inspires you, gives you energy to keep going' and then asked, 'Why is it important to you to "give parents a chance to recharge" / "offer opportunities parents and children would not get"?' This line of inquiry brought forth a lively energy from the consultees as, assertively, they shared their strong personal, social and political commitments that included, 'I want to pass on learning opportunities I have been given to benefit others who have not had the opportunity' and 'This is a good use of public money'.

Towards the end of this first consultation, we agreed that I would share the maps we had created (Figure 4.2) with Eileen, the manager. When I asked the consultees, 'What is one thing that has particularly stood out for you from our talking together today – that you want to hold onto?' I heard, 'We do a lot in our job... I feel lucky to have this work ... We do an important job ... We have a lot in common'.

Positive talk creates good emotions and, reflexively, good emotions can facilitate progress. Through affirming and appreciating practices, the process of AI generates new possibilities for cooperation and creates opportunities for sharing commitments and dreams. Thus Amaal, Lena and Shahara show us how, through valuing their everyday activity and generating descriptions of what gives life to their work, their 'relationships grow and feel warmer and safer. They grow deeper and more cooperative' (McAdam and Lang, 2009:4).

Appreciating what works

Guided by the AI principle that 'there is always something that works: we can learn from and build on successes', we join consultees on a journey of *discovery* of what is working well. This usually involves interviewing consultees about a piece of work where there was a good outcome, a moment or episode where they feel proud, pleased or satisfied with what happened in order to bring forth stories of competence in relation to the topic they have identified as the focus for the consultation. Therefore, at the end of our first session, intending to build on the cooperative spirit, sense of optimism and shared commitments in the group, I (Nicola) suggested we use our next consultation to 'focus on helping parents with settling their children when leaving them in crèche'. As the consultees welcomed this proposal, I left them with a task:

'To help us prepare for our next meeting, let's look at what you are already doing with settling that works well. So, between now and next time we meet, notice times when the settling goes well, when you are pleased with how you have managed a situation or when a parent is satisfied with what you have offered. Pay attention to

- What happened;
- Who else was there;
- What and who made the best possible.

Bring back stories of your best examples to share with us here so we can look at what works and build on what is already happening that is working well'.

Implicit in the communication, 'look at what you are already doing … that works well … when a parent is satisfied with what you have offered' is the message that Nicola has no doubt that the child-care workers were already doing good work. Our intention is to study in detail examples of what makes them their best so we can enable consultees to take these abilities forward to use with intention in their future practice.

Appreciative interviewing to bring forth ability stories

To invite consultees to share their 'exceptional' stories to bring forth the best in their practice, we usually begin with an open question like 'Tell me about a time when you were successfully involved in [helping a parent to settle their child in the crèche]' or 'Describe a moment when things were not going well, and [settling] turned out much better than you expected'. If consultees are unable to find an example of what worked well, we suggest they find an instance 'when you participated in preventing the situation from getting worse'.

We go on to call forth a detailed account of the 'best' outcome, with questions like

- What happened to make the best possible? What else did you do? Tell me more about what you did to get the best from the situation?
- Who or what gave you the idea to do this? Who else was involved? Who else noticed and supported what you did? What did they notice? What did they do?

Shahara, Amaal and Lena welcomed me (Nicola) warmly to our second consultation. Amaal began with her story of settling two-year-old Ellie: 'When I asked if she had ever left Ellie before, the mother said, "No, but she'll be fine". I was going to ask her, "What do you imagine she might feel?" but I was worried the mother might think I was criticising her – like I was saying she doesn't think how her child feels – or something like that. So I just asked, "What helps Ellie to settle at home? What helps comfort Ellie? What does she like playing with?"' Amaal went on, 'Ellie started to cry when her mother was leaving. I was so pleased I had asked what comforted her because that's how I learned that Ellie and her grandma do "hug-a-bug" when Ellie is fretful. So I just held Ellie and said, "We're doing hug-a-bug and it's going to be ok". And her mother smiled and she seemed to be more relaxed. Ellie was clinging to me and she was crying but she was also ok'. Amaal appreciated Shahara's support with settling Ellie, 'Without me asking, Shahara went off to get the toys the mother said were Ellie's favourites ... And then she took care of all the other children we already knew so I could concentrate on Ellie, and comfort and distract her after her mum left'.

We interview each consultee to bring forth stories from which we can generate examples of what enables the best outcomes. As we interview, we listen carefully with appreciative ears, tuning in to abilities that contribute to the successes.

Ability spotting

We interview in fine detail, inviting consultees to recall the episode frame-by-frame as if replaying a video slowly. We spot the abilities, skills and values they demonstrate, unpacking and exploring these to see what other abilities are involved. We note these abilities on Post-it notes to give to the consultee we are interviewing after the interview. Having spotted abilities, we amplify times when the skill is being used, bringing it into view. Through this interviewing process, the consultees discover that they already have skills to address the issue they have brought for consultation. Realising they have these skills creates a confidence to use the abilities and skills more frequently and in other contexts. Thus, these never-before-noticed abilities can become part of the new identity of the person (McAdam and Lang, 2009).

When we are working with more than one consultee, we position the other consultees present as 'Ability Spotters'. We invite them to listen to the interview and write on Post-it notes all the abilities, skills, attitudes, actions or relationships that made the best possible in their colleague's story. (See Chapter 7 for more examples of how we use the group as a resource to the consultation process.) Our intention is to identify abilities, draw attention to them and name them so that they can become part of the consultees' identity.

At the end of each 'interview' with me (Nicola), the two listening workers gave the Post-it notes to the storytelling consultee. Lena and Shahara spotted many abilities Amaal had demonstrated through her story, including '... respecting the parent ... putting herself in the mother's shoes ... kindness ... sensitivity ... awareness that parents can be sensitive to criticism ... using knowledge of child development'.

Collecting, clustering and mapping abilities

Once we have witnessed key stories that demonstrate the best of consultees' practice, we collect all the abilities we have discovered, connecting them together into wider themes. We invite consultees to stick all their Post-its onto a large sheet of paper and to cluster the abilities according to themes which may include resources, capabilities, relationships, partnerships and positive hopes. Sometimes we offer to start with an example, but it is important that the consultees identify the themes in their own words, not the consultant's.

> Once we had heard all three stories, I asked the consultees, 'What enabled the successes? Let's collect all your abilities ... We can stick them on one page so we can pool all your skills and see what we have here'. Lena asked cautiously, 'Can we get these back at the end – I'd like to hold on to mine – to remind myself of what I can do when I forget'. Spontaneously, they started writing their names on the back of each Post-it before they added it to the large sheet of paper.
>
> Amaal, Shahara and Lena enjoyed moving the Post-its around into clusters and together settled on six themes[2]: 'Talking and listening with kindness, sensitivity and respect';'Drawing on our training in child development and using questions to help parents get into the shoes of the child'; 'Recognising parents have expertise about what works with their child'; 'Showing empathy for parents and recognition it can be hard to separate'; 'Showing curiosity about parents' concerns about separating without judging'; and 'Working with colleagues as a team and supporting each other'.

By bringing together into themes all consultees' abilities that made the successes possible, we could move from individual to team abilities. Through clustering the abilities to create a shared visual map, a consensus began to emerge whereby the consultees identified the abilities they valued and aspired to; individual appreciation became collective appreciation and individual vision became collaborative or shared vision. Thus discovering the best of what is by appreciating what works, ability spotting and collecting and clustering and mapping the abilities orients the consultees' looking towards the future, bringing into view images of their dreams.

Dreaming: Stories of what might be

Once consultees *discover* their abilities, their *existing resources*, the next step is to imagine and envision what their practice might look like if they carry forward their current strengths, 'what might be' the implication of their existing resources for their future practice. Guided by the principle, 'our positive images of the future lead our positive actions' (Cooperrider and Whitney, 2005:52), therefore, we invite consultees to develop a bold vision of their preferred future that embodies their hopes and dreams by imagining their practice or service at its best.

Tapping into frustrated dreams

During the *dreaming* phase, participants are encouraged to talk about (and dream about) not what is, but what might be even better in their practice and their service. However, we frequently encounter times when consultees are so overwhelmed by problems in the present they find it difficult to step away and accept our invitation to journey to the future to dream. We have found that 'what we complain about most has within it what we value most and therefore what we most want' (Anderson, 2017). Therefore, as consultants, we always acknowledge the problems consultees identify, to witness their experience and appreciate their values. The problems they describe also offer opportunities for dreaming.

Peter Lang coined the phrase 'every problem is a frustrated dream' (McAdam and Lang, 2009:25) and encourages us to work with the dream since the dream comes first; that is why there is a problem: 'it is usually because we would like life to be different, or it would not be a problem' (McAdam and Lang, 2009:10). Therefore, we pay careful attention to consultees' descriptions of the problem, listening out for the frustrated dreams. We tune in to words that have positive visual images or point to hope or possibility and use these words in subsequent questioning. For example, when the manager named 'demotivated ... undervalued ... lacking skills ... lacking energy', Nicola inquired about what 'inspired' the child-care workers and helped them feel 'valued'; she heard that the manager and the workers wanted to develop 'skills' and asked whether the manager 'would like to see their energy and creativity grow'. When the child-care workers worried 'we're not up to it' and 'parents are complaining', Nicola connected their concerns to their dreams and their manager's vision for 'working excellently with parents'. Thus approaching problems as frustrated dreams offers another entry point into future dreaming conversations.

Envisioning positive images towards positive action

Future questions enable people to construct possible future worlds (Boscolo and Bertrando, 1996); imagining 'can awaken people's longings and stimulate recollection of forgotten hopes and dreams' (Whitney and Trosten-Bloom, 2010:185), and stories of the future create the present more than stories of the past (McAdam and Lang, 2009). Therefore we ask 'imagine' or 'future dreaming' questions like:

- Imagine parents are regularly complimenting your centre about the way staff help children into crèches and are nominating it to the commissioner as the best in the borough for settling children into crèches. What is happening? What are parents saying? What is your manager's response? What else do you notice?

We purposefully frame these questions in the present tense to invite consultees to experience the future state as present (as described in Chapter 3) so they can begin to live the dream as if it were happening now. We explore in great detail to bring the vision into view. To stretch the imaginations of consultees, we may invite them to imagine other people's perspectives with questions like 'What are your colleagues saying about this?' 'What is your manager pleased with?' Sometimes we invite consultees to draw on others' ideas or practices they admire, aspire to or might want to incorporate into their own practice.

'Dream talk allows the imagination to create the seemingly impossible and in this it gives freedom ... creates hope and a close connection to life-giving energy' (McAdam and Lang, 2009:9). Inviting the child-care workers to dream in this way was invigorating and generated many bold images of their preferred future practice and service, including:

> 'children are thriving ... parents like the way we work alongside them ... we show we are professional ... parents are confident they are helping their children to develop as well as possible ... parents are really happy with the way we help to settle their children in crèche ... parents telling us they have new ideas about what to do with their children at home ... we feel much more satisfaction with our work ... we are full of energy ... Eileen (manager) is so proud of our centre'.

Designing how we get there

Visualising a future in which they are drawing on existing abilities gives consultees a glimpse of how the future could be and how they might get there. Thus, the purpose of dreaming 'what might be' is for consultees to take their existing resources that we have collected into their future so they can imagine what they can create with it. We can then go on to craft 'design statements' or 'possibility statements' (Mohr et al., 2003; Watkins et al., 2011) using their own ability stories to bridge 'the best of what is', 'what gives life' (existing resources identified in *Discovery*) with 'what might be' (possibilities and hopes imagined in *Dreaming*) in order to present clear, compelling pictures of how things will be when the existing resources are put into practice. It is important that the design statements fully integrate the best of existing abilities and possibilities and that they are consistent with the intended outcome or topic of the inquiry.

Crafting possibility statements

We craft the possibility statements by returning to and refocusing consultees' attention on the ability themes we had clustered and mapped during *discovery*. Then we invite them to contemplate 'what if' they continue to perform this set of abilities.

> Therefore I (Nicola) reminded the child-care workers, 'This is what you are already doing – these are all your existing skills and abilities that you have been using in your work with the children and parents. What if you continue to do this – to use these abilities of yours? Which of your dreams will be possible if you continue to do this? For example, what if you continue "talking and listening with kindness, sensitivity and respect with parents" and you "make use of parents' expertise about what works with their child" – what will this make possible?' Lena said, 'We will be working in partnership with parents ...' and Amaal added, '... so they appreciate we are working alongside them'.

We invite consultees to frame these statements in the present tense, as if the future dream is already present. We support them to create *written* statements so they can have bold, provocative and motivating statements to return to that connect their dreams to the roots of their success. Thus Nicola went on to generate the possibility statements (in Box 4.1) with the consultees.

> ## Box 4.1 Possibility statements generated with child-care worker-consultees
>
> - *When we show empathy for parents, recognise that it can be hard to separate and when we are curious about their concerns regarding separating without judging, then parents feel we are listening and are really happy with the way we help to settle their children in crèche.*
> - *When we show curiosity and respect to parents and make use of their expertise about what works with their child, then we are working in partnership with parents and they appreciate we are working alongside them.*
> - *When we draw on our training in child development and use questions to help parents get into the shoes of the child, we show we are professional and parents are confident they are helping their children to develop as well as possible.*
> - *When we are working together with colleagues as a team and supporting each other, then we feel much greater satisfaction with our work and we are full of energy.*
> - *When we talk and listen with parents with kindness and sensitivity and share honestly any concerns about safeguarding, then we are working safely.*
> - *When we treat each parent and child as unique individuals, then parents feel respected and confident we know their child.*

We write the possibility statements in the present tense. They describe where consultees want to be, based on their stories of what actually took place, examples of what they are already doing well and their best practice. Thus we design statements of possibility, affirmative statements that describe the consultees' preferred future as if it is already happening. The statement can also function as a symbol, a reminder of what is best in their practice and can regenerate the energising moments from the consultation.

Developing and delivering

In the process of creating their possibility statements, the child-care workers were already generating ideas about next steps, including developing a leaflet; creating books for individual children with photographs of them playing and some of their creations; and meeting with Eileen, their manager, and other centre staff to hear their visions and think about how they could make these possible.

Co-constructing plans and prioritising to enable delivery

We go on to invite consultees to consider what kinds of actions and relationships will best support their dreams and wishes with questions like

- Who will be involved [in writing the leaflet]?
- Who will take responsibility for what?

Co-creating structures and processes to sustain development

In this phase, we also engage with consultees in in-depth dialogues about the best structure and processes to support their plans or design. Our intention is to invite consultees to reflect on how to keep living their dreams and using appreciative principles. Therefore we ask

- Who/what will support you?
- How will you help and encourage each other? How will you draw attention to each other's successes?

If we are working with an individual consultee, we might ask

- What inner dialogue will support you?
- Who will you invite to encourage you?

> The child-care workers decided to 'have a five-minute conversation' as they packed up after crèche sessions 'to tell each other stories of what has worked well that day'. They also agreed to share abilities they had spotted in each other's work with children and parents. They said they were going to put the maps we had created of their dreams and possibility statements up in their office. They had also agreed to meet monthly with Eileen and other team members to review parent feedback to continue to 'make more dreams'.

Outcome of the consultations

Over the course of three consultations with the child-care workers, I (Nicola) witnessed a boost in their energy and a growing excitement. I noticed them coming back to each meeting with examples of their excellent work with parents. Their manager told me 'what a huge change' she had seen in Amaal, Lena and Shahara, and that she felt they were 'walking tall again'. A few weeks after our final consultation, Eileen invited me (Nicola) to join a team meeting where I witnessed her asking the child-care staff to share 'examples of excellent work' with parents. She also read out feedback from parents' evaluation forms highlighting what they appreciated and framing their criticisms in terms of 'what they want from us is …'. The team spontaneously applauded after each positive comment and Lena suggested they add them to their 'ability map'.

Final reflections

Inviting consultees to *discover* and *dream* often enables enough momentum to provoke change and for transformation to unfold. Therefore we do not always need to rigorously go through each of the stages of the appreciative consultation cycle we have outlined. We have noticed that it is essential to consider the context in which the consultees work. For example, having the support and 'cheering' of the consultees' managers and leaders is central to an appreciative approach working well. We have also learnt that it is crucial to remain 'energetically positive' ourselves (Whitney, 2010:83) throughout the consultation process, always looking for ways in which we can bring out the best in consultees.

We have seen the dramatic and transformative effects that inviting appreciation can have on consultees and have been fascinated to witness how the 'spirit' of appreciation can mushroom to inspire managers and also the clients of our consultees. As consultants, we feel privileged to participate in the almost immediate energising effects of appreciative consultation on both our consultees and ourselves.

Guide 4.1 Appreciative consultation: A practice guide

Defining and clarifying a topic for consultation

Planning for appreciative consultation with people commissioning the work
Co-creating a positive focus for consultation with consultees

Discovering the best of what is

Valuing everyday practice
Bringing forth what gives life
- What do you appreciate in your work?
- What inspires you?
- What is precious? Why is this important to you?

Appreciative interviewing to bring forth ability stories
Invite consultee to:
- Share a story of a precious moment when you participated in or witnessed an episode of [helping a parent to settle their child in the crèche*]' or 'Describe a moment when things were not going well, and [settling*] turned out much better than you expected.
*Consultant use the name of the topic identified for consultation.

Call forth from the consultee a detailed account of what made the best possible, with questions like:
- What happened to make the best possible? What else did you do? Tell me more about what you did to get the best from the situation.

- Who or what gave you the idea to do this? Who else was involved? Who else noticed and supported what you did? What did they notice? What did they do?

Ability spotting
- Treat what you hear from consultees as a gift
- Identify the qualities, skills and abilities that contributed to that best moment and note on Post-its

Collecting, clustering and mapping abilities

Dreaming what might be

Tapping into frustrated dreams
Envisioning: positive images towards positive action

Designing how we get there

Crafting possibility statements
- When we ... then we can ... make possible ....

Developing and delivering

Co-constructing plans and prioritising to enable delivery
- Who will take responsibility for what?

Co-creating structures and processes to sustain developments
- Who/what will support you?
- How will you help and encourage each other? How will you draw attention to each other's successes?

Notes

1 The original Appreciative Inquiry model, often referred to as the '4-D cycle' (Cooperrider and Whitney, 2005), involves four processes: *Discover*: grounded inquiry to identify the best of what is; *Dream*: envisioning to identify ideals of what might be; *Design*: planning and prioritising processes that would work well, and *Destiny*: implementing the proposed design. We have adapted the 5-D cycle (https://www.neasc.org/downloads/annual.../What_is_Appreciative_Inquiry.pdf, accessed 9 January 2017) for our approach to appreciative consultation which incorporates *Defining and Clarifying* the topic for consultation as part of the process.
2 Lewis, Passmore and Cantore (2011:47) recommend six to twelve themes: 'fewer than 6 means that items don't get separated out sufficiently; more than 12 and people struggle to remember what the themes were'.

References

Anderson, E. (2017) Personal communication.
Anderson, H. (1997) *Conversation, Language and Possibilities*. New York: Basic Books.
Boscolo, L. and Bertrando, P. (1996) *Systemic Therapy With Individuals*. London: Karnac.
Bushe, G.R. (2007) Appreciative inquiry is not (just) about the positive. *OD Practitioner,* *39* (4), 30–35.
Bushe, G.R. (2013) The appreciative inquiry model. In E.H. Kessler (ed.) *Encyclopedia of Management Theory*, Vol. 1, Los Angeles, London, New Delhi: Sage Publications.
Cooperrider, D. (2001) What is appreciative inquiry. In D.A. Hammond and C. Royal (eds.) *Lessons from the Field: Applying Appreciative Inquiry. Revised Edition.* Plano, TX: Thin Book Publishing Company.
Cooperrider, D.L. and Srivastva, S. (1987) Appreciative inquiry in organizational life. In R.W. Woodman and W.A. Passmore (eds.) *Research in Organizational Change and Development*, Vol. 1, Stamford, CT: JAI Press.
Cooperrider, D, and Whitney, D. (2005) *Appreciative Inquiry: A Positive Revolution in Change*. San Francisco, CA: Berrett-Koehler Publishers.
Hammond, S.A. (1998) *The Thin Book of Appreciative Inquiry*. Plano, TX: Kodiak Consulting.
Lang, P. (2003) Personal communication, cited in Hedges, F. (2005) *An Introduction to Systemic Therapy With Individuals: A Social Constructionist Approach.* Basingstoke, Hampshire: Palgrave Macmillan.
Lewis, S., Passmore, J. and Cantore. S. (2011) *Appreciative Inquiry for Change Management: Using AI to Facilitate Organisational Development.* London: Kogan Page.
McAdam, E. and Lang P. (2009) *Appreciative Work in Schools: Generating Future Communities.* Chichester: Kingsham Press.
McAdam, E. and Mirza, K.A.H. (2009) Drugs, hopes and dreams: Appreciative inquiry with marginalized young people using drugs and alcohol. *Journal of Family Therapy,* *31*, 175–193.
Madsen, W.C. (2007) *Collaborative Therapy with Multi-Stressed Families*. New York: The Guildford Press.
Mohr, B.J., McLean, A. and Silbert, T. (2003) Beyond discovery and dream: Unleashing change through the design phase of an AI intervention. *AI Practitioner,* 1–3.
Oxford English Dictionary (2016). [Online] Available from: https://en.oxforddictionaries.com/definition/appreciate. Accessed 18 April 2016.
Shotter, J. (2010) *Social Construction on the Edge: 'Withness'-Thinking and Embodiment.* Chagrin Falls, OH: Taos Institute Publications.
Watkins, J.M., Mohr, B.J. and Kelly, R. (2011) *Appreciative Inquiry: Change at the Speed of Imagination*. San Francisco, CA: Pfeiffer.
Weingarten, K. (1998) The small and the ordinary: The daily practice of a postmodern narrative therapy. *Family Process,* *37* (1), 3–15.
Whitney, D. (2010) Appreciative inquiry: Creating spiritual resonance in the workplace. *Journal of Management, Spirituality and Religion,* *7* (1), 73–88.
Whitney, D. and Trosten-Bloom, A. (2010) *The Power of Appreciative Inquiry: A Practical Guide to Positive Change*. San Francisco, CA: Berrett-Koehler Publishers.

Chapter 5

Consultation in contexts of ending and transition

When teams change or people leave

Emma Worwood

In this chapter, I describe some of the practices we have used in individual and group consultation to address ending and transition when the consultant or consultee is leaving a group, when a consultee is leaving their post, when a group with whom we have been consulting is ending and when a team with whom we are working is going through a significant change. In the current UK financial and political climate of budget cuts, restructuring or closure of services, we are often consulting to practitioners in contexts of change that involve endings and transitions, both expected and unanticipated. How people leave and how a team or service ends or reorganises affects not only the staff leaving but also those who remain. Hence the process of change has important consequences for staff relationships and morale as well as for clients using the service. This chapter offers consultation practices to create a context for talking about endings, to help consultees become observers to their own relationships to ending and to bring forth preferred stories of endings that enable consultees to value and take forward their skills, abilities and learning.

Making time and space for talking about ending

It was my penultimate consultation with a group of child mental health practitioners. We had been meeting every six weeks for the past two years to develop their work in children's centres. The group was ending because the organisation was in the process of restructuring, which had been confirmed only the previous month. While waiting for the consultees to arrive, I was going over some ideas I had put together to review with the group their joint learning over the course of our consultations. I was also contemplating the effects of the forthcoming changes on them. 'Will they want to make time for this?' I pondered. As this thought crossed my mind, Rhiannon, a group member, popped her head round the door to give her 'apologies', explaining she did 'not have time' to attend as she felt 'under pressure' to finish her administrative tasks. Like several others in the consultation group, Rhiannon was moving from one part of the service to another because of the restructuring. She was ending with clients, and picking up new work.

We commonly encounter practitioners like Rhiannon who are concerned or reluctant to 'take' or 'make' time to address change, ending or transitions in their work because of 'pressure to get on' with other tasks. Sometimes they doubt 'the point' of talking about an inevitable change, as 'it's going to happen anyway', or question their, or others', entitlement to 'waste time' or 'indulge' in talking about ending.

We find that working with practitioners to make sense of change and to reflect constructively on the challenges and opportunities of transitions can enable them to find ways to go on in their work and to take their skills and experiences into new work situations. However, we do not assume that consultees should address or want to reflect on ending or forthcoming change in their services with us in consultation. Therefore, we always begin by asking ourselves, as consultants, whether we have created a suitable context for talking (Fredman, 1997), and then go on to explore consultees' perspectives on whether and how we might address the ending together. Hence, when the rest of Rhiannon's consultation group arrived, I asked whether taking time to talk about the ending of our group could be useful. Trying not to make assumptions, I opened the conversation with 'What do you all think about spending some time today talking about the ending of this group? I am interested to hear all your different ideas', and went on to explore their beliefs about talking about ending with questions like: What are your (different) ideas about talking about the ending of this group? Who thinks it might be useful to spend some time considering the ending of our group? Why? Why not? What are your views about the effects of talking/not talking on yourself/others/clients/relationships in your service?

> Having gladly accepted my invitation to join briefly for a piece of cake 'to mark the end of our group', Rhiannon participated in this conversation. Group members shared different perspectives, including: 'Talking about what we're losing is really important'; 'I have so much to do, it feels an indulgence talking about ending, I just need to get on'; 'I'm going to miss this group – but I'm not sure that talking about this will help in any way?'; and 'I don't want things to change'. I added a few of my own ideas, including: 'We could use some time to consolidate what we have learned together so you can take this forward to your new role' and 'to celebrate what you have achieved in the work you have been doing'. One group member suggested, 'It would be weird to just close the door without acknowledging all the work we have done together'. Rhiannon provoked shared laughter from the group when she responded, 'It is important to mark the ending in some way – even if only by eating cake!'
>
> Susan, a committed group member, remained silent while her colleagues talked about talking about ending. When I invited her to contribute her ideas, she said our discussion was 'making me think about how I should end my work with the West Park children's centre'. Susan had been working one day a week for almost two years with the staff and families with young children using this centre. She was 'moving on' from this post and wondered whether 'anyone would even notice if I

were gone? Maybe I should just slip away, that might be easiest. I do not want to make a big song and dance of it'.

When Susan finished speaking, several group members agreed it was 'important to think with Susan about her ending ... and we can get some useful ideas for our own changing posts'. Therefore, we used the consultation to focus on Susan's ending and agreed to return to marking the ending of our group in our final session.

Talking about talking about ending in this way can open space for consultees to reflect on different beliefs about their rights as well as their duties or obligations to address the effects of ending and change on themselves, their service and clients. As practitioners, we all hold varied and even contradictory beliefs about the value, usefulness or perhaps appropriateness of talking about ending, which we draw from the different personal and professional contexts of our lives. For example, many members of this group were uncertain whether they should give any time at all to addressing the ending, questioning their entitlement to take time to 'indulge' in more than a piece of 'farewell cake'. Others perceived talking about ending as a necessary requirement to 'mark' an important transition or as valuable use of the time to consolidate learning and an opportunity to celebrate good practice. Susan doubted whether her departure would even be noticed. *Talking about talking* about ending invited consultees to become observers to their own relationships to ending and to their beliefs about talking about change. It also opened space for Susan to begin contemplating how she might manage ending her work as a consultant with the children's centre.

Our picture of organisations informs our approach to ending

The wider political, social and organisational contexts in which we work inform the varied ways we picture our services and organisations, which shape how we see relationships, how we understand change and how we respond to ending within the workplace. Table 5.1 presents four pictures or metaphors of organisations: 'machine', 'living organism', 'human system' and 'culture' (Lewis, Passmore and Cantore, 2011; Morgan, 1997a, 1997b). These metaphors are not an exhaustive or mutually exclusive list and there is no one 'right' metaphor or 'one picture fits all' for organisations. For example, Elkind (1998) offers metaphors of 'religion' and 'marketplace' for the British National Health Service (NHS) and Morgan (1997b), adding the further metaphors of 'psychic prison' and 'brain', notes that each metaphor highlights particular interpretations of the organisation. The four metaphors in Table 5.1 reflect the range of ways the consultees above were engaging with their service. Each metaphor has different implications for relationships and approaches to change, including the beliefs and the meanings we attribute to endings and how we act or respond.

The consultation group above was working in a service that was consumed by serious financial cuts, which had led to 'deleted posts', 'restructuring' and a new service 'configuration'. Consistent with this language of technology, Rhiannon and

Table 5.1 Metaphors of organisations shaping approaches to ending

Metaphor	View of relationships	Meaning of ending/change
Machine	People are cogs in the wheel of the machine. Parts are exchangeable and replaceable. Efficiency and productivity of the 'machine' is a priority. New and cheaper parts can do the job better.	People come together to do a job; when the task is complete they move on. Change is seen as an interruption to normal smooth running of the organisation. When one person leaves the 'part' can be replaced.
Living organism	The organisation is alive; it has the potential for growth and renewal. Each person is a necessary part of the 'body' providing a unique/significant function. Therefore, parts/people are not exchangeable or replaceable. The body parts need sustenance to give life to the organisation.	The loss of a person is like an amputation; the 'body' does not function the same way. Through nurturing the life-giving aspects of the organisation, people can grow and take something forward to their next transition.
Human system	People create the organisation. People are in relationship with each other, interdependent and have an effect on one another. Without people working together the organisation would not exist.	Change is embedded in patterns of human communication and relationship. A change in one part of the system has effects on all people and relationships.
Culture	People create and are connected through culture (including shared assumptions, collective values, beliefs, principles and visions) transmitted through language, symbols, stories and practices or rituals. Thus culture guides how people interact with each other.	The stories told about change and transition within the organisation inform meanings of ending and shape how people behave and interact with each other and manage change.

several of her colleagues seemed to be construing their service as a 'machine', relating to themselves as cogs or parts contributing to its smooth running and productivity. Hence these practitioners were prioritising efficiency and productivity, perceiving time to reflect on ending as a 'waste' and an interruption to the smooth running of the service. Susan seemed to have positioned herself as an exchangeable cog in the wheel of the children's centre where she worked, believing that the centre staff would be unlikely to notice her absence, especially if she were 'replaced quickly'. We can see how talking about endings could be construed as 'indulgent' or not permissible for practitioners who position themselves as parts in the organisational 'machine'.

When I suggested that the consultees might use the time to 'consolidate their learning' from each other to 'take forward' to their new roles in the service, I was relating to the service as a 'living organism'. Thus I invited people to 'celebrate' their achievements in their work, intending to nurture the life-giving aspects of the organisation so that people could take something forward into the next phase of their professional development.

As consultants, we have found it useful to ask ourselves what picture of their service or system consultees hold; what metaphor informs how they explain their organisational life. We can also reflect on what metaphor we, as consultants, are focusing on and intentionally shift or add alternative metaphors to offer us different language and bring forth new perspectives. I recognised that the 'machine' metaphor was giving meaning to Susan's relationships and forthcoming departure from the children's centre, leaving her feeling devalued. Mindful that the 'living organism' metaphor was shaping my approach to the ending of the consultation group, I chose a different metaphor, 'human system', to inform the next part of my conversation with Susan with the intention that this metaphor might open space to approach the centre staff as interdependent, where each person's actions affect the others. Thus I invited Susan to map her relationship to ending with the centre. Together we explored the effect of her leaving on people and relationships.

Mapping the relationship to ending

Susan had the idea that leaving her post at the children's centre would have little or no impact on the people with whom she was consulting so that she may as well 'slip away quietly' without making a 'song and dance of it', unsure whether 'anyone would even notice if I were gone'. When I asked Susan whether she preferred to end by 'just slipping away' and whether it would make a difference to her if her departure were acknowledged in some way, she responded wistfully that she had 'worked really hard' with the staff at the centre, 'they use me so well now … I think as long as someone replaces me soon they'll be OK?' Since Susan was asking for help with how to approach her ending and had a sense that nobody would be affected by her absence, I invited her to help me draw a map of the children's centre system so we could look at the effects of her leaving, not just on herself but also on those with whom she had been working. Suggesting we begin by putting herself on the map, I went on to map her system with questions like those presented in Box 5.1.

Box 5.1 Questions to map the effects and views of ending

- With whom do you work in the centre? With whom do you have contact?
- Who else is involved/connected with you?
- Who will notice you are gone?
- Who will be affected by your leaving?
- What effect will your leaving have on them?
- Who will have an opinion or a view on your departure?
- What will they say or think? What ideas will they express?

Susan rapidly identified a number of 'key staff' at the centre: two health visitors – Joan, who 'regularly refers families with young children to me' and Alice, who had been in the post six months and 'often asks for my help with family's concerns or difficulties in relation to their children'. When I asked, 'Who else connects with you?' Susan added Michelle, a family support worker: 'we ran a parenting group together', and Iraj, an outreach worker: 'we often discussed creative ways to support parents' play with their children ... some of the families I work with attend her play sessions'. I invited Susan to add the families with whom she worked on the map. When I asked, 'Who will notice you are gone?', Susan added David, the receptionist, to her map, explaining, 'He has such a warm way with the families... and makes them feel very welcome when they arrive'.

Exploring effects and views of ending

Suggesting Susan 'step into the shoes' of each person in her map (Figure 5.1), I went on to invite her to consider the effects of her leaving on each person by asking 'Who will be affected by your leaving?' and 'What effects will your leaving have on them?' Thus Susan was able to take different perspectives and include the voices of many people in the centre, including the children and families.

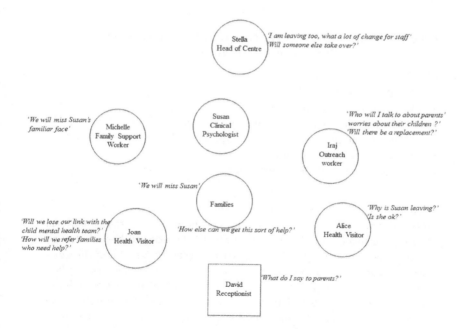

Figure 5.1   Mapping Susan's relationship to ending

Susan wondered whether the support workers and nursery nurses may be 'disappointed' that they no longer have a 'named person ... a familiar face' with whom to talk about parents' worries concerning their children. She said the health visitors may feel that 'our service is further away', and she contemplated whether the centre staff 'might not be aware that there will be someone new replacing me'.

Focusing on the effects of her leaving brought significant relationships into view for Susan so that she noted another significant ending about to happen in the centre: 'The head has to leave shortly without much notice because of a serious health problem'. As Susan added Stella, head of the children's centre, to the map she gasped, 'Oh ... maybe the staff will think *I* am ill! I need to let them know ... but where do I begin?'

Creating a context for knowing and telling about ending

When consultees like Susan are unsure how to begin to 'let people know' about a forthcoming ending, we find it useful to explore what each significant person in their system knows about the ending, their awareness of what each other knows and the beliefs that they hold about people knowing and telling others about the ending. Thus I set out to explore 'who knows what, who wants who to know what, and who believes what about who knows what' (Fredman, 1997:25) with questions like those presented in Box 5.2.

Box 5.2 Questions to create a context of knowing and telling about change/ending

- What do you know?
- What do you think ... knows?
- Where do they get that idea from?
- What does that suggest to you about their understanding?
- How do you think they might be explaining this to themselves/others?
- What do you think she wants to know?
- What do you think others want her to know?

When I asked Susan 'Who, do you think, would want to know you are leaving?' and 'What would they want to know?', Susan thought Stella, the centre head, would 'be quite upset if I did not tell her'. Although Stella 'may be preoccupied by her own leaving and have a lot of things to organise for the centre in the meantime', she had been an important link and very supportive of Susan's family clinic. 'Stella might be worried that the clinic will fold ... She definitely would want to know if someone else is taking over'. Susan thought the health visitors would want to know why she was leaving and where to refer families in her absence.

Through mapping the system of relationships in the children's centre and including herself in the picture, Susan gradually noticed connections between significant people in the system. For example, she noted that David, the receptionist and 'first face the families see when they visit ... the person who puts people at ease', would want to know what to tell the parents.

As the conversation unfolded, I explored what Susan knew about the arrangements for after she left. I invited her to reflect on when it would be helpful to let people know of her leaving and what story she wanted to tell others of why she was leaving and what would happen next. One consultee in the group mentioned the 'need for transparency' and another said it 'could raise anxiety if there is no clarity' about what was happening to Susan's post.

> Reverting to the language of efficiency and 'machines', Susan began, 'Someone new will replace me', but she did not know who or when he or she would be able to start, so there may be 'a gap in service'. Then she paused and, re-engaging with a relational perspective, reflected, 'It is making me think I should talk to our manager about how we can best keep the staff in the picture' and 'a timescale for when we will know more'.

This process helped Susan think about how she would go on with talking about her leaving with the centre staff and with whom she would communicate. It enabled Susan to consider what information she had already and when and how she and others could learn more, thus viewing the 'telling' of her leaving as something that would take place over time.

Coordinating multiple stories of ending

Just as organisations hold a range of beliefs about endings, so individuals, groups and teams will have multiple stories of endings. For example, Susan shared her own personal belief that people at the children's centre were unlikely to notice her absence and it would be 'better to slip away ... the least said the better'. She thought centre staff might tell different stories of her leaving, including that she was going due to 'ill-health', 'because of dissatisfaction with the way the centre was run' or was 'losing (her) job' in the current economic climate. The story that she was 'being redeployed' because of service restructuring seemed relatively weak in comparison.

Therefore, when consultees ask for help with what to tell or how to explain the termination of a service or someone leaving, we begin with inviting them to generate multiple stories, explanations and understandings of the ending as in the consultation with the manager, Clare, and her children's centre team below.

> Clare's eyes welled up with tears as she told me she was leaving her post at the end of term following a restructuring of the service. She felt 'so sad having to leave' her team and the centre that she had 'worked so hard to build up over the past five years'. Clare asked if I could offer a consultation to 'help the team cope with the loss ... some of the staff are reacting badly'. I was working as a psychologist in the centre, offering consultation to staff. When I explored how Clare preferred to

leave her team, she insisted, 'I don't want them to feel sorry for me; they have a job to do and they do it well ... we've worked so hard here to make this an excellent centre for the children and the parents. They are a great team. I really want them to know how good they are; really (touching her heart) know it ... and carry on with their excellent work'.

Clare's acknowledgement of the effects of her departure on staff ('reacting badly') suggests she was relating to her service as a 'human system', acknowledging that people are interdependent and connected in relationships, so that what one person does will affect others in the system. Engaging with her service as a 'living organism', she also expected that the staff would 'feel' the effects of her leaving 'badly', as a 'loss', and therefore need sustenance in the form of 'support'. Choosing the metaphor of 'organisation as culture' opened space for me to consider the cultural assumptions and practices of termination in Clare's organisation and what stories were being told about her leaving.

Discourses of ending

The stories we tell of ending are connected with different discourses which include our beliefs and values and have different implications for how we talk about and approach ending. Fredman and Dalal (1998:3) organised ideas about ending therapy according to different discourses of 'loss', 'cure', 'transition', 'relief/release' and 'metamorphosis', 'each representing a cluster of stories and beliefs about endings which give meaning to the therapeutic relationship'. In consultation, we have identified different discourses of ending that practitioners draw upon from their personal, professional and wider social political contexts to approach transition and ending in organisations. The picture or metaphor people hold of the organisation and their discourses creates contexts which give meaning to relationships, influence practitioners' approach to ending and change and thus inform how people go on. Thus there is a reflexive relationship between the 'ending discourse', organisational metaphor, relationships and the approach to termination.

Table 5.2 summarises how different discourses inform meanings, relationships and approaches to ending in organisations. We do not propose these discourses as an exhaustive or mutually exclusive list of approaches; rather they represent a range of themes and narratives about endings which have different implications for relationships and practice. As consultants, we draw on these discourses as a resource to guide our conversations with consultees to address ending or transition in consultation. For example, 'transition' and 'metamorphosis' discourses shaped my approach in the consultation with Rhiannon and the child mental health practitioners above.

In preparation for addressing termination in consultation, we ask ourselves what ending discourses those significantly involved (including consultees, clients, managers and the organisation) might be privileging: what language are they using to talk about the ending and how will the different narratives they draw on affect their approach to ending? Clare (p. 83) seemed to be moving between discourses of 'loss', as she spoke tearfully of her own 'sadness' at having to leave

Table 5.2 Discourse, meanings, relationship and approach to ending

Discourse	Approach to ending	Ending practices
Ending as loss	Important to mourn the end of the relationship and acknowledge the loss.	• Actively address the loss; • Mourn the ending; • Support staff to work through loss;
Ending as completion and closure	The work is done. Practitioners are relieved of responsibility and free from commitment.	• Move on to the next job.
Ending as transition	Ending is a new beginning; we move forward and hold onto development. Important to mark the transition.	• Mark the transition; • Celebrate and witness changes / achievements; • Rituals and rites of passage.
Ending as metamorphosis	Skills and abilities are not lost; they are transformed and carried forward. Opportunity to review and evaluate developments / learning. Need an audience to witness and sustain preferred developments.	• Review and evaluate learning and development; • Explore transport to new contexts; • Reflect on new views of self/stories of identity.

her team, and then 'metamorphosis' and 'transition' when, talking animatedly with optimism, she expressed her wish for them to 'really know' their excellence and 'carry on'. Acting out of a discourse of 'loss', she called forth 'support' for her team; informed by a 'transition' discourse, she was seeking the opportunity to celebrate and witness their achievements.

Different discourses about ending inform the sorts of questions a consultant might ask to explore termination with consultees (Table 5.3). We always connect our questions with feedback from consultees. Therefore we present the questions below as examples and not a checklist or interview schedule.

Initially connecting with Clare's discourse of 'loss', I had explored what sense staff were making of Clare's leaving and how they were affected. When I asked what the staff already knew, what stories they were telling and what they would want to know, Clare feared that 'all sorts of rumours are flying about causing havoc'. She wanted staff to know the 'service is not being lost' and that she was leaving because of restructuring as a result of 'budget cuts ... beyond the control of anyone working here'.

Clare was aware that scattered or sparse information can leave people filling in the gaps with flights of imagination and harmful rumours to manage confusion. Inviting consultees to generate their 'preferred story' about a forthcoming change can help develop explanations that people *want* told and that will enable, rather than disable, their service or organisation. Since Clare wanted to focus on the

Table 5.3 Ending discourses inform the sorts of questions a consultant might ask

Discourse	Questions to explore ending
Ending as loss	• What effects will your leaving have (on individuals, relationships)? • How will others make sense of this ending? • What are you leaving behind? • Who will miss what?
Ending as completion / closure	• Where are you moving on to? • What are you looking forward to? • What do you see yourself doing in six months?
Ending as transition	• How would you describe (the situation) then/now? • What developments are you pleased with? • Who else has seen these changes? / How would they describe (the situation) now? • What opportunities does this change offer? • What will you do to remind yourselves of these changes if things are difficult in the future? Who else might remind you? • Who is most pleased with the changes that have occurred? • Who is most likely to support these changes? • What aspects of (the situation) do you want to retain / change / develop as time goes on?
Ending as metamorphosis	• What have you learnt from (this consultation)? • If you were to face the same situation what would you do differently now? • What will you take with you from this experience into your new post/team? • What effect have [the changes] you have made here had on (yourself, others, relationships, views of self)? • What do [the changes] you have made tell you about (self, others, relationships)?

service 'not being lost' and did 'not want (staff) to feel sorry for her' so they could 'carry on … their excellent work', I agreed to her request to meet with her and the staff team to generate preferred and enabling stories of the forthcoming transition in their service. Clare was keen to join the consultation and have the opportunity to contribute her perspective.

Opening space for preferred and enabling stories of endings with consultees

'Talking about talking' about Clare's leaving with the staff team provoked a sigh of relief from Sibel, a support worker. She told us that a mother who used the service regularly had asked her the previous day whether Clare was leaving 'because she was a bad manager'. Sibel tried to reassure the mother that this was not the case, but 'what should I say instead?' Sibel said she felt responsible for telling parents 'what is happening', which opened space for me to invite the group to participate in an exercise to 'think together about what to tell families using the centre about Clare's leaving'.

Like the mother who spoke to Sibel, we all try to make sense of unexpected or unusual events, as in the sudden news of a manager leaving. A narrative or story offers a way of holding together complex and possibly ambiguous, contradictory or conflicting information. Since unusual events trigger narrativising or storying (Bruner, 1990), we aim to work with consultees to construct coherent narratives which make sense of their experience, do not blame or criticise self or others, fit with the stories told by other significant people in the service or organisation and create opportunities for adaptive action and relationships for everyone involved.

Generating a repertoire of stories about ending

The principles guiding our approach to coordinating narratives are informed by a systemic approach that involves generating and elaborating a repertoire of stories about the forthcoming change, choosing and evaluating preferred stories and reflecting on the effects and meanings of new stories for people, relationships and action (Fredman, 1997; Fredman and Fuggle, 2000). Therefore I began by inviting consultees in the staff team to generate a repertoire of stories about Clare's leaving with questions like those in Box 5.3.

Box 5.3 Questions to invite stories and meanings of ending and transition

- What have you understood about [Clare] leaving?
- What [stories] are you/others telling about [Clare's leaving]? What theories/explanations do you/they have? What has [Clare] told you?
- What do others (families/children) say?
- Where do the ideas come from?
- Are there other/different ideas you have/would like them to know?
- What would you like to say to staff/families? What do you want them to understand? What explanation or story do you prefer to tell?
- What sense will they make of this?

As consultants, we do not position ourselves to evaluate consultees' ideas or stories about ending. Our intention is to bring forth multiple ideas by asking all people present for their own views and to consider the perspectives of other significant people who are not present. Thus I invited the staff team to share their understandings of Clare's impending departure.

> Laura, an outreach worker, thought they were 'cutting [Clare's] job ... because the funding has run out', and Amina, a bilingual worker, wondered if they were 'moving [Clare] to teach others ... because we have been so successful'. Esther, a health advisor, wondered whether all family activities were going to continue if there were cuts. Inviting perspectives from the position of parents using the children's centre generated other stories, such as the existing 'funding needs to be spread out so services can reach

more children' and 'the next step will be to close the centre'. Clare said she wanted everyone to know she was leaving 'because there has been a decision to reorganise the management structure across the whole of children's centre services ... the service is not being lost'. She was pleased the staff team 'could carry on the excellent work we have developed for the children and parents'. As we went along, I wrote up all the ideas we had collected about Clare's leaving on a flipchart. When I asked 'And what might the children say?', Sibel, a nursery worker, responded enthusiastically, 'They will want a graduation party like we do for all the children when they move on ... with balloons'. 'Esther added 'And a card for Clare and a cake with her name on'. At this point, Clare looking embarrassed, jumped up from her chair and said 'Oh I'm touched but I'm not sure I can hear this at the moment ... I may get upset ... you carry on without me' and quickly left the room. After a few moments of silence, I asked the group if they would like to continue the meeting. This was met with positive responses and I suggested we could think about how to connect Clare to our discussion at the end.

Evaluating and coordinating preferred stories

We go on to invite each person to evaluate the different stories the group has generated about ending, identify their preferred explanations and consider which versions of which story fits most suitably for themselves and with the other people involved, including parents and children.

Therefore I invited the team to get into pairs and discuss the different ideas we had collected about Clare's leaving, with questions like

- Which ideas have you been using to explain Clare's leaving to yourself?
- Which ideas have been most and least useful to you?
- Which of these ideas do you like/fit well for you/suit you best?
- Which bits of the stories do you like/want to hold onto/get rid of/change?
- Do you have other ideas you would like to add?

All the consultees were adamant they did not like the 'bad manager' explanation and were pleased that they could 'scotch any rumours' that the centre was closing. They said they wanted parents to know that 'restructuring' and 'spreading services fairly' was the reason for Clare going. They also wanted to hold on to the view of their work as 'successful' and 'excellent'.

Inviting people to generate a range of stories enables them to construct a narrative which helps make sense of previously unexplained experiences or makes new connections between old meanings. Exploring which versions fit most suitably for everyone involved enables consultees to make connections between their preferred explanations, opening space for the emergence of narratives 'never-before-told'.

Towards the end of this consultation, Esther, a very warm, softly spoken health advisor and one of the older members of the team, went on to say 'I can't believe Clare is leaving us. It is not going to be the same without her'. The nurturing, warmth and safety of this group seemed to make it possible for Esther to reflect on the 'loss' of Clare, which opened space for me to explore with the group, 'What will you miss when Clare leaves?', thereby inviting a generous contribution of appreciative comments from all the staff.

> When I asked if they wished to 'do something to show Clare how much you appreciate her ... and what she has done for the centre before she leaves', they all enthusiastically launched into suggestions that included 'cake ... a card ... a graduation ceremony ... the children can sing a song ... should we buy a thank you present?' Amina followed with, 'So we must show Clare how we carry on the good work she has taught us'.

Appreciating, celebrating and taking forward contributions

The 'ending as transition' discourse locates endings on a continuum, or part of a larger cycle where endings can become new beginnings (Relph, 1985). This discourse construes people's leaving as moving from one context to another, with some people departing, others remaining and the whole service changing. Thus the process of ending involves moving forward, leaving something behind and holding onto developments we have made. By approaching ending as transition, final sessions can offer an opportunity for consultant and consultees to mark the forthcoming change, witness developments and celebrate achievements with validating practices and affirming rituals like prize–givings and certificates (White and Epston, 1990), as Clare and her team used to mark her leaving.

> With agreement, I told Clare that her team wanted to 'mark' her leaving by 'doing something together to show you how they will carry on the good work they have learned from you'. They suggested 'something like the centre's graduation ceremony when the children leave'. Clare 'loved the idea ... I can see this is important for everyone and I can't shy away from this', and suggested having 'a ceremony with certificates ... that gives me the chance to praise each person's talents ... leave it to me!'

Rituals and ceremonies

We often use rituals in consultation to mark significant transitions in organisations or teams. Rituals gather us together, mark important moments and allow us to notice and comment on significant changes. Ceremony and ritual connect people emotionally, help to slow us down and focus energy on the values and culture of the organisation, thus allowing people to feel stronger and ready to move on to the next stage in their lives (Singer, 2009).

As consultants, we take care not to impose rituals and try to carefully co-create them with all the people involved, so they fit with their relationship and cultural contexts. Thus Clare and her team created versions of rituals familiar to the children's centre culture: a 'certificate ceremony', a 'smiley face cake' with the words 'Sorry to see you go Clare', and a beautiful card incorporating the children's drawings, starting with 'We will miss you because …' followed by a long list of statements of appreciation of Clare. Thus rituals can offer the opportunity for expression beyond the verbal domain, simultaneously embracing multiple meanings, including contradictions. Hence rituals fit well with a process of transition that includes feelings of loss and sadness for someone leaving, celebrating developments as well as moving on (Imber-Black et al., 2003).

> Clare elected to begin this ritual by reading out certificates she had made for each member of staff, thereby opening space for the team to talk enthusiastically about what they had learnt from each other, their hopes for their future professional development and also about their wishes to keep in contact with Clare. The staff team went on to present Clare with her card. Laura read out all the staff's appreciative comments that completed the phrase 'We will miss you because …'.

The certificate ceremony and farewell card created opportunities for Clare to witness each staff member's 'talents' and for the staff team to appreciate Clare's contributions to their development. Appreciating and witnessing the contributions of each person to the team, to the service and to each other resonates with the 'ending as transition' discourse. Documents like the certificates Clare presented are enduring; by bearing witness to achievements and acknowledging abilities, they enhance the positive stories consultees can tell of themselves (see ability spotting, Chapter 4). Recognising that preferred developments need witnessing to sustain consultees, as consultants we often invite consultees to identify how they might draw attention to progress: who can give witness to the changes they have made, and who can participate in their preferred developments and views of themselves which were generated in the course of consultation?

Acknowledging transport to new contexts

The 'ending as metamorphosis discourse' encourages us to see ending as a transformation from one form into another, whereby people's skills, abilities and knowledges are not being lost with the ending but carried forward into future practice, relationships and responsibilities. Therefore we invite consultees to consider how they will transport their developments, learning and the contributions they have received from each other to their new contexts. As the name suggests, 'transport' implies movement; by 'acknowledging transport', we invite consultees to consider where their developments and the contributions they have received from each other have taken them and can transport them. Therefore I could have asked the team, 'What [from Clare] do you want to make sure you keep hold of for this team?', 'How will you use this in the future to continue the success of this service?' or 'What would you like to share with new team members when they join?' And [to Clare], 'What will you take with you from this experience into your new post/team?'

Conclusion

I have outlined an approach to consultation in contexts of ending and transition and invite you, our reader, to consider these principles as guidelines rather than prescribed techniques and therefore to prioritise the consultees' feedback and agenda rather than assume this as an established method. For clarity, the practices are presented as if they follow a logical progression. The construction of narratives, however, is rarely such an ordered affair. Narratives are created in conversation and in relationship and are continually evolving and changing as the context changes. People may hold several different stories to account for the same experience and how or whether a story is used is influenced by the contexts of relationship, time and place.

We have found that these steps can give consultees confidence and energy to begin something new and transform endings and change into times of accomplishment, new discovery, hope and memories that linger.

Guide 5.1 Consultation in contexts of ending and transition: A practice guide

Making time and space for talking about ending

- Explore consultees' perspectives on whether, when and how to address the ending.
- Enable consultees to become observers to their own relationships to endings.

Mapping 'relationship to endings' to bring significant relationships into view

- Reflect on pictures and metaphors of the organisation informing approaches to change.
- Invite consultee/s to take the different perspectives of people in the mapped system.
- Explore the effects of leaving on relevant people and relationships.

Create a context of knowing and telling about ending

- Explore: Who knows what? Who wants who to know what? Who believes what about who knows what?

Coordinating preferred and enabling stories of ending

- Generate multiple stories and explanations of the ending or transition with consultees.

- Draw on different discourses of ending to bring forth multiple stories of ending.
- Invite consultees to evaluate the stories generated.
- Explore the use and fit of different stories for consultees, their clients and others involved.

Appreciating, celebrating and taking forward contributions

- Co-create rituals and ceremonies with consultees to mark transitions.
- Witness and celebrate contributions and developments to sustain consultees.
- Explore the transport of developments and learning to new contexts.

References

Bruner, J. (1990) *Acts of Meaning*. Cambridge, MA: Harvard University Press.

Elkind, A. (1998) Using metaphor to read the organisation of the NHS. *Social Science and Medicine*, *47* (11), 1715–1727.

Fredman, G. (1997) *Death Talk: Conversations With Children and Families*. London: Karnac.

Fredman, G. and Dalal, C. (1998) Ending discourses: implications for relationships and action in therapy. *Human Systems: The Journal of Systemic Consultation and Management*, *9* (1), 1–13.

Fredman, G. and Fuggle, P. (2000) Parents with mental health problems: Involving the children. In P. Reder, M. McClure and A. Jolly (eds.) *Family Matters*. London: Routledge.

Imber-Black, E., Roberts, J. and Whiting, R. (2003) *Rituals in Families and Family Therapy, Revised Edition*. New York: Norton.

Lewis, S., Passmore, J. and Cantore, S. (2011) *Appreciative Inquiry for Change Management: Using AI to Facilitate Organizational Development*. London: Kogan Page.

Morgan, G. (1997a) *Images of Organization 2nd ed*. Newbury Park, CA: Sage.

Morgan, G. (1997b) *Imaginization: New Mindsets for Seeing, Organizing and Managing*. Thousand Oaks, CA: Sage.

Relph, A. (1985) The last time: a metaphor for leaving. *A.N.Z. Journal of Family Therapy*, *6* (3), 23–127.

Singer, J. (2009) *Birthrites: Rituals and Celebrations for the Child-Bearing Years*. East Meon, Hampshire, UK: Permanent Publications.

White, M. and Epston, D. (1990) *Narrative Means to Therapeutic Ends*. New York: Norton.

Chapter 6

Evaluating collaborative consultation

Emma Worwood and Glenda Fredman

In this chapter, we approach evaluation as a joint activity for the consultant in collaboration with the consultees. We show how we have made evaluation an integral part of our consultation practice and provide guiding questions and measurement tools for evaluating consultation that our readers can use or adapt in their own work settings.

> Victoria Mattison was convening consultation groups with staff at a school for children with learning disabilities (Chapter 2). Six months after these groups began, the head teacher who commissioned the consultation questioned whether the teachers were making use of the consultation and whether she could justify its continuation with so many competing demands on the staff.

In this age of accountability, with expectations to demonstrate outcomes for resources invested, people commissioning mental health services, like the head teacher above, want to know what they are 'getting for their money'. We cannot assume consultation is valuable and justifies the resources invested in it; we need to evaluate and demonstrate the impact it has and the contribution it is making.

We have identified several definitions and descriptions of evaluation relevant to the practice and outcome of collaborative consultation: 'to determine the importance, effectiveness or worth of' (American Heritage *Dictionary of the English Language*, 2011); 'an appraisal of the value of something' (WordNet 3.0, 2003–2008); and 'to gain insight, enable reflection and to assist in the identification of future change' (del Tufo, 2002). We evaluate 'effectiveness', 'worth' and 'value' in relation to the goals and intended outcomes of consultation. These include enabling consultees to develop their thinking, knowledge, skills and confidence, and hence their practice and relationships with clients to enhance client outcomes (Chapter 1; Rosenfield, 2012). Thus measuring outcomes and drawing on feedback from consultees enable us to clarify how useful the consultation is, identify how to improve or develop it and provide feedback about effectiveness for commissioners and other significant audiences. We also evaluate in order to review, and thereby enhance our working relationship with consultees. Clarifying what is working, what consultees appreciate and what to adapt or change gives us useful feedback to develop our own consultation competence.

We have recognised three activities necessary to the evaluation of consultation: determining a baseline for the intended outcomes of the consultation to be evaluated; obtaining systematic, ongoing feedback through conscious monitoring of these outcomes over extended periods of time; and deliberately tracking, reviewing and then adjusting practice, plans or next steps based on the ongoing feedback (Miller, Hubble and Duncan, 2007; Miller et al., 2015). We try to initiate the process of evaluation from the start, when we contract with the people commissioning the consultation and when we first meet with consultees. We clarify 'who are the key stakeholders and audiences', 'who is asking for what from this consultation' and 'who wants what feedback' (see also Chapter 2).

The timing of evaluation will vary depending on what is being asked or measured. We try to establish baselines as early as possible. Gathering feedback to help us review and adjust our practice can take place 'in each moment' during a consultation, as a routine activity at the end of the consultation or at the start of the following session.

Who participates and contributes to the evaluation of consultation

The people with and for whom we are evaluating will influence what and how we evaluate as well as the timeframe (e.g. ongoing review, annual reporting). The following questions help us identify who participates in evaluation, significant stakeholders and audiences:

- To whom are we accounting or reporting?
- Who is interested/wants to know the outcome, impact or effects of the consultation?
- Who wants to contribute?/Who notices what?/Who wants to offer feedback?
- Who will be affected by/benefit from the evaluation?

Therefore, from the start, we try to clarify the outcomes of most value to each stakeholder and how the consultant will participate in contributing and communicating feedback so we can build this into the contracting process.

> Victoria Mattison identified a number of significant stakeholders and audiences for her consultation with the staff at the school for children with learning disabilities: the local authority commissioner funding the child mental health team's work in schools (including Victoria's consultation time); the head teacher of the school; Victoria's manager of the child mental health team who set up the original service level agreement; the teacher-consultees; and the client-children, as well as Victoria herself, as the consultant.

Who wants what from the consultation

We always try to establish the goals, hopes or intended outcomes from the perspectives of all key stakeholders when setting up individual or group consultation.

We document the goals, which provide a useful baseline to refer back to when evaluating over time (see Chapter 2).

> The 'stakeholders' had different goals and expectations of the consultation Victoria was offering; therefore, they had different perspectives on what would demonstrate a good outcome of the consultation. The local authority commissioner wanted an indication of how the consultation was 'making a difference for the children' in the school; she also wanted annual feedback about 'what help was offered to staff' in the school to review whether the service was meeting guidelines for the required provision of continued professional development to all staff in schools. The head teacher and Victoria's manager wanted evidence that the teacher-consultees were developing competence to deal with difficult situations with children in the classroom. Furthermore, the manager hoped the consultations would enable staff to make sense of children's problems from a psychological perspective and support their confidence to 'try problem solving in the classroom before referring' to the child mental health team. The teacher-consultees wanted to feel 'less stressed' and 'more confident' working jointly with parents. Victoria could not directly elicit the perspectives of the client-children as they were non-verbal, but she could use the teacher-consultees' observations of their behaviour to evaluate changes at school. As the consultant, Victoria was focusing on her working relationship with the consultees and their transfer of skills from the consultation to similar problems in other work contexts. She wanted to know in what ways the consultation was proving useful and whether her collaborative approach was enabling consultees to 'draw on each other as a resource' rather than only look for an 'expert' view.

A multi-level approach to evaluating consultation

The multi-layered impact of consultation and the diverse expectations of multiple stakeholders leave many practitioners daunted by the task of evaluating consultation. We also hear consultants expressing concern that the distance between the consultation and the client outcome makes it difficult to reliably confirm any direct effect of the consultation on clients, since interpreting any client outcome data requires inference regarding which interventions (if any) contributed to change (Crothers et al., 2011). Hence consultants have told us that they often avoid evaluating their consultation practice because capturing the outcome of consultation seems so complex.

In an attempt to address this complexity, we take a multi-level approach to the evaluation of consultation. Recognising that consultation can have an impact at many levels, we have identified four levels at which to evaluate[1]:

- *consultant-consultee partnership*;
- *consultees' development and learning*: understanding/conceptualisation in relation to the issue brought for consultation; development in skills and practice; transport of learning to other work situations; confidence and well-being in relation to the work;

- *consultees' progress with the client*: the consultee–client relationship and client outcomes;
- *outcomes for the service or agency.*

Evaluating the consultant–consultee partnership

We view consultation as a work in progress that is constructed with consultees. Hence the working partnership between consultant and consultee is key to the success of consultation and we want to keep what is working, to change what is not and to try out new ideas. Therefore, as consultants, we continually check in with consultees about how well the way we are working fits with what they want, with questions like 'Am I getting this? Is anything new/useful coming out of this? Is this useful to you? In what way?' We use their immediate feedback to inform whether and how we recalibrate to create the best possible fit with consultees.

We also try to set aside dedicated time to stop and reflect with consultees on their experience of our working relationship and how well the method, approach and focus of the consultation fits with their goals and preferred ways of working.

The Consultation Partnership Scale

We have developed the Consultation Partnership Scale (CPS)[2] (Figure 6.1) to help us obtain a baseline and monitor the ongoing progress of our partnership with consultees.

Introducing the CPS to consultees

Below, Emma introduces this scale to Lynne and Carole, two family support workers with whom she was starting consultation sessions to support their work with families in a children's centre.

> In our first session, I (Emma) explained that I would be asking for feedback on 'how we are working together ... to help me make sure you are getting what you want from this meeting. So if this is OK with you, at the end of our session I would like to take the temperature of how you are finding our work together'. (Pointing to the scales on the CPS), 'For example, how well you feel I have listened, understood and respected you; whether we have talked about what you wanted to talk about; how the way we have worked today fits for you and whether there was anything missing. Your feedback is critical to the success of our meetings and will help me to learn what to keep doing that is useful and, importantly, what I might need to do different next time to make it better for you ... This is a way for me to check in, to get your input about what we did here today to keep me on track and let me know when I am off track and need to make some changes for you'. Carole said she thought this was important and was open to trying anything. Lynne was more hesitant; she said she did not want us to 'get bogged down with lots of form filling or questionnaires' and asked, 'Can we keep it simple?'

Consultation Partnership Scale (CPS)

Name of consultant: Date:

Name of consultee:

Please rate this consultation by placing a mark on the line nearest to the description that best fits your experience.

_____

Relationship

I did not feel heard,   I felt heard,

understood and respected   understood and respected

|--|

Goals and topics

We did not work on or talk   We worked on and talked

about what I wanted to   about what I wanted to

work on and talk about   work on and talk about

|--|

Approach or method

The way we have worked was   The way we have worked

not a good fit for me   was a good fit for me

|--|

Overall

There was something   Overall the consultation

missing in the consultation   was right for me

|--|

Group consultation

We did not work well   We worked very well

together as a group   together as a group

|--|

Figure 6.1   Consultation Partnership Scale (CPS)

Using CPS feedback to inform the consultation partnership

We invite consultees to place a mark on the 10 cm line (range 0–10) between the polarities of each question. We try to score the CPS in the presence of the consult-ees. Using a ruler, we measure the distance of consultees' markings from the left, scoring to the nearest millimetre and noting the scores as we do so.

> Noting, at the end of our second session, that Lynne and Carole's scores on the four scales ranged from 7.1 to 10, I (Emma) thanked them for their 'clear feedback': 'That is really helpful to me. I can use your feedback to help us work together in the best possible way'. Then I averaged Lynne and Carole's scores on each scale and, pointing to the 'Relationship' scale (aver-age rating 9.2) and then the 'Approach or method' scale (average rating 8.7), I noted, 'These scores suggest you feel I have listened to you and under-stood and that the consultation approach we are using seems to fit for you. Is that right? ... Can you think of anything else I might do differently to make these meetings even better for you ... to move your ratings closer to 10?'

In the early stages of building a partnership, consultants commonly receive high scores from consultees. Therefore, we take care with how we introduce the CPS and how we phrase questions so consultees feel comfortable offering frank and honest feedback (Bertolino and Miller, 2012). We stress that the aim of using the scale is to make the experience as good as possible for the consultee. If a consultee rates 10 on all four scales, we may respond by saying, 'Ok let's say 10 is an A, then can you help me do even better? What do I need to do to reach a distinction?' To assure consultees that we are open to their candid responses, we might suggest: 'It is early days and we are learning how to work together so I am concerned I might miss something; I am hoping you will help me keep on track'.

When we receive lower ratings from consultees, we always try to adopt an atti-tude of appreciation rather than disappointment, treating the feedback as a gift from consultees as they give us the opportunity to learn and adjust how we are working.

> Therefore, pointing to the 'Goals and topics' scale, I went on, 'We have an average of 7.1 for whether we talked about what you wanted to work on. Thank you for showing me that I could be doing better here. I am grate-ful for the opportunity to try to make some changes. So what could I do next time to make the necessary adjustments to improve how we work together? To help me move from a 7 to 8, what could I do differently? What would you like more of in the future? Less of? What have we not included that you think could be useful?'
> Carole said that, while we had agreed an agenda at the start, we had not checked back to it and as a result we had used up all the time discussing the first request. Lynne said she liked having the chance to sit back and listen to Carole and I reflect on her work dilemma but she would have liked to hear more from me about the literature and research on bereave-ment, an important theme with the family she presented for consultation.

The CPS provides us, as consultants, with a useful measure of how well we are doing in the consultation; Lynne and Carole's feedback would not have come to light in such an accessible way had Emma not formally evaluated the process. When we monitor process in this way on an ongoing basis, we have found enhanced effectiveness of consultation, like Miller et al. (2007), who report an improved client outcome consequent to monitoring the *therapeutic* alliance.

Reviewing the CPS opens space for collaborative dialogue, enabling both consultant and consultees to become observers to the consultation process and thereby to better coordinate. Hence I (Emma) paid more attention in the next consultation with Carole and Lynne to clarifying their agenda and checking how they wanted to prioritise the time. I also checked partway through that consultation that we were still on track with what they wanted. Completing the CPS also helps consultees clarify for themselves what they want from the consultation. In following consultations, Lynne and Carole put a lot of thought into how they would like to use the consultation sessions and what they would like to be able to take back into their work.

Evaluating outcomes of consultation

Consultee-centred consultation aims to improve consultees' competence by developing their understanding and 'new ways of conceptualising' work problems and by expanding their repertoire of skills in order to improve client outcomes so they can go on to benefit similar clients in the future (Caplan, 1970). Therefore we evaluate consultees' development and learning, their progress with clients and the outcomes for their service or agency.

Evaluating consultees' development and learning

We evaluate whether there has been development in the consultee's thinking and understanding, their skills and practice, whether they can transport their learning to other work situations and the consequences of the consultation for their confidence in the work.

Changes in consultee's understanding of the issue: Conceptual development

A consultation is effective when the consultation process promotes 'conceptual changes in the consultee' (Lambert, 2004:17). A conceptual shift or 'turning' occurs when the consultee 'has framed the problem in another way' (Hylander, 2004:45). Thus, a consultation is successful when consultees take away a different representation of the problem from how they first viewed it and/or consultees have made progress in their knowledge and confidence to address the problem presented for consultation. Therefore we evaluate the effects of the consultation on consultees' thinking and understanding at the end of a consultation or at the start of the following consultation with questions like:

• How has the consultation influenced your thinking about the issue you brought?

- What new ideas/understanding have you taken from the consultation to address this issue/dilemma?
- What sense are you making now of the issue you brought for consultation compared to when we first started talking about it?

Sometimes the initial issue or what was important to a consultee changes as the consultation progresses, so we may also ask: 'Do you have different questions now – from when we started?' or 'Has what was important to you changed?'

> When I met with Lynne and Carole two weeks after their first consultation, Lynne said that, 'Understanding what the family is doing as their grief reaction to a significant bereavement has helped me see that what I was calling "overprotection" could be them wanting to keep their child safe and close and be together as a family ... I feel so much more empathic ... they seem more relaxed with me'.

Skills and practice developments

To evaluate consultees' use of the consultation once they are back in their work environment, we ask consultees questions like:

- What new ideas do you have about how you might go on?
- How did/will you use the ideas from this consultation? What did/might you do next?
- What did/will you do differently as a result of this consultation?
- What impact has the consultation had on your confidence to [manage the situation]?

> Victoria and the teacher-consultees had agreed to 'use the initial ten minutes of each meeting to discuss developments and outcomes since the previous school consultation ... to capture feedback more rigorously'. Omar, a newly qualified teacher, had used the previous consultation, two weeks before, to address his 'struggles' in class with a child called David.
> When Victoria asked, 'What stayed with you from the last consultation?' and then, 'What ideas were useful?' and 'How did they help with what you did next?', Omar explained that David had 'been in my thoughts a lot' since the consultation; Omar had 'been paying a lot more attention to how David is struggling in the classroom ... and so I've noticed much more'. When Victoria explored, 'So what are you doing differently – from before?' Omar went on, 'I'm staying calm when David reacts angrily ... And I've been talking to David more – well, showing interest in him – like what he enjoys when he is more settled ... and I've also spoken to David's mother about how he has been at home'. Omar had also shared ideas from the consultation with Georgina, the teaching assistant, and she was now 'understanding David a lot better'. Omar reflected, 'I am beginning to feel confident we can really help David with his behaviour'.

We evaluate developments in skills and practice through interview and observation, commonly drawing on feedback from the consultee and observations made by fellow consultees, other staff and managers.

> Victoria asked the other teacher-consultees in the group: 'Did anyone else notice an impact on Omar following this consultation?' and 'Did this consultation offer any benefit for anyone else?' The teaching assistant, Georgina, said she was pleased Omar had shared his ideas with her; it made her feel they were working 'more as a team' to understand and support David. Victoria was sure the head teacher would be very interested to hear examples of the staff's increased confidence in dealing with difficult situations and their team work and she asked the group if they could start to keep a 'log of all these positive developments you are making'.

Transport of learning[3]

Since our intention is for consultation to have an effect on consultees' practice in situations beyond the one brought for discussion (Caplan, 1970; Chapters 1 and 3), we evaluate how consultees might develop, learn and use the ideas, knowledge or skills acquired in the consultation in other areas of their work. Therefore, at the end of a consultation session, we explore how consultees might transport their learning from the consultation to other contexts, asking:

- What ideas/practices are you holding onto from today's conversation?
- Which ideas most connect with you/seem most useful?
- Where might this take you in your work?
- How will you take the ideas and practices from today and use them in other situations at work?
- What might you use in another context/situation with other clients?

We also explore transport of learning at the start of subsequent consultations or when evaluating after a period of time. For example, we might ask 'What ideas have you taken from these meetings into your work?' 'How have you used them in other situations?' In group consultation, we might ask other group members 'What have you learned from our conversation with [the consultee]?' 'How might you use this learning in your own work situation?' 'Where has this experience taken you that you would not otherwise have arrived at, if you had not been listening to this conversation?'

Confidence and well-being in relation to the work

When consultees' understanding of a work issue starts to shift through consultation and new ways forward begin to emerge, we often see a change in the emotional atmosphere or feelings of the consultees. We have witnessed the impact of this on consultees' well-being and their relationship to their work. For example, consultees start seeing themselves in a more appreciative light; their expectations of what is possible shift; their worry, stress or feelings of 'stuckness' begin to dissipate; and they express or act with more confidence. Following consultation, managers have also reported that staff appear 'less stressed' or that there is a 'calmer atmosphere' in the workplace. In Chapter 8, Selma Rikberg Smyly and Sarah Coles noticed a 'markedly different atmosphere in the room' following the consultants' sharing of their reflections; consultees 'seemed to express their feelings with more confidence' (p. 145). In Chapter 10, Eleanor Martin and Alison Milton give examples of how consultation 'softened self-criticism, [and] invited more appreciative perspectives on [consultees'] own competence' (p. 179).

To capture the effects of the consultation on consultees' confidence and well-being, we explore whether and how the consultation helped relieve pressure or ease stress for the consultee, to what extent the consultation reduced anxiety or 'stuckness' about a situation or enhanced confidence with questions like 'What difference has this consultation made to your experience of [stress/anxiety/stuckness] that you described when we started?' 'What effects has the consultation had on how you see yourself/feel about your work?'

Evaluating consultees' progress with clients

As well as exploring progress with consultees, we try to invite the contribution of significant stakeholders and audiences, whether present or not in the consultations. We have often invited managers to join part of a consultation to share their perspectives, or the consultant has documented their feedback and taken it to a review with consultees. Many managers have appreciated the changes in staff's language, actions and relationships with clients following the consultation.

Consultee–client relationship

Practitioners frequently request consultation to address their relationship with the people with whom they work. For example, we have had requests for help with difficulties in engaging clients and unwanted feelings or attitudes towards clients. A hope of changing or improving this relationship is often at the heart of what is wanted from a consultation (Caplan, 1970). For example, in Chapter 10, Eleanor Martin and Alison Milton offered consultation to staff in a nursing home to address their concerns about Antonio, an older man with dementia who had been 'threatening staff with a cutlery knife', hitting and scratching them. The staff felt unsafe and no one wanted to work with Antonio. They were 'upset ... stressed ... constantly coming to [the manager] with complaints and worries about Antonio', so that the manager had to 'keep calling the community psychiatric nurse' (p. 171). At the one month follow-up, the team manager informed Eleanor that, although the consultation had not resulted in a change in Antonio's *behaviour*, there had been a significant improvement in the staff's *relationship* with Antonio: 'the staff are fine ... I have not heard any complaints from them about Antonio'.

To evaluate the impact of consultation on consultees' relationship with the clients, we ask consultees and significant audiences questions like 'Has the consultation helped in your/consultee's relationship with this client?' 'How have things changed between you/consultees and [client] since the consultation?' 'What difference has the consultation made to your view/feelings/attitude of [irritation/dislike/frustration] towards [the client]?' 'What effect has the consultation had on how consultees are being with [the client]?'

When Eleanor explored with the team manager the effect of the consultation on how the staff were 'being with' Antonio, with questions like 'How have things changed between staff and Antonio?' 'What differences have you noticed in their attitude or how they feel about him?', she learned that there had been a shift in how they felt towards and how they communicated with Antonio: 'they used softer, more compassionate tones and less critical language' (p. 171).

Client outcomes: Consultation goals

At the start of the consultation process, we try to invite stakeholders, audiences and consultees to identify their intended outcomes or goals for the consultation (Chapter 2) and to help us name the goals.

> When I (Emma) contracted for consultation with a day nursery, the children's centre head commissioning the work wanted day nursery staff to be more 'aware of parental mental health and its impact on the child'; the day nursery manager wanted nursery staff to be 'able to identify when to refer to child mental health services' and to 'identify a child at risk of emotional or behavioural problems'; and the nursery worker-consultees wanted help with 'improving the children's behaviour or emotional well-being'. I therefore prepared the following short questionnaire for a review with nursery staff following a term of consultation groups:
>
> To help us review the consultation groups this term, please tick if the consultation helped with any of the following (give an example):
>
> 1   Improving a child's behaviour or emotional well-being   [ ]
> 2   Identifying a child at risk of emotional or behavioural problems   [ ]
> 3   Identifying the need for referral to the child mental health service   [ ]
> 4   Recognising a parent's mental health difficulty   [ ]
> 5   Noticing the impact of a parent's mental health on the child   [ ]

The nursery worker-consultees' responses to the questions opened space for us to share stories and examples of developments staff had made since the start of the consultations as well as improved outcomes for the children in the centre.

Client outcomes: Proxy measures

Stakeholders like commissioners and managers frequently want to know if the consultation makes a difference for clients. While it may not always be possible to directly link observed or measured client outcomes with the benefits of consultation (Crothers et al., 2011), we can use indirect or proxy measures by asking consultees questions like 'What effects/benefits do you think this consultation has had for [the client]?' 'How do you know?' and 'What impact have others observed on [the client]?'

> When Victoria reviewed the impact of the group consultation at the end of term, she asked the teacher-consultees: 'Is the impact of our work here showing in any way with the children? Can you give some examples?' One consultee shared a striking observation that, since starting the consultation with Victoria, 'we are keeping many more children in the classroom rather than excluding'; his observation was substantiated by several others who confirmed that exclusions had fallen dramatically. When Victoria started working with the staff team, she had noticed 'there were often children in the corridor, excluded from class'. On reflection, she realised this was 'now a rare sight'. When Victoria invited staff to review records of daily exclusions before and after the consultations, they found there was a reduction of internal exclusions of children from two or three a day to one or two a week.

The Consultation Outcome Scale

There are times when we have found it useful to use a more structured evaluation method, or we are specifically requested to provide quantitative measures of the outcome of consultation. For this purpose, we have developed the Consultation Outcome Scale (COS) (Figure 6.2) which comprises seven separate scales to enable us to establish baselines and monitor progress in relation to the levels of consultation outcomes we have identified. These are *consultees' own development and learning* (ideas and understanding, skills and practice, transport of learning, well-being and confidence in relation to the work issue) and *consultees' progress with the client* (relationship with the client; outcomes for clients; consultation goals).

We use the information we gather from the COS ratings as feedback to inform and develop our work with consultees. We do not treat the scores as data or evidence of success or failure of the consultation and especially not of the consultees. Thus we approach consultees' feedback as the beginning of a conversation, not as the end, and try wherever possible to create the opportunity to respond to and accommodate consultees' feedback to improve the outcomes. Therefore, we usually invite consultees to complete the scales with us so we can bring forth examples and stories to contextualise their ratings, explaining, 'I would appreciate your help with reviewing the impact this consultation has had on [your thinking/your practice/how you are using the consultations in your work with clients/outcomes with the people you work with/the progress you have made with the issue you brought to consultation]'. We rarely use all the COS scales at one time, trying to select scales that fit the context and focus of the consultation and that address outcomes most relevant to significant stakeholders in the consultation. When we are working with

Consultation Outcome Scale (COS)

Name of consultant: Date:

Name of consultee:

Please place a mark on the lines to mark what best fits your experience
_____

Ideas and understanding

The consultation/s have given me new understanding / changed my thinking to help me

address the issues brought

|--|

Not at all   Very much

Please give examples

Skills and practice

The consultation/s have helped me learn new ideas or skills to address the issues brought

|--|

Not at all   Very much

Please give examples

Using your learning in other situations

I have used / can use the ideas and practices from the consultation/s in other situations at

work

|--|

Not at all   A great deal

Please give examples

Well-being / relationship to the work

The consultation/s have helped ease stress about work related issues / improved my

confidence

|--|

Not at all   A great deal

Please give examples

Figure 6.2   Consultation Outcome Scale (COS)

Relationship with client

The consultation/s have helped improve my relationship with clients

|---|

Not at all   Very much

Please give examples.

Outcomes for clients

The consultation/s have enabled positive effects / outcomes for clients

|---|

Not at all   Very much

Please give examples

Consultation goals

What were your hopes or goals at the start of the consultation/s?

-- -------------------------

How has the consultation/s met your hopes / goals?

|---|

Not at all   A great deal

Please give examples

Figure 6.2   Continued

large groups in consultation, we may distribute the COS to all consultees and then summarise or theme the feedback to share with consultees and commissioners.

> At the end of term, Victoria decided to use this more structured tool, rather than ask the questions in conversation with the teacher-consultees, to ensure she gathered feedback from everyone in this large group. Victoria invited each teacher-consultee to complete the COS by themselves, discuss their feedback in pairs and then share with the wider group. The teachers fed back that they were able to 'make more sense' of the children's difficulties. They offered several examples of their

improved confidence in managing tricky situations in class. One teacher, Michael, spoke of how he 'kept hold of the idea more strongly' that he was 'a role model' for the children at times of conflict with their peers; he now saw this as an opportunity for the children to learn 'through my example and encouragement'. Several other teachers talked about 'not feeling alone' and the benefits of hearing their colleagues' ideas which they could 'try out with other children'.

The consultation context: Organisation, service and agency

We frequently observe effects beyond the client and consultee when we provide consultee-centred consultation, reminding us of the recursive relationship between client or consultee developments, the client-consultee relationship and the practices and relationships within the service or agency. Therefore, even when we offer consultee-centred consultation rather than whole system consultation, we evaluate the effects of the consultation on the agency or service and review how the organisation context is enabling or constraining the quality and outcome of the consultation.

Evaluating outcomes for the service or agency

When we have asked consultees, managers or commissioners questions like 'What effects has this consultation had on your service?', we have learned about changes in the quality of communication and enhanced appreciation between colleagues. They have reported staff 'feeling more of a team' and 'working better together', enhanced staff retention and shifts in agency culture from focusing solely on clients' deficits to noticing strengths and possibilities. For example, in Chapter 10, Eleanor Martin shows how consultee-centred consultation opens space for staff to address their relationships with management, and in this chapter, Victoria Mattison shows the effect of consultation on the whole school's practice of exclusion.

Reviewing the organisational context for consultation

A common challenge to the effectiveness of consultation is consultees' ability to access the consultation. Therefore, we review consultees' satisfaction with our availability for consultation and with the length, frequency, number of sessions and convenience of the venue.

When we have explored *what* enabled consultees' ability to use the consultation we offered, their common responses have included *support from the organisation and managers* to attend the consultation and *managers expressing an interest in the outcomes* of the consultation. Barriers to the usefulness or effectiveness of the consultation have included *inadequate time for attending* consultation, the burden of 'workload' and *'resource pressures'* like 'staff shortages' and 'lack of staff cover'. We therefore review and evaluate whether and how the culture and management of the organisation enable or constrain consultees' use of the consultation. When we have asked 'What changes to your organisation would help you make [even better] use of the consultation?' or 'What arrangements would you like to see in your organisation to make your attendance as easy and convenient as possible?', consultees have generally identified 'planned and protected time' to attend, 'adjustment to caseload' and 'clear permission and support from management'. At times we find the service context has changed, rendering consultation no longer useable, relevant or fitting, so that we need to review and re-contract with managers and commissioners whether and how to continue providing consultation (see Chapter 2).

Spreading the news: Disseminating the findings of evaluation

Feeding back the findings of evaluation ensures accountability. Through this process we are able to describe 'what works'; demonstrate and celebrate developments and achievements; draw attention to strengths and needs in a system; build partnerships and collaboration; and plan, shape and sustain the provision of future consultation as well as satisfy requirements for funding (Hepburn et al., 2007). How and to whom we communicate the findings of our evaluation has implications for decision-making about resource allocation and policy and hence may have significant consequences for clients, consultees and services. Therefore, we take care how we document and communicate the outcomes of our evaluation.

Once we are clear about the stakeholders, we consider how each interested party might prefer to learn of the impact or outcomes of the consultation, what ways of giving feedback would be most meaningful, what language and presentation style would fit best with their discourse and which outcomes and in whose voice (clients and/or consultees) we present the feedback. For example, we may engage the manager of the consultees in mutually agreed ongoing conversations, set up more formal reviews of the consultations with commissioners or senior managers in the service or invite managers or commissioners to join a 'review' session with consultees and/or clients.

We also provide written documents and reports. We try to include qualitative descriptions in our reports to convey the experience of consultees and their clients through stories and case studies that emerge through the evaluative process with consultees. To capture these 'lived' experiences, we invite consultees to share and record their learning, practice developments and client outcomes at the end of each consultation or the start of the next. We usually allocate one or two consultees in the group to take on this 'record-keeping', 'log' or 'minutes' task for the whole group each time, inviting the consultees to agree how they would like to do this.

Conveying outcomes through 'storied experience' in this way brings the impact alive so that it 'touches the heart' of the receiver. Inviting managers or commissioners to join a consultation 'review' with consultees in the position of 'witness' to the consultees' developments and accomplishments has not only touched the hearts of the commissioners but has also had the effect of boosting morale and enriching the consultees' perception of their own developments.

We also provide quantitative 'data' about the consultation activity, for example, the number of sessions, number of consultees attended, number of clients discussed and scores collated from measures like the CPS and COS about the use and impact of consultation on consultees' practice. We have presented this sort of numerical 'data' visually using tables and graphs to convey findings simply as part of the process of annual reporting.

We try to make reports concise, easy to understand and tailored to the audience, to convey messages that can engage, educate and enrich stakeholders. Our key intention is that the audience can easily understand what the presented information means and what the implications are for consultees, clients and the service (Child Trends and SRI International, 2002; Perry et al., 2007). We have also shared feedback through newsletters, articles and poster displays on service websites and offered presentations and training sessions to communicate what we have learned from the evaluation.

Following the production and distribution of an annual report on work we provided in children's centres, Emma attended a meeting with stakeholders to discuss key findings and implications for service delivery over the coming year. We learn much about the outcomes of most interest to different parties in these sorts of meetings and can get feedback about the reporting itself, what has been particularly useful, what was less so and what was missing that the audience would have liked to have known to inform future reporting. Contributing to and reviewing annual reports and evaluation documents within our own team has also helped to develop a shared understanding of the consultation work we are doing, explore the similarities and differences in our practices and consider ways to improve, shape and enhance our consultation skills.

Closing comments

Evaluation has enabled us to foster our professional development as consultants and give an account of and demonstrate the worth of our practice to commissioners, managers, consultees and ourselves. We recognise that there are different opportunities and challenges with each method of evaluating consultation we have presented in this chapter and that you will want to take into consideration issues such as the 'user friendliness' of the method and the time involved to use it. We try to use the approach and methods we describe in an ethos of collaborative practice to create a fit that is as good as possible for consultees, commissioners and the culture of the agency. We hope this chapter has encouraged you, our reader, to evaluate the impact of your consultation practice on consultees and clients and has offered you some 'tools' for taking and following feedback and adjusting your practice to generate the best outcome and fit for consultees.

Notes

1 There are few consultation evaluation measures available in the published literature. Two scales we have drawn upon are the Child Outcome and Research Consortium Consultation Feedback Questionnaire (CORC, 2002) and the Satisfaction with Early Childhood Mental Health Consultation (ECMHC) scale (Hepburn et al., 2007).
2 Adapted from Miller and Duncan (2000) and Miller et al. (2005) Session Rating Scale (SRS) created to provide feedback on the therapeutic alliance.
3 We use the word 'transport' rather than 'transfer' of learning to connote the dynamic movement implicit in 'transport'. Consultees do not simply 'carry over' the ideas and skills they have taken from the consultation to other clients; they make use of the new skills they have acquired and develop their new understandings to fit with their different contexts. Thus they are moved to create new opportunities.

References

American Heritage® Dictionary of the English Language, Fifth Edition (2011) Available from: http://www.thefreedictionary.com/evaluation. Retrieved 24 October 2016.

Bertolino, B. and Miller, S.D. (2012) *ICCE Manuals On Feed-Back-Informed Treatment*, Vol. 1–6. Chicago: ICCE Press.

Caplan, G. (1970) *Theory and Practice of Mental Health Consultation*. New York: Basic Books.

Child Outcomes Research Consortium (2002) *Consultation Feedback Form*. Available from: http://www.corc.uk.net/resources/measures/practitioner/corc-evaluation-questionnaire-15-11-06-6/. Retrieved 31 October 2016.

Child Trends and SRI International (2002) *First 5 California: Child, Family, and Community Indicators Book*. Menlo Park, CA: SRI International.

Crothers, L.M., Hughes, T.L. and Morine, K.A. (2011) *Theory and Cases in School-Based Consultation: A Resource For School Psychologists, School Counselors, Special Educators, and Other Mental Health Professionals*. New York: Routledge.

del Tufo, S. (2002). 'WHAT is evaluation?' *Evaluation Trust*. [Online] Available from: https://en.wikipedia.org/wiki/Evaluation#References. Retrieved 24 October 2016.

Hepburn, K.S., Kaufmann, R. K., Perry, D.F., Allen, M.D., Brennan, E.M. and Green, B.L. (2007) *Early Childhood Mental Health Consultation: An Evaluation Toolkit*. Washington, DC: Georgetown University.

Hylander, I. (2004) Analysis of conceptual change in consultee-centered consultation. In N.M. Lambert, I. Hylander and J. Sandoval (eds.) *Consultee-Centered Consultation: Improving the Quality of Professional Services in Schools and Community Organisations*. Hillsdale, NJ: Lawrence Erlbaum Associates.

Lambert, N.M. (2004) Consultee-centred consultation: An international perspective on goals, process and theory. In N. M. Lambert, I. Hylander and J. Sandoval (eds.) *Consultee-Centered Consultation: Improving the Quality of Professional Services in Schools and Community Organisations*. Hillsdale, NJ: Lawrence Erlbaum Associates.

Miller, S.D. and Duncan, B.L. (2000) *The Outcome and Session Rating Scales*. Chicago, Il: International Center for Clinical Excellence.

Miller, S.D., Duncan, B.L., Sorrell, R. and Brown, G.S. (2005) The partners for change outcome management system. *Journal of Clinical Psychology, 61*, 199–208.

Miller, S.D., Hubble, M.A., Chow, D. and Seidel, J. (2015) Beyond measures and monitoring: Realizing the potential of feedback-informed treatment. *Psychotherapy*, *52* (4), 449–457.

Miller, S.D., Hubble, M.A. and Duncan, B.L. (2007) Supershrinks. *Psychotherapy Networker*, *31*, 26–35, 56.

Perry, D.F., Woodbridge, M.W. and Rosman, E.A. (2007) Evaluating outcomes in systems delivering early childhood mental health services. In D. F. Perry, R. K. Kaufman and J. Knitzer (eds.) *Social and Emotional Health in Early Childhood: Building Bridges Between Services and Systems*. Baltimore: Paul H. Brookes.

Rosenfield, S. (2012) *Becoming a School Consultant. Lessons Learned.* New York and London: Routledge.

WordNet 3.0, Farlex clipart collection (2003–2008). Available from: https://www.learnthat.org/dictionary/92663_WordNet.html. Retrieved 24 October 2016.

Part II

Extending consultation practices

Chapter 7

Working with the group as a resource to the consultation process

Glenda Fredman and Andia Papadopoulou

We commonly witness impressive expertise among practitioners participating in group consultation. Therefore, starting from the premise that group members bring a wealth of knowledge and expertise from their professional and also personal experience, we approach all the members of group consultation not as 'accidental bystanders' but as active participants in and a rich resource for the consultation. Hence we try to facilitate a process of collaborative participation whereby group members can share and make use of their collective expertise and experience with each other, enhance the abilities and confidence of consultees through a process of exchanging and valuing all views as potential contributions to the consultation questions, and extend the learning and competence of all group members to other similar issues encountered in their practice.

This chapter describes some of the ways we actively involve the whole group in collaborative consultation so that members can be a resource to each other by contributing to the process of the consultation as well as offering a repertoire of ideas and new ways to go on. From the start, we aim to involve everyone in the group, whether they are bringing the issue for consultation or not, since participants who view themselves as significant players in the ongoing process of change are more likely to become actively and enthusiastically engaged (Anderson and Burney, 1997). We describe the steps we take to prepare and build the group. We explain how we position the consultees who bring work for consultation, the group participants and ourselves, the consultants, to facilitate group collaboration.

Building a cooperative group partnership

Some consultation group participants have told us that they prefer to 'sit back and enjoy' the opportunity to observe a stimulating exchange between the consultant and consultee or be with their own thoughts after a hard working day rather than be called upon to participate. Others have expressed fear of being 'evaluated' by the consultant, 'judged' by the group or concerned about 'feeling deskilled'. Since the position of 'passive observer' risks isolating and disconnecting group members from the purpose of coming together as a group and excluding them from the creative process, we try to position all from the start as active members of a 'work group' (Bion, 1961; Granville, 2010) by inviting them into a state of readiness to engage together with the agreed tasks of the group consultation and by setting the expectation that they all have something of value to bring to the consultation.

From the start of the work, therefore, we try to build a collaborative partnership where consultants and group members experience themselves and each other as contributing to a 'joint project' in which we are all working and developing together. We ask ourselves, as consultants, the following questions to guide us throughout the process (Fredman, 2014):

• How can we work together towards a joint achievement where we are all on the side of the project?
• How can we engage in the activity so that we all value and benefit from each person's contribution and abilities?
• How can we be together in ways that appreciate and respect everyone involved?
• How can we position ourselves so that we all experience ourselves and each other as competent?
• How can we open space to develop each person's abilities?

Preparing the group for collaborative practice

Whether we are working with an ongoing regular group or a one-off session, we always co-create a contract with the group members to help us establish contexts of safety, comfort and respect for all attending the consultation; appreciate the culture and the practices of the organisation; clarify the relationships between consultees and consultant in terms of their rights, duties and responsibilities; and agree a clear focus for our work together. (Chapter 2 offers practices for co-contracting.)

To make the most of our time with groups, especially when we are offering one-off consultations or when there is limited time allocated for consultation, we begin co-contracting by sending a letter or email of welcome to all those attending the group consultation. We clarify the context for the consultation by introducing ourselves, explaining the request and contract for group consultation that has been negotiated with the people commissioning the consultation and confirming the arrangements that have already been agreed, for example, date, time and venue. We often attach a brief questionnaire to help us start the process of preparing the ground and creating a focus for group consultation. For example, when I (Andia) was invited to offer consultation to a group of health visitors, I sent them the following letter with the questionnaire in Box 7.1.

To: Health Visiting Team
From: Andia Papadopoulou, Clinical Psychologist

Re: Monthly Health Visiting Team Group Consultation
Dates: 7th March, 4th April, 9th May, 23rd June
Time: 9.15 am to 11.15 am
Venue: The Health Centre

I am pleased to be invited by your locality manager, Jane Simmons, to work with you all on developing your practice with families.
To help me prepare so we can make the most of our time together in our first meeting, I would be grateful if you would complete the following questionnaire before Thursday 12th February.
I will use your responses to the questions to identify common themes and a focus for our first meeting. I will not share or identify the specific content of each person's feedback with the group.

Please send your response to my email address above.
Looking forward to working with you all.
Many thanks
Andia

Box 7.1   Example questionnaire to begin preparing the group for consultation

Health Visiting Team Consultations

Please complete this brief questionnaire to help us prepare

1   What do you want to create as an outcome by the end of our four consultation sessions?
2   Imagine you are at the end of our sessions and you say to yourself, 'That consultation was really worthwhile. I got what I wanted'.
   a)   What issues have we addressed in our meetings?
   b)   What have you added to your existing repertoire of skills/ knowledge?
      What are you able to do?
   c)   What is clearer for you?
3   What is most precious to you in your work? What most inspires you in your work?
4   What do you think that I, in the position of consultant, may overlook in our meetings?

5   What do you not want from our meetings?
6   Any other comments?

(I will use your responses to the questions to identify common themes and a focus for our first meeting. I will not share or identify the specific content of each person's feedback with the group.)

By sending the letter and questionnaire to all group members before we meet for the first consultation, we intend to engage them, from the start, with the process of building the group by communicating that we are 'looking forward to working' with them all, we are committed to 'making the most of' this work, we value everyone's perspectives and contributions, and that this is a joint project. By taking time to respond to the questionnaire, group members also begin to imagine, as consultees-to-be, what they would like our 'coming together' to look like. Their responses can enable us to get to know the culture and language of their organisation and tap into their expectations and hopes for the consultations.

Collaborative contracting using mind-maps

Prior to our first meeting, we collate participants' responses to our questions and group them together into themes. We go on to organise the themes into two mind-maps[1], 'what is precious' (or 'what inspires') the group members and 'what [they] want' from the consultation, with a view to using this feedback with the group at the first meeting. To represent all voices in the group, we take care to place the group members' own words and expressions on the mind-maps. This process makes an important contribution to establishing a common language of agreed shared goals and values for the group.

> I (Andia) was pleased to greet seven health visitors for our first consultation. Following a round of brief introductions, I explained that we would be using the first part of this meeting to 'clarify and agree how we work together'. I took time to thank them all for their email feedback that 'helped me get a sense of what is important to you in your work as health visitors and what you would like to get from our sessions'. I went on to share the mind-map I had previously drawn up from their responses on a flipchart (Figure 7.1), noting, 'I am using your own words here. If you do not see your responses here, please let me know so I can add them'. Then I read aloud from the mind-map, using their actual expressions and pointing to their words on the map as we went along, 'I learned that "making a difference" to the "lives of young children and their families" is precious to you and you appreciate it when you do this as "a team effort" since you particularly value "working as team."' I repeated this process with their other themes such as 'family focused working' and 'opportunities to develop our practice'. As I named each response aloud, I noticed the participants nodding or smiling as they recognised their own expressions.

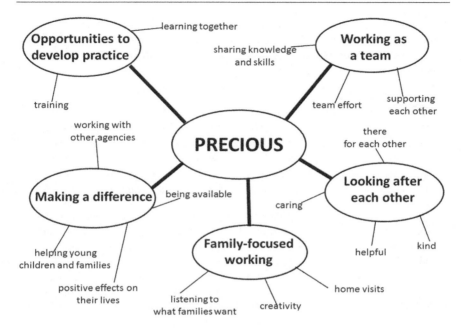

Figure 7.1 Example of a mind-map of 'What is Precious'

We pay careful attention to how group members respond to our sharing their expressions, noticing who nods in agreement and recognition to the words or who appears disengaged. We try to maintain eye contact with all participants, positioning ourselves in the room to avoid excluding or marginalising anyone. We intend to show that our listening is open and accepting by summarising and clarifying what we have heard, using the language of the persons and avoiding assuming too quickly through checking our understanding of the meanings of words they use. When we have named all participants' responses on the map, we always check with the group, 'Is there anything else I have missed that we could add?' to ensure that we have captured all their perspectives. We include new phrases and themes they offer in their own words, checking where they prefer to put them on the map.

> Sharon, one of the senior health visitors, responded, 'I value how we are there for each other … like back in the office after a difficult visit'. When I (Andia) asked, 'Where would you like to put this on your map … for example, is it part of "working as a team"?', Sharon reviewed the themes on the page and pondered, 'This may be different … It's more about how we look after each other'. So, with Sharon's direction, I added, 'Looking after each other' to the mind-map and then drew a line to connect it with 'Precious'.

Building the group involves co-creating a group culture of collaboration, acceptance and respect that will enable group members to work together as equal contributors and appreciate each other's different perspectives as valuable offerings to the consultation. Asking questions about what is precious and important to participants in their work enables us to bring forth, in their own language, their values and what they stand for in their work. Thus we are able to incorporate the shared language we have co-created as a group when we go on to co-contract.

> Thus I (Andia) went on, 'Would you like us to pay attention to these values in this group? [Pointing to the mind-map] for example, "Looking after each other" by offering help and taking care with kindness? And do you want the group to "share knowledge and skills" and "support each other" as a "team effort" … and to try to keep the work "family focused" … so we are all "listening to what families want"?'

We use this same mind-mapping process (on another flipchart) to collect and collate 'what [the participants] want' from the group consultation. By placing the actual words and phrases from their questionnaires on the mind-map, we can include all their voices.

As individual members recognise their personal contributions on the map and witness their hopes and expectations being linked with those of their colleagues, the group has a lived-experience of valuing all contributions. Thus we can ensure that what we agree reflects the perspectives of all group members and connects with individual as well as group hopes and expectations.

Explaining how we use the group

When we contract, we describe 'how we will work as a group'. We usually explain briefly that we will invite one or more participants to 'bring a work issue for consultation' to the group. We outline the different positions group members can take during the consultation, clarifying and agreeing the respective responsibilities and rights that go with each position.

> Therefore I (Andia) explained to the health visiting group, 'Each time we meet, I will invite you to decide who wants to use the group for consultation on a work issue. If more than one of you is involved in that work, you may choose to bring the issue together. I will begin by asking the persons bringing the issue for consultation some questions to clarify what you want from the conversation with me and the group. We refer to the people bringing work for consultation as the "consultees". The rest of you will be listening to this conversation. I may ask some of you to work with me as "co-consultants" to help me listen and then share what you have heard. I will offer suggestions on how you can listen and what to listen out for at different points in the conversation. Is that clear? Do you have any questions?'

Positioning of consultants, consultees and the group

In group consultation, we identify the positions of consultant and group members. Consultants can take the positions of convenor of the consultation, conductor of the session and interviewer of the consultee. Group members can take the positions of consultee, co-consultant and group participant, who may also be positioned as observers. Each position carries rights, duties and responsibilities for how practitioners can/cannot and should/should not act in certain contexts. Thus, in group consultation, the positions of consultant, consultee and group participant signal something about the person's differential power, informing their respective rights and abilities to speak and to contribute.

Positioning ourselves as consultants

When we engage with each other, each person takes up positions and offers or calls the other person into positions according to a storyline. The storyline may or may not be shared by the persons relating with each other and we may accept or refuse a position (Davies and Harré, 1990; Harré and van Langenhove, 1999). For example, we commonly experience the tendency for consultation group members to position us, the consultant, as the expert with all the answers, who will solve the problem or instruct the consultee. Often there is an assumption that group participants will not be actively involved in the consultation, taking a back seat while the consultant works with the consultee (Granville, 2010). In Chapter 2, we describe how we try to position ourselves in a 'cooperative partnership' with consultees, and in Chapter 3, we address our attempts to 'resist the pull towards an expert position' within a collaborative consultation relationship.

In this chapter, we describe how we also take a 'decentred and influential' position (White, 2005) whereby we try to centre the knowledge, experience and expertise of consultees and group participants and still remain influential as consultants. In the positions of *convenor* and *conductor*, we are 'influential' in engaging the group in building a cooperative partnership; we take responsibility for involving all group members and we facilitate the consultation process by explaining how we work in group consultation, clarifying our different positions in the consultation process (for example consultant, consultee, co-consultant or observer) and agreeing the responsibilities and rights of each position.

As *conductor* and *interviewing consultant*, throughout the consultation, we also try to hold a 'decentred' position in relation to both the consultees' and co-consultants' knowledge and skills on the issues brought for consultation. Therefore, from the start, we dispel any assumption that the consultant is the only one to do the 'thinking' or to provide answers to the consultees' dilemmas while the group takes a back seat. As *interviewing consultant*, we guide the consultee through the steps of the consultation process that include co-creating a focus for the conversation together, exploring what the consultees have already tried and other ideas they have, inviting multiple perspectives of the wider system involved as well as sharing our specialist knowledge and expertise. (We describe these practices in detail in Chapter 3.)

Positioning consultees to engage with the group as a resource

To bring forth the expectation of collective participation, we try to position group members not as competitors but as collaborators contributing to their clients' well-being *and* each other's mutual learning. Therefore, we usually start by asking the whole group

- 'Who wants to use the group for some ideas today? Who would like the group's input with some issues?'

This opening question calls participants into different positions: 'consultees' (who use the group for consultation) and the 'group' (who offer 'ideas' or 'input' to the consultees on the work issue). With this question, we intend to invite consultees to value their group as a resource that can offer support and different perspectives. Thus our intention is to foreground the collective expertise of the group, orient the consultees towards the group for ideas and positively promote the group's knowledge and experience in the eyes of the consultees.

As consultants, we go on to interview the consultees, repositioning ourselves as 'interviewers' and the group participants as our 'co-consultants' who will join us in centring the knowledge and skills of their 'consultee-colleagues'. We orient the listening of the 'co-consultants' so they can contribute to the process of co-creating a focus with their consultee-colleague and then capturing the consultee's abilities and solutions or generating a repertoire of new ideas and possibilities. Thus the co-consultants are a resource to the consultation process.

Separating talking and listening

We adopt the practice of separating listening and talking (Andersen, 1995), with the intention of opening a reflective space for all participants whether they are in the position of *consultee, co-consultant* or *group member*. When participants shift between 'inner talks' while listening and 'outer talks' when talking, they can experience being in different positions (as a listener or as a talking contributor), witnessing and generating different ideas and perspectives which, when juxtaposed, enable new connections and new possibilities to go on. With the perception of difference, new contexts can evolve, giving new meanings to old ideas (Bateson, 1972). (Chapters 8 and 9 provide detailed examples and explanations of how and why we separate talking and listening.)

> Therefore I (Andia) explained to the health visitors, 'We find it works well for everyone in the group when we separate talking and listening. In this way, we can give those of you requesting consultation a chance to talk and say what you want us to hear without the group interrupting. This also gives the rest of the group the chance to listen carefully to what you are telling us and to have their own thoughts while they are listening. So at some points during my conversation with [consultee bringing the work issue], I will ask those of you listening to share what you have heard. While you are talking, [consultee] can listen and have your own thoughts, so you don't feel you have to reply to the group. At the end I will come back to [consultee] to find out what you found useful and what you are taking away with you from this consultation ... Usually this becomes a lot clearer when we give it a go ... Is that OK with you all?'

Involving the group as co-consultants

I (Andia) began our third group consultation by asking the health visiting staff, 'Who wants to use the group today? Who would like the
group's input with a work issue?' Sharon, one of the senior health visitors in the group and an enthusiastic attendee, suggested that Suzie, the
health visitor student for whom she was responsible, ask for 'strategies'
to 'help a mother with her son's peculiar eating habits'. We learned that
three-year-old Sam had been 'eating non-food items from the floor' and
recently had been 'chewing the bottom of his shoes'. Also attending the
group that day were Fatimah, a very experienced family health advisor
and manager; two other experienced health visitors, Jo and Rachel; and
another health visitor student, Hayley, who had been with the team for a
year. Suzie was joining the group for the first time.

Mindful that this consultation approach may be a new experience for
Suzie and recognising that talking on her own in front of the group could be
quite daunting for any new and junior staff member, I went on to ask Suzie,
'Who else here has been working with Sam and might be able to contribute?
Is there anyone else in the group who also knows Sam and could join Suzie?'
Suzie turned to Sharon, who nodded and agreed to join our conversation.

Orienting the group's listening to what the consultees want

We go on to position group members as co-consultants to help us co-create a
focus for this consultation with the consultees. Therefore I (Andia) invited the
group to 'help me listen for what Suzie and Sharon want from our conversation
today' and to 'hold on to any advice or solutions you have for the moment'. To
orient their listening, we suggest the co-consultants 'write down the actual words
or phrases' the consultees use 'so you can give *their* actual words back to me'.

To help the group tune in to the consultee's key words, we ask them to attend
carefully to the consultees' language. We suggest that 'each of us is likely to
connect with different expressions' and that certain 'phrases may touch us, move
us' or seem to 'call a response from us'. Therefore we invite the group to 'note
which expressions touch or move *you*' or seem to be 'particularly meaningful for
[the consultees]'. We invite them to listen for 'words that could serve as good
names for projects', that might connect to what the consultees want to get from
the conversation and that 'point to hope' (Chapter 3). Our intention is to bring
forth what the consultees want to take from the consultation and to connect the
group actively with this process of co-creating a focus and shared language that
everyone can use in a collaborative exchange of expertise later on.

Having oriented the group's listening, I (Andia) repositioned myself as 'interviewer' and went on to ask Suzie and Sharon future-focused questions such as
'Imagine you have got exactly what you want from this conversation: What are
you clear about? What are you able to do?' (See Chapter 3 for more examples).
After ten minutes or so, I paused the interview and explained to Suzie and Sharon,
'Now I will ask the group what they have heard *you* want from the consultation',
inviting them to listen to the group's discussion.

In response to my questions: 'What did you hear Sharon and Suzie say they want from this conversation? What is important for each of them to be able to do?' Jo and Rachel, their health visitor colleagues, suggested that Sharon and Suzie both wanted to 'make sense of Sam's behaviour' and were pleased for 'a space to think about Sam'; Hayley, the health visitor student, added, 'Suzie wants to understand more about Sam's difficulties so she can feel more confident and help his mother manage better'.

Inviting co-consultants' own connections with what consultees want

When co-consultants share their understandings of what the consultees want from the consultation, we often invite them to connect their own experiences with the consultee's question or dilemma. Thus I (Andia) explored whether they had encountered issues in their work, similar to Suzie's, asking 'Is this a familiar issue for you? Have you had similar dilemmas in your work with families?' Jo responded that she was often 'not sure how to make sense' of clients' difficulties, and Rachel added, 'There are times I don't know what to make of some families' problems and this makes me wonder if I am giving them the right advice and help'.

Checking with consultees whether we have understood what they want

We always check with consultees that we have captured what they want from the consultation. Therefore, I asked 'Suzie, has the group understood what you want from this discussion ... to "make sense" of Sam's difficulties so that "you feel more confident" to "help his mother manage better"?' Suzie seemed to relax; glancing briefly at Sharon, who was looking at me and nodding, she breathed out, saying, 'Yes that's it'.

Tuning the group's listening to consultees' abilities, achievements and initiatives

Having clarified what consultees want from the consultation, we go on to bring forth their solutions, ideas and abilities as potential resources by exploring what ideas they have already had, what they have tried and what they have achieved or are doing. At this point in the consultation process, we brief our co-consultants to capture everything the consultees say that points towards progress with the issue they have brought for consultation. Our intention is to orient the group's listening towards resources, achievements, abilities and initiatives the consultees have shown that point towards hope, possibility and potential projects before asking group members to generate their own ideas on the issue.

Therefore I (Andia) continued, 'At this point we are trying to notice abilities rather than look for solutions or plan strategies ... so make a note of what you hear is working or going well; anything that stops things getting worse; any good ideas you have heard that Sharon and Suzie have tried out; anything you have learned from Sharon and Suzie'.

By inviting the group to tune their listening towards abilities and achievements, we are asking them to suspend their familiar professional tendency to give advice. Instead, we are positioning them as 'ability spotters' (McAdam and Lang, 2009; Webb and Fredman, Chapter 4) and 'opportunity watchers', to take time to capture and name the ways consultees have been able to go on.

> I (Andia) went on to interview Suzie and Sharon for another ten minutes with questions like 'What has worked well in the past few weeks?' 'What ideas have you (already) had to "make sense" of Sam's behaviour?' 'What have you already tried to "help" him/his mother? What effect has this had?' 'What sense do you make of this?' 'What other ideas do you have?' Who else has a view on this situation?' 'What would they suggest?' Our conversation brought forth a repertoire of initiatives and ideas Suzie and Sharon had already used to address their consultation question.
>
> I paused again and invited the consultees to listen to the group: 'Now I am inviting you to listen to us all reflecting on what you have told us so far. This is a chance for you to think and note whatever seems most relevant to you? After we finish talking, I'll come back to you so you can let us know your thoughts of our conversation'.

Facilitating co-consultants' feedback

We go on to invite the co-consultants to share the abilities, achievements and initiatives they have captured from the consultee's feedback. When co-consultants are new to the process of collaborative consultation, we may prompt their feedback with questions such as

- What have you heard that points to what is going well in the work?
- What did you pick up that Sharon and Suzie have already been doing [to help the situation/stop it getting worse]?
- What other good ideas have you heard that Sharon and Suzie have considered?

> Inviting the co-consultants to capture and name what Sharon and Suzie were already doing with Sam generated many examples from the group that included Suzie's 'calm style' and 'containing influence'; her ability to 'notice that Sam had difficulties with unstructured times in the day' and was 'less likely to swallow bits and pieces when he is engaged in an activity that grabs his attention', and her 'ingenious ideas for distracting Sam' from eating inedible items. When the co-consultants noted what the consultees were already doing to ameliorate the situation, Suzie and Sharon were able to re-connect with their skills and abilities that may have been out of their awareness at the time and go on to use them with a renewed sense of intention and purpose. Sharon told us that 'telling us what we are already doing well is like finding treasured items that we have forgotten we have'.

Inviting perspectives and connections from the group

We also invite the group to offer alternative perspectives, connecting with their own personal and professional experience. We remind them to share their reflections as tentative and speculative offerings, to avoid blame or criticism and to use the consultee's language when connecting with their own experiences. (Chapter 8 offers guidelines for reflecting.)

> When I (Andia) asked 'What ideas would you like to offer that might be useful to Suzie and Sharon?' Hayley noted Suzie's link between Sam's 'tummy bug' and his chewing the bottom of his shoes. She wondered whether 'giving information' to Sam might 'help him understand'. Rachel remembered, from her nursing training that, 'people eat peculiar things when they lack iron or magnesium'.

We take care, as consultants, to facilitate the group's sharing and connection with each other's ideas first, before we offer our own perspectives, since we are mindful that as a 'perceived expert' our input may overshadow their contributions or restrict the flow of exchange when our intention is for them to 'liberate each other's expertise … in such a way that the problem being explored can be looked at anew, with people assisting each other in finding their own workable alternative solutions' (Steinberg, 1989:24).

We do also offer our professional contribution by connecting our specialist theories and concepts with the knowledge and skills we have generated with the group (as we describe in Chapter 3). Thus I (Andia) saw the opportunity to *capture and name* Rachel's knowledge about 'lacking iron and magnesium' and connected this with my specialist knowledge about the condition pica. Seeming pleased with the ideas I was offering, Rachel said, 'That's the condition that I was thinking of!' When Hayley asked for my experience, as a clinical psychologist, of children with pica, I connected her idea of 'giving information to children about their condition' with the recommendations in the literature that 'it can be a useful first step for managing pica to "give information" to the child about, for example, what is food and not food'.

Inviting consultees' responses to the group's reflections

With the reminder that 'there are no right or wrong ideas … rather, what is more or less useful in the situation', we invite the consultees to evaluate the usefulness of the offerings from the group and to choose what fits for them and their clients with questions like

- Sharon and Suzie, what ideas do you like or connect with you from the group's reflections?
- What can you use? How will that effect what you do next?
- Is there anything that does not fit for you?

> Sharon was interested in 'following up pica' and possibly discussing this with Sam's mother. They did not think Sam would be able to make the connection between the 'tummy bug' and eating his shoes as they

felt it may be 'a bit difficult to grasp' due to 'some language difficulties'. However, these ideas sparked new perspectives; for example, Sharon suggested 'using a visual social story[2] with Sam', enthusing Suzie who became very animated as she talked about photos and pictures she could use to develop that story. Before I could ask what might be their next step, they were planning how to include Sam's mother.

Opening space to develop each person's abilities

The purpose of consultation is to enable consultees to resolve the particular issue they bring for consultation and also to work better with similar situations so as to benefit many other clients in the future (Caplan, 1970). In group consultation, we further intend that all group members, not only the consultees, develop their own practice through this mutually informing process in which they are sharing and learning from each other's contributions.

Inviting group members' connections and resonance

To facilitate this process, we invite group members to share their resonance and connections with the consultees' experience, with questions like

- From what you heard from Sharon and Suzie today, what struck a chord for you/what were you drawn to?
- What connections do you make with your own work [or your life]?

Exploring transport of learning to develop practice

We go on to explore how the participants will take these connections into their practice with questions like

- What have you learned from our conversation with Suzie and Sharon?
- What new ideas have you now that you would not have had without hearing our conversations today?
- How might you use this learning in your own work situation?
- What will you take forward into your own practice?

(See Chapter 6 for more examples of exploring transport of learning.)

> Most of the group were taking away ideas, skills or principles to guide their practice. For example, Hayley said she had 'learned so much'. She had been thinking of a lot of children on her 'case load' and was keen to 'start visual social stories with them – I think their mums would love that – it's so positive'.

Exploring how consultees and group members will use their learning from the consultation in their own practice is one way we evaluate the outcome of group consultation. Chapter 6 offers a range of approaches to evaluating group consultation with examples. We have found the question in Box 7.2 from the Consultation

Partnership Scale (CPS) (Worwood and Fredman, Chapter 6) particularly useful to invite group members to become observers to the group process and to draw their attention to the group as a resource.

Box 7.2 Question from the Consultation Partnership Scale (CPS) to review group collaboration

Group consultation

We did not work well   We worked very well
together as a group   together as a group

I--I

Some common challenges we meet in group consultation

We see it as an integral part of building the group to cultivate a culture of collaboration, acceptance and respect that will enable members to come together as equally valued contributors who can share and receive each other's different ideas as generous offerings and thereby experience the group as a valuable resource. When we, the authors of this book, have joined with each other for consultation on our own consultation, we have benefitted from each other's experience to address common challenges we have encountered in group consultation. To conclude this chapter, we offer you, our reader, some of the joint learning we generated to address these challenges.

When group members seek advice or request direction from the consultant

Adding our contributions to the pool of ideas

When group participants ask for our advice or specialist knowledge, we often position ourselves alongside the co-consultants and add our contributions to the pool of ideas and practices we have already been generating with the group. We invite the consultees to evaluate the various contributions from the group and consultant, according to their own personal and professional contexts and those of the clients with whom they are working. (See Chapter 3 for detailed steps and examples.) Thus, once Sharon and Suzie's group contributed their thoughts and ideas about Sam's peculiar eating habits, Andia added her knowledges and experience, placing them alongside the group's ideas and perspectives as equal possibilities for the consultees to consider.

Connecting known and familiar ideas with new concepts

As consultants, we also contribute our specialist expertise by connecting consultees' known and familiar knowledge and skills that we have generated together with theories and concepts new to them that we draw from our own specialist trainings or professional expertise, with the intention that this new perspective might move them to a new level of conceptualisation. (See Chapter 3 for detailed steps and examples.) Therefore, later on in the conversation, Andia tentatively offered 'pica' as a further perspective to add to the ideas the group had generated already, connecting with Hayley's ideas about 'giving information to children about their condition'. If she had offered her knowledge of pica as an expert opinion earlier in the consultation, Andia may have interfered with placing the group's creative and 'ingenious' ideas at the heart of the group conversation and thus risked undermining their resourcefulness and competence.

Positioning consultees to interview the consultant

Sometimes we take requests for our advice or professional opinion as an opportunity to position the consultee as the 'interviewer' and offer: 'You are welcome to ask me any questions that you think could be useful to you with this piece of work/ issue. For example, you may be curious about what I have done or what I have learned from my own practice with similar issues. Or you may want to hear about what theories or ideas have informed my approach. Then I will ask you what you can use from our conversation in your work with [the client]'.

After the consultee has interviewed the consultant for no more than ten or fifteen minutes, the consultant changes position and goes on to interview the consultee and the group about how they might make use of what they have heard, with questions to explore transport (on p. 127) as well as questions such as

- Where have my answers taken you to in relation to your initial dilemma/ own practice with similar issues? What ideas do you have now about how to go on?
- What steps might you take as a result of this conversation? (Redstone, 2009).

Therefore, having first invited the consultees to centre our (consultant's) knowledge and experience while they interview, we return to re-centring the consultee's knowledge and experience of their client and their work context.

When group participants give advice or criticism

When I invited the co-consultants to reflect on what Suzie and Sharon were already doing with the family, I was inviting them to share their perspectives within a discourse of possibilities (Madsen, 2006; see also Chapter 3). This is not always an easy shift to make for practitioners whose training is based on problem-focused models of intervention and whose services are oriented towards protection against risk. So, I was not surprised when Fatimah, one of Suzie's experienced colleagues, offered direct advice.

> 'It's obvious to me', sighed Fatimah, 'that the family got what they needed from Suzie. How long do we persist with entrenched problems like this when we have so many other families to see? Suzie has done as much as she can – she can't go on with this family forever. She must close or refer on'. I (Andia) was taken aback by Fatimah's blatant expression of irritation and the sharpness of her retort. I noticed the long silence that followed and wondered how Suzie was hearing this.

We have noticed that advice or criticism coming from a 'deficit discourse' ('entrenched problems', 'limited resources') often brings collaborative exchange of ideas to a standstill as consultees and group members take up positions of justification, rationalisation or even self-protection and appeasement and move away from curiosity and mutual respect. It was not the first time that the pressure of limited resources had been raised in this health visitor consultation group and I was aware of the constant demands on the team to meet targets in the face of significant cuts in staffing.

Madsen (2006) points out the importance of recognising deficit discourses and encouraging reflection on the effects these have on practice. Questions like 'Can you share some of your thinking about this – what informs your ideas about this?' 'How have you come to support this view?' 'What has influenced you practicing in this way?' can locate critical comments or unsolicited advice in wider contexts and discourses and thereby open space for the group to reflect on these discourses.

> Fatimah was able to connect her comments with her position as a manager and to reflect on her 'competing struggles to be supportive to [her] staff' while managing long waiting lists for services. Fatimah's reflecting on the resource-led discourse informing her views, and her 'struggle', opened space for the rest of the group to participate in a collaborative conversation in which they shared their own 'struggles' with similar ethical dilemmas.

When there are differences in status and power between group members

Consultees bring to the consultation group their own experiences of groups which they have described as 'positive' and 'affirmative' as well as 'threatening' and 'invalidating'. They will also have varied personal and professional relationships to each other that extend beyond the group, for example supervisor-supervisee, manager-trainee, colleague-friend. Therefore, their previous experiences of groups and their differential status and power within the group will have an impact on how they engage with each other and the group. We try to enable an atmosphere where each person can contribute their views, irrespective of their status or position in the organisation.

Inviting group members to move to different positions

One way we do this is by inviting participants to take different positions. For example, when Sharon volunteered Suzie to discuss a dilemma with one of her client-families (p. 123), I (Andia) noticed Suzie's nervous smile. I wondered if this was a sign of apprehension and whether Suzie perceived this as helpful and supportive or exposing and disempowering. Mindful that junior staff do not usually feel empowered to refuse a senior's request or suggestion to 'present' their work, as consultants we commonly take the initiative to invite a senior to join in the consultation interview with the intention of shaping the context for collaborative practice. Thus Andia offered Suzie the opportunity to invite another group member to join her for this consultation. Including Sharon in the interview repositioned Sharon from manager and supervisor to supportive co-consultee with Suzie.

Hearing and valuing all voices

In most groups we have convened, we have encountered loud and forthcoming members as well as participants who are quieter and more pensive. To encourage, involve and value all voices, therefore, we may invite group participants to discuss their ideas in pairs or smaller groups first, before they offer contributions to the pool of ideas generated in the larger group. We find this works particularly well when the consultation group is larger than six members.

Paying attention to differences in power within the group, we usually check with the participants which groupings are most likely to enable contribution from all members or constrain participation; for example, whether they would prefer to talk first with colleagues of similar grade or experience or in mixed groups. Participants have told us that sharing first with colleagues of similar status tends to afford junior and less experienced members the freedom to share their ideas without concerns about being evaluated by their seniors; junior staff have also told us they like joining with senior colleagues in mixed groups since 'this is not about having the best or right answer – but sharing ideas and learning how each other thinks'.

When new members join ongoing group consultation

Staff turnover is high in many services with which we consult and most services take on new trainees at regular intervals throughout the year. Therefore, when we are contracting with the group, we ask from the start how they would like to 'help new colleagues join our consultations' so that they can become 'active participants' and 'contribute with confidence'. Group members have suggested sharing our group contract to induct new members to the working of the group, either before they join or at the beginning of their first session.

To give new members space to get to know the group and a chance to connect with its culture, we usually invite them to participate 'in whatever way you feel comfortable for this first meeting'. To actively engage and value the new member, we point out that they will be 'bringing a fresh pair of eyes and ears to the group' and we 'would really like to hear any of your ideas' so 'we can all benefit' from 'your unique position'. Therefore, towards the end of their first session, we often ask questions like 'What was this first group consultation like for you today? What do you make of it? Anything you particularly appreciated or did not fit for you? Do you have any questions?'

Inviting an established group member, well-acquainted with our group's approach to consultation, to 'accompany' a new member the first time they take the position of consultee can also help to familiarise the new member with the consultation approach we are using. Thus Andia invited Sharon to share the 'spotlight' with Suzie, thereby supporting Suzie and scaffolding her experience of the consultation process.

Wherever possible, we invite members of the group familiar with our collaborative approach to explain to the new member how we work and why we work like this. We spent some time welcoming Suzie to the health visitor consultation group (p. 123) by inviting the other group members to introduce themselves and explain 'how we have been working together' and 'how we are using the group'.

> Rachel explained, 'One of us talks about our work with Andia. The rest of us listen and tell Andia what we have heard the person wants help with'. Sharon added, 'What that person wants to be able to do ...'. Hayley offered, 'We all put our ideas in the pot – and the person who brings the case takes what they want. It's like potluck!' (All the group members laughed).

In this chapter, we have offered a repertoire of ideas and practices to use the group as a resource to the consultation process. We invite you, our reader, to take what fits to enable you to build a group through which the participants can draw on the rich resource of local knowledge and expertise of their colleagues and support the consultant in the consultation process so that together you can create new possibilities for the whole group and their clients. To quote Hayley, we invite you to select and enjoy the 'potluck' this chapter offers.

Guide 7.1   Using the group as a resource: A practice guide

Building a cooperative group partnership

Prepare the group for collaborative practice
Co-contract using mind-maps
Explain how we use the group

Positioning consultants, consultees and the group

Position ourselves as consultants
Position consultees to engage with the group as a resource
Separate talking and listening

Involving the group as co-consultants

Orient the group's listening to what the consultees want

- Invite co-consultants' own connections with what consultees want, using actual words or phrases that touch or move them.
- Check with consultees whether the group have understood what they want.

Tune the group's listening to consultees' abilities, achievements and initiatives
Facilitate the co-consultants' feedback

Inviting perspectives and connections from the group

Invite consultees' responses to the group's reflections

Opening space to develop each person's abilities

Invite group members' connections and resonance
Explore transport of learning to develop practice

Notes

1 A mind map is a diagram used to visually organise information.
2 A visual social story is a short story accompanied by visuals to help people make sense of or anticipate a situation, social interaction, skill or concept. The story usually describes the situation and then scripts the appropriate response.

References

Andersen, T. (1995) Reflecting processes; acts of informing and forming: You can borrow my eyes, but you must not take them away from me! In S. Friedman (ed.) *The Reflecting Team in Action. Collaborative Practice in Family Therapy.* New York: Guilford.

Anderson H. and Burney J. P. (1997) Collaborative inquiry: A postmodern approach to organizational consultation. *Human Systems: The Journal of Systemic Consultation and Management*, 7, 177–188.

Bateson, G. (1972) *Steps To An Ecology of Mind.* New York: Ballantine.

Bion, W. (1961) *Experiences in Groups.* London: Tavistock.

Caplan, G. (1970) *Theory and Practice of Mental Health Consultation.* New York: Basic Books.

Davies, B. and Harré, R. (1990) Positioning: The discursive production of selves. *Journal for the Theory of Social Behaviour*, 20, 43–64.

Fredman, G. (2014) Weaving net-works of hope with families, practitioners and communities: Inspirations from systemic and narrative approaches. *Australian and New Zealand Journal of Family Therapy*, 35, 54–71.

Granville, J. (2010) Minding the group: Group process, group analytic ideas, and systemic supervision – companionable or uneasy bedfellows? In C. Burck and G. Daniel (eds). *Mirrors and Reflections: Processes of Systemic Supervision.* London: Karnac.

Harré, R. and Van Langenhove, L. (eds.) (1999) *Positioning Theory.* Oxford: Blackwell.

McAdam, E. and Lang P. (2009) *Appreciative Work in Schools: Generating Future Communities.* Chichester: Kingsham Press.

Madsen, W.C. (2006) Teaching across discourses to sustain collaborative clinical practice. *Journal of Systemic Therapies,* 25 (4), 44–58.

Redstone, A. (2009) Narrative practice and supervision – the re-population of identity. *Context,* October, 23–26.

Steinberg, D. (1989) *Interprofessional Consultation: Invitation and Imagination in Working Relationships.* Oxford: Blackwell Scientific Publications.

White, M. (2005) Michael White Workshop Notes. Available from: www.dulwichcentre.com.au. Accessed 13 June 2017.

Chapter 8

Working with two consultants

Reflecting conversations to create new ways to go on in staff consultation

Selma Rikberg Smyly and Sarah Coles

In this chapter, we describe how we work with two consultants in the room in consultation with a staff team in a supported living setting for people with intellectual disabilities. We take you, the reader, through our approach to consultation including how we plan our sessions; take turns to talk, listen and share reflections; and invite consultees to comment on these reflections. We discuss how this process of separating talking and listening creates reflecting conversations and opens space for new meanings and shifts in thinking which enable new possibilities and solutions to emerge.

Our community-based multidisciplinary team for adults with intellectual disabilities receives many referrals from group homes where support staff work together with a small number of residents with intellectual disabilities. The residents in these homes have had years, sometimes lifelong experiences, of professional input; they rarely refer themselves for help and the problems are usually identified by staff.

> Annette, the manager of a support service for people with intellectual disabilities, contacted me (Selma) for help with Jane, a fifty-two-year-old woman living on her own in a staffed home. Jane had been referred to the multidisciplinary team many times in the past. 'Long-term mental health problems' and an 'institutional history', had contributed to Jane being offered a twenty-four-hour one-to-one service, so that she had one of the 'most expensive care packages' and 'most intensive staff input' of any of the clients known to the service. Annette wanted help with Jane's 'aggressive outbursts … happening every day'. She explained that staff were 'struggling' at the end of their shifts when Jane would 'physically and verbally attack' staff as they were about to leave the house. Annette wanted support to help the staff team develop 'a consistent approach' to deal with these situations 'more effectively'; she was concerned that staff did 'not want to work with Jane' and it was hard to keep staff in their posts due to 'burn out'.

Over the years of our practice as clinical psychologists, we had noticed that most progress made in our work with individual clients tended to get lost when the sessions ended without the support of the staff team, and that it could be difficult for residents to find enough of a voice to be able to change outside of the therapy room (Coles et al., 2012). We are also mindful that organisational changes such as alterations in shift patterns or the departure, or even death, of significant staff or co-residents can have a profound impact on the well-being of residents (Rikberg Smyly, 2006). Therefore, we recognised that we needed to think beyond the individual referred person, like Jane, when responding to requests from group homes, to consider not only what might be happening for the referred person with intellectual disabilities, but also the contributions and effects on the situation of the referrer and the group home staff and the impact of significant transitions in the organisation.

I (Selma) was aware that Jane's staff team were very experienced, which led me to be curious about their views on this referral. Would they see it as helpful to have another professional coming in to offer support, or would they perceive it as undermining? Or maybe they would view it as a form of evaluation of how well they were doing their jobs? I was also aware, from what staff had said before, that lone working over long shifts with Jane could be very demanding. I was therefore curious to find out what the rest of the staff team thought about the referral.

Responding to the request for consultation

We usually phone the referrer to 'clarify the nature of the request for consultation' (Mattison and Fredman, Chapter 2). Thus I (Selma) explored with Annette, the team manager, who wanted or decided to make this referral; whether the staff team were aware of this referral; whether everyone agreed there was a problem – or who saw it differently; their different views and understandings about how the problem came about; and who and what had been helpful in the past, and what they thought we, as consultants, could offer. We also discussed the organisation of the first meeting, including whom to include, who would invite whom and other practicalities such as venue and time.

We try to offer consultees some idea of what to expect before they come to a consultation. Therefore, I explained to Annette that 'two of us will work together with the staff team … to give us more than one set of eyes and ears to pay attention to everyone in the room and hear all your contributions … so we can offer more than one set of ideas'.

> I learned that four staff members were particularly concerned about Jane and that all wanted this consultation. The consultees were Tracey (54) and Sharon (49), who were experienced in working with people with intellectual disabilities: they had worked with Jane for over two years. Amy (35) had recently begun this work, since her children had started school, and Adam (26) had been there a few months having recently returned from travelling abroad following completion of university. We agreed to join the team at their next staff meeting in order to maximise the number of staff present.

Inspirations informing our consultation practice

Recognising the limits of individual work beyond the therapy room, the impact of organisational changes and the importance of involving staff in the work, we have extended our ways of talking and listening in consultation with staff teams to open up conversations between staff, residents and professionals to create more mutual and shared understandings of the referred resident and the perceived problem. A key influence on our practice has been the work of Tom Andersen, a Norwegian psychiatrist and family therapist (Andersen, 1987, 1991, 1992, 1993). Like many family therapists of that time, Andersen interviewed client-families in the therapy room while a team of colleagues (and trainees) sat behind a one-way screen to observe and give feedback to the therapist to take back to the family in the room. In the early 1980s, he introduced the novel idea of bringing the therapy team from behind the one-way mirror into the same room with the client-family for '*open talks*', where the family members were able to hear the team's *reflections* on the family's conversation with the therapist.

The aim of both the therapist's interview with the client and the reflecting conversation between team members is to create multiple understandings of the situation, of what has happened and what is desired for the future. All perspectives are 'neither right nor wrong'; the intention is for all involved 'to engage in a dialogue in order to understand how the various persons came to create their descriptions and their explanations' (Andersen, 1991:38–39). These conversations are guided by what the participants are offering in the room and we explore everyone's explanations and understandings. Thus the conversation includes what is said, how it might be interpreted by different listeners, how these ideas came about and how they fit or not with what has already been spoken. The task of the reflecting team is to create ideas in the 'hope that they will trigger a small change' in the consultees' picture or understanding of the problem (Andersen, 1987:421).

Inviting inner and outer talks to open space for new understandings

Tom Andersen described how these *reflecting conversations* involve shifts between talking about an issue with others in an *outer dialogue* and then sitting back and listening to others talk about the same issue. During that listening, the listener engages with an *inner dialogue* as he or she talks with oneself (Andersen, 1993). In this sense, the issue under consideration can be said to be talked about from two different perspectives – one from the *inner* and one from the *outer* dialogue. According to Andersen, it is this shift between inner and outer dialogues that has the potential for bringing in new perspectives. By moving between talking and listening, and talking about the listening, there are opportunities to share the inner as well as outer conversations. This sharing of the *outer and inner* brings in new ways of understanding.

Having witnessed and experienced the transforming effects of these sorts of reflecting conversations, we wanted to make both the *outer* and *inner* conversations part of our consultation process. Introducing these sorts of reflecting practices into our consultations has had a considerable impact on the quality of the conversations we create and the possibilities for change in our sessions.

In our services, we do not have the resources to work with (reflecting) teams of people but we have been able to include a second consultant in some sessions so that one person could interview the consultees in the position of Interviewing Consultant (IC) and one person could listen to the interview and offer reflections from the position of the Reflecting Person (RP). Thus, we adapted Tom Andersen's method to working with two consultants in our consultations with staff teams, to offer consultees an opportunity to engage with the IC in outer talks about how they see and understand their current situation, and reflect on their inner talks while listening to the RP and IC share their perspectives in a reflecting conversation with each other.

Preparing for working with two consultants

Before joining consultees for consultation, we (the IC and RP) usually spend fifteen to thirty minutes planning, to help us share and co-ordinate our thinking with each other.

Agreeing the positions we take in the consultation

We use the pre-session discussion to agree which positions we will take in the consultation, IC or RP. The IC talks directly with the staff team; the RP usually sits slightly outside the conversation circle in the room and listens to the interview without contributing to the interview conversation between the consultees and IC (see Figure 8.1). The RP sits physically distant enough to emphasise her listening position and so that the consultees do not try to engage her in the interview talks.

The IC has the dual role of conducting the interview as well as taking an active part in the reflecting conversation. The IC takes charge of the timing of sessions and the timing of reflections and usually invites the RP to contribute when the interview has generated the consultees' picture or description of the situation and explanations of the problem, or when the IC is feeling unsure about how to proceed in the interview.

> We decided that I (Selma) would take the IC position and Sarah the RP position. I had worked with Jane and this staff team before and we were aware there had been several referrals to our multidisciplinary team concerning Jane in the past. Acknowledging the manager's concern about 'staff burnout' and that I (Selma) held opinions about this staff team from my previous contact with them, I therefore asked Sarah, in her position as the RP, to notice and comment on any signs of hope or opportunities for optimism.

Pre-session hypothesising

We also use this time to reflect on the assumptions we are making about the request for consultation, our views about the presenting concerns and possible alternative explanations, our emotional response to the situation and the emotional postures (Fredman, 2007) in which we might enter the consultation. This practice of 'pre-session hypothesising' was originally developed by the Milan school of systemic family therapy (Selvini Palazzoli et al., 1980) and developed

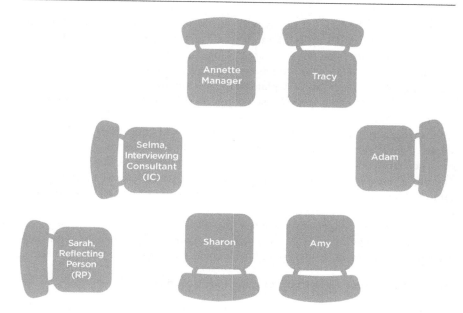

Figure 8.1   Position of Interviewing Consultant and Reflecting Person

further by Cecchin et al. (1994), Lang and McAdam (1995), Reder and Fredman (1996) and Fredman (2007; 2017).We have found hypothesising helps us consider how our professional knowledge and personal prejudices might influence our ideas, how to orient our listening, what questions might be useful to ask and how to share our perspectives (Rikberg Smyly, 2012).

> Through pre-session conversations, we recognised that we knew very little about Jane's life outside of the difficulties staff identified. We wondered about her experience and views of the problem and how her voice might be represented in the room.

We often agree that the RP will introduce into the consultation conversation the perspectives of other people not present, such as family members, other services, absent staff members and the client, by wondering what they might think or say. This is to introduce a number of different voices, a 'multiverse', into the room (Andersen, 1991). Therefore we decided that Sarah, in her RP position, would hold Jane in mind while listening, and if appropriate, ask questions about Jane's views and understanding when reflecting.

The consultation interview

When we start a consultation, we explain how we will talk in the interview and the reflecting conversations, in particular who talks when and the opportunities and intentions for the listening. For example, the IC says something like, 'I will talk with you all first, to get a picture of the issues you want to address in this consultation. We would really like to hear all of your ideas about the situation. Sarah (the RP) will listen while we are talking. Then I will turn to Sarah and we will talk with each other while you listen and have your own thoughts on what we are talking about'. We further explain that the RP might also offer ideas during the interview, suggesting to the IC something like, 'I have an idea that might be useful' or 'I wonder if we might talk a bit while the others listen?'

We have learnt to be clear about our expectations of consultees from the outset since there can be a temptation for everyone to talk at once or for consultees to comment on the reflections before the consultants have finished talking. Therefore, we clarify, 'We would like you to hold your ideas on what we have said until we finish talking and then we would like to hear your thoughts and ideas'. Mostly we have found people to be genuinely interested and appreciative of listening to the conversation between the two consultants (Rikberg Smyly et al., 2008), and that this process has made the sessions more engaging, with staff members becoming more involved in the conversation following the reflections.

From picture and explanation to new understandings

We have adapted Tom Andersen's (1987) interview and reflecting team structure for creating new understandings with families in therapy. This involves moving between three levels during the interview: *picture (P)*, *explanation (E)* and *alternatives (A)*; inviting and exploring the client-family's picture and explanations of the problem; and generating alternative understandings of the situation and how it has come about (Figure 8.2). An important task of the reflecting team is to offer acceptable *alternatives (A)* for the client's *picture (P)* or *explanations (E)*; the clients choose those ideas that fit. The intention is that alternative perspectives will elicit a small change in the client's picture and their understanding of the picture which could help them understand the connection between 'what they understand and how they understand', their 'understanding of this understanding' (Andersen, 1987:421).

Elaborating pictures (P) of the situation

The IC begins by inviting an account of the issues the consultees are bringing for consultation, their descriptions of what is happening and the feelings they have, to

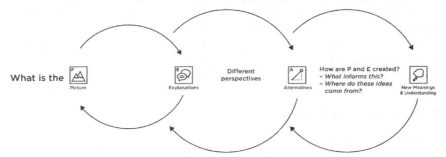

Figure 8.2 Moving from picture to understanding

get a *picture* (P) of the situation from the perspectives of different staff members and other significant people.

Selma:	What would be most helpful to talk about today?
Annette:	Well, I thought we could discuss how we can support Jane better.
Tracey:	It can be really hard to know what to do, especially at the end of shifts.
Staff team:	Oh yes.
Selma:	Can you tell me a little bit more about that?
Amy:	I get quite worried about leaving Jane; even when we have a nice time together, she can get like angry – screaming. I know that Sylvia [a former support worker] left because she was so upset that Jane would not let her leave at the end of the shift.
Sharon:	It's so hard leaving Jane at the end of the shift because she shouts at me. Sometimes she even kicks me. You never know when she is going to do it. I worry a lot of the time I'm at work …
Amy:	We do so much for her … she has so much attention and care from all of us … no other residents do that.

This exploration gave me (Selma) a picture of the distress staff members were experiencing with Jane. I wondered if they were becoming afraid of her. I always try to acknowledge and bear witness to the difficulties staff face in these sorts of situations and explicitly value the difficult work they do before going on to ask further questions to elaborate the picture of the situation.

Selma:	I have heard how worrying and upsetting this can be for all of you. It sounds quite frightening. I imagine it must be really hard to be on shift knowing it might all end in such a distressing way. I know you often work on your own – how difficult that can be with no breaks and sole responsibility for someone who can be as challenging as Jane. I wonder how that has been for you?
Adam:	You can have a good shift … and then out of the blue … just to spite you … she gives you hell before you go.
Sharon:	Other days, she can be difficult while you are on shift and nothing you do will change that and you know you will have a difficult time leaving.
Selma:	Are there staff who are not present who might describe this in similar or different ways?
Tracey:	I think most of us have the same problems, but for some staff it is easier to leave than others.
Amy:	I think it depends how well she knows you, like she lets you go easier if you are new.

To elaborate the picture, we ask for all views, exploring similarities and differences among the staff team. We might ask if there are any changes people would like to make in the picture and the possible consequences of change. Sometimes we trace the development of the picture over time; noticing that the problem has varied or changed can suggest it might also change in the future.

Exploring explanations (E) of the situation

The IC goes on to ask what *explanations (E)* consultees have for the problem, shifting from the 'what is' (picture) level to a 'how come' (explanation) meta-level. Therefore, as the IC, my (Selma's) intention was to both witness the consultees' dilemmas and also to move the conversation from the detail of *what was happening* to the sense or *meaning* consultees were making of the situation they were describing. Thus, using Adam's words, 'changing out of the blue', to frame my question in the consultees' language, I went on, 'It sounds very tricky that Jane often changes "out of the blue". What ideas do you have about why she is distressed when you leave?'

Aware that people with intellectual disabilities often have their emotional lives simplified, with the result that their complex emotions can become minimised as simply 'anger' without consideration of the complexity of their feeling or action, I used the word 'distress' to introduce a possible different explanation for what was happening with Jane in those moments. This question also introduces the idea that there may be different explanations for Jane's reactions that have not yet been explored.

Tracey:	I'm not sure. I sometimes think she is just attention-seeking.
Amy:	Really? I think that she likes being with people, and is scared somehow about losing you … hmm … maybe she thinks she will be left with someone she doesn't like.
Adam:	I always feel like she wants to punish me for leaving her, like she wants to be with me all the time and can't cope with the idea I have a life away from her.

Bringing forth alternative (A) explanations to generate new understanding

The IC can bring forth alternative explanations for the picture, with questions like 'Who has a different idea?' 'Do you have any other theories about/ways of making sense of this?' 'What would happen to the problem (situation) if we made sense of this (picture) in another way?'

The IC can also explore how the different ideas have come about (Does anyone have ideas about why some days are more difficult than others?) and where the ideas come from (How do we know she is just attention-seeking? Who else might know? Where does that idea come from?).

Sometimes, as IC, we introduce into the conversation alternative explanations from our professional knowledge. We always frame these as questions to ensure they are received as a tentative idea rather than a fact. For example, it is often the case that people with intellectual disabilities who also have mental health difficulties have few people outside of their paid network of support in their lives. Therefore, connecting with Amy's explanation that Jane 'gets scared' when people leave, I explored:

> Selma: What does Jane think about you leaving? You were wondering if she may be worried about losing you. Do you think she ever feels lonely? Does anyone else apart from staff visit her?
>
> Tracey: I think that she sometimes does this because she wants attention from staff; she might be lonely, and she doesn't want us to leave.
>
> Selma: That's interesting. How would Jane ask for attention in other situations? (connecting with our pre-session discussion about how people with intellectual disabilities, like Jane, communicate their needs) Hmm ... How would any of us in this room ask for attention if we were afraid or lonely?

When the IC starts offering alternative explanations, this suggests to us it is time to bring in the RP to share her alternative perspectives, affording the consultees an important break from their outer conversation and the opportunity to engage with their inner talks.

The Reflecting Person listens

During the interview, the RP is free to listen and be touched by the consultees' talks with the IC without the pressure to manage the process of the conversation. Thus the RP is in a unique position to be able to listen to the conversation, have her own thoughts, engage with her inner talks while listening and then bring her thinking into the room. We have also found we can be more adventurous from the RP position, expressing ideas which might feel too challenging to mention directly as the IC (Smith et al., 1993).

From the start, I (Sarah) tried to tune in to the consultees' language so that I could use their words and styles of talk in the reflecting conversation. As I was listening, I was struck by the emotional effect on me of the language the consultees used when talking about Jane. My first reaction was, like Selma, to want to reframe 'challenging behaviour' as 'distress', not because this was true but to try and soften the words to make the problem less like a diagnosis, easier to identify with and hence to open space to create alternative meanings. I was also struck by the helplessness and frustration consultees felt at the end of their shifts. Therefore I was aware of my need to both acknowledge the challenges and hold hope by witnessing the difficulties staff were facing and drawing out strengths and opportunities. I wanted to reflect on Jane's position and the staff's position and the connections between them. As the RP, I (Sarah) also wanted to voice alternative views from the perspectives of others in the network.

The Interviewing Consultant and Reflecting Person talk while consultees listen

Introducing the reflecting conversation

We often introduce this part of the consultation as an opportunity for consultees to listen to us talk about the ideas we have had while listening to them. The IC asks the consultees, 'I wonder if Sarah [the RP] has some ideas that might be helpful? May I ask for her ideas now?'

Sharing reflections

The RP and IC talk with each other to generate a repertoire of different ideas. Trying to keep the conversation dialogical and tentative, they ask each other questions such as 'Where did that idea come from?' 'How does that influence your thinking?' 'Do you have any different ideas from mine?' When in the reflecting position, we are mindful of how much we are saying and how long we are talking for. We find that five minutes focusing on a couple of key ideas is usually plenty.

We have found that the impact of a reflection is closely linked to how well it is grounded in the conversation in the room. Therefore the RP usually begins with what she has heard expressed in the consultation interview and connects these expressions with what this has made her think about. Thus I (Sarah, the RP) began, 'Hearing what happens at the end of shifts and the level of distress Jane is showing, I wonder what Jane would say if she was here?'

We always try to situate our ideas within our personal and professional contexts (Andersen, 1992). This transparency in sharing where ideas come from is a very important aspect of what the RP offers and the ability to locate where an idea has come from takes practice in self-reflection. Thus I (Sarah) went on, 'I was reminded of my experience as a support worker with adults with intellectual disabilities – how sometimes when someone doesn't have many words, they might express themselves in unusual and unexpected ways. This got me wondering what Jane is trying to say about not letting staff leave at the end of the shift. If I were working with Jane, how would I know if Jane was or wasn't distressed or upset? What would I notice?'

It is easier to hear and listen to reflections when they are embedded in a conversation (Andersen, 1987). Monologues are more susceptible to producing lists of suggestions or opinions from the reflecting person, whereas in dialogue, the IC and RP can ask each other where their ideas come from and can also suggest different points of view, for example, 'In addition to this way of seeing ... I was wondering about ...', thereby sharing multiple possible meanings. In this way, a conversation is created whereby issues may have several possible explanations and hence a number of different ways to go on.

> Thus, situating my ideas about Jane in the contexts of my gender, age and family, I (Selma) responded to Sarah (the RP).

> Selma: From my own position as a woman similar in age to Jane, I have been most struck by the differences in our lives. I live with my

husband and children, and it makes me think about how lonely I would be in Jane's position.

Sarah: So I am wondering how Jane might understand her relationships with her carers. When Adam suggested maybe she can't cope with the idea that he has a life of his own separate from her, I wondered if Jane considers the staff as her employees, friends, family or something else. I didn't really get a sense of who else was important to her, and whether she had other people around who aren't paid to be in her life.

Selma: I wonder what Jane thinks when the support workers leave; how does she understand this? Does Jane know when they will be next on shift? What if they are going away on holiday? Or what happens when a member of staff leaves for good, like when Sylvia left?

Sarah (repositioning to introduce the perspective of staff):

I was particularly struck by everyone's descriptions of trying to leave after a shift ended. I sat here wondering, if I were a member of Jane's staff team, how uncomfortable and anxious I would have felt. I know I would find it very hard to be detained in such a forceful way. And I wonder how Jane's support workers felt when they left after a shift which ended so stressfully?

We try to ensure we leave enough time after the IC and RP have reflected (at least twenty minutes) to continue the conversation with the consultees so that everyone can participate.

Consultees respond to reflections

Following the IC and RP's reflecting conversation, the RP takes up her listening position again. The IC, resuming the lead, returns to the consultees, who have been listening, to invite their comments, and the conversation continues between the IC and the consultees. The IC says something like, 'How did you find our conversation?' 'Did anything strike you or resonate with you?' 'Was there anything surprising or different from what you were thinking?' The IC does not ask the consultees what they thought about specific ideas in the reflections. We want consultees to feel free to comment or not on what resonates with them without their feeling obliged to respond to each reflection. Thus, I (Selma, the IC), thanked Sarah (the RP) for her reflections and turned to the consultees, asking 'Has anything resonated or surprised you about our conversation?' At this point, the IC and RP say very little.

Immediately we noticed a markedly different atmosphere in the room. The discussion was lively and invigorated. All the consultees made more contributions to the conversation and seemed to express their feelings with more confidence.

They described feeling 'embarrassed' if Jane 'made a scene' at the end of a shift, negatively judged themselves as 'can't do my job properly', 'unprofessional' or 'not competent enough'. Some staff were worried managers would criticise them for Jane being 'too dependent' on them since the ethos of the organisation was to strive for the independence of all residents with intellectual disabilities.

As staff expressed their embarrassment and sense of incompetence, we noticed they became less blaming of Jane. The focus of the conversation shifted to include not only what was going on for Jane ('I didn't know much about Jane's life … maybe she's missing her family … maybe she thinks we are her family … and doesn't want us to leave') but also what was going on for the staff group ('I didn't know others had felt as bad about ending shifts as I had'.)

We frequently notice shifts like this in the quality of conversation after reflections; many more ideas are generated and the conversations become livelier and more animated.

Offering more than one reflecting conversation

We often include more than one reflection during a consultation, particularly when consultees are unable to move from describing the problem (picture) to explanations, when they attribute overwhelmingly negative or critical explanations to the client, when the consultees remain very distressed or unhappy or the IC is unsure how to go on. I (Selma) felt unsure whether to continue exploring the meanings for Jane's distress in more depth or to continue with the theme of staff's feelings of 'incompetence'. Therefore I invited Sarah to reflect with me again.

Talking from my different personal and professional positions and trying to use the consultees' language, I (Sarah, the RP) resonated with the consultees' experiences.

Sarah: I noticed that I became very interested in the conversation when staff were talking about 'not feeling competent' or feeling that they might be 'unprofessional' if they said they did not know what to do. This reminded me of when I began my job and was new to my team. I felt very much that I didn't know what to do, while others expected me to know.

Selma: And sometimes that feeling about competence doesn't change, even when you have worked for a long time! It can be difficult to know what to do, and sometimes something works only a bit of the time. What ideas did you have about what to do when you felt like that?

Sarah: I think because I was new, it felt really hard. I wasn't sure how safe it was to tell others that I didn't know what to do.

Tentative offerings

Sometimes we introduce new ideas as tentative offerings through questions, in particular 'not yet asked' but 'not too unusual' questions (Andersen, 1987:420).

For example, moving on to the staff's challenge with ending shifts, we reflected on ideas we had drawn on in our work (Mason, 1991).

Selma: I wonder what ideas Jane would have about how she would like shifts to end?

Sarah: It reminds me of a conversation with another client who didn't like the idea of 'handovers' being held behind a closed door where she was not included. I wonder what Jane would think about that? Would she want to be part of a conversation around the time when staff are leaving, perhaps with the new staff coming in? Or would she want something else?

Selma: I was also wondering whether maybe the better the shift, the more upset Jane will be when it comes to an end?

Planning the next steps

As the IC, we try to avoid the pressure to move too quickly to 'solutions'. Therefore, staying with the new meanings and understandings that were emerging in the consultation, I (Selma, the IC) invited the consultees to consider whether anything might have changed for them as they listened to our talks: 'Have you had any new ideas or different thoughts while you were listening?'

The staff appreciated having others recognise that they were doing a challenging job and agreed when Sharon said, 'It's not always possible to get it right; there will be days when whatever we try, Jane will be unhappy'.

To move towards a plan of action to explore what staff want to do from here, the IC usually asks, 'Having had this conversation, what might you do differently?'

At this point, the staff team were talking more quickly with each other, suggesting different ideas to try.

Annette: We could review the guidelines and see what is no longer helpful.

Tracey: I wonder if Jane would like to meet up with some friends she used to have at the day centre she attended a couple of years ago?

Adam: Maybe we need to ask Jane what she wants to happen when staff leave at the end of their shift.

Using reflections to explore: Who does what?

Towards the end of a session, we frequently resume our reflecting positions to negotiate *our* future involvement and to offer ideas about who takes responsibility for what actions and relationships. If time allows, we put forward these ideas in a conversation between the IC and the RP.

Selma: What ideas do you have about next steps?
Sarah: I noticed that the staff team have had lots of different ideas and possibilities about things to try. I am wondering what they think might be worth trying first? I am also interested who they think would be best placed to talk with Jane about ideas from today's discussion, and what she would like to happen next?
Selma: I am wondering if they would want a key worker to take that on or if they would like support from us with that?
Sarah: I was also thinking about what next in terms of our input. For example, we could offer another consultation, or wait and see how the ideas the staff team have already come up with work out.

Tentatively offering possibilities in the form of questions enables us to suggest different options to take forward without consultees having to 'accept', 'refuse' or respond. The sorts of questions we might ask include 'How can we add to what they are already doing?' 'What might [the staff team] want us to be involved in?' 'If we were to meet Jane, how would we do that?' 'Should someone else be present?' 'Should someone who has not been present today be included in our conversations?' 'What might get in the way of this work?' 'Would [staff] like further consultation sessions?'

We ask the consultees for their feedback. Consultees always have the last word.

Post-consultation discussion between the IC and RP

The IC and RP usually have a discussion after each consultation to reflect on the process and outcome of the consultation. We review the themes in focus in the consultation, new ideas that have emerged in the conversation and those not addressed. For example, we noted that witnessing the staff team's distressing and frustrating situation and resonating with our own feelings of professional incompetence and self-doubt opened space for the creative exploration of alternative pictures, explanations and new understandings and more hopeful conversations around possibilities for change. We might draft a letter to the consultees to highlight alternative explanations, new ideas and plans for next steps that emerged in the consultation.

Outcome of the consultation

Some months after this consultation, the staff team produced a 'staff training video' with Jane in which she explained her 'moods' (times when nothing helps), what staff did that helped or did not help to support her and how she preferred staff to be with her. This video changed the staff's perception of Jane to someone who 'can contribute to her own care plans if we create the right conditions for her' and led to more hopeful conversations where staff felt more enthusiastic about working with Jane.

Our final reflections

Talking and listening in reflecting conversations has energised all of us taking part in consultations and freed us to have new ideas, new ways of thinking and hence new ways of doing something different. When a consultation goes well, the tone of the conversation changes – people feel more engaged and lively. It is infectious! As consultants, we feel this positive energy and hope that has been generated in the session and often notice changes in our relationship with the staff team. We are also encouraged that many staff teams who have taken part in these sessions ask for more consultations involving reflecting conversations (Rikberg Smyly et al., 2008).

Working this way has also invigorated us in our work as consultants within a public health service setting, keeping us feeling more purposeful, positive and hopeful about the possibilities of change and better futures for the client group we are working with. As Tom Andersen pointed out, let's keep looking for all those other ways of seeing, hearing and understanding 'there are other words in the words, sometimes sounds and music in them, sometimes whole stories, sometimes whole lives' (Andersen, 1996:6).

Guide 8.1 Guidelines for reflecting

- The aim of the reflecting conversation is to create ideas. The consultees select what fits.
- **Talk with each other**, avoiding eye contact with consultees. Talk about the client and consultees in the third person (he, she, they).
- **Embed your ideas in a genuine conversation** where you listen to each other, valuing each other's different ideas rather than each presenting a series of discontinuous ideas. You can keep the conversation dialogical by asking each other questions.
- **Keep the conversation brief**, 5–10 minutes. Slow the pace; a few ideas can be more useful and easier to hear.
- **Use consultees' language,** words and conversational style. Try to avoid jargon and specialist terms.
- **Reflections should flow from the interview**. Therefore, begin with what has been said and heard, using specific examples that have emerged during the interview, connecting with what consultees want from the consultation.
- **Introduce a difference.** Ideas should be new to consultees but **not too unusual** in content or the way they are covered. Drawing out themes from the interview can connect ideas in a new way.
- **Let consultees know where your comments are coming from** by situating your comments within your personal and professional contexts. Make the theories you use overt. Avoid interpretations from grand theories.

- **Introduce new ideas as tentative offerings**, not as 'pronouncements, interpretations or supervisory remarks' (Andersen, 1987:421). To avoid sounding like you are giving instruction or advice, frame your comments as questions, or present ideas as one way of seeing, such as 'I am not sure but …', 'perhaps …'.
- **Remain respectful and sensitive** by pointing out achievements, abilities and competencies as the listening position tends to magnify criticism and remarks like 'why-did-they …'. Therefore, avoid criticism, blame and normative judgement by
  - presenting ideas from an affirming, non-critical position;
  - expressing in terms of what people do, think, believe and feel and not what they 'are';
  - offering circular and relational rather than linear and causal explanations like labels and diagnoses.
- **Take and offer multiple perspectives.** Talk in terms of **both/and rather than either/or** to increase, rather than limit, possibilities. Reflect from both sides of a dilemma and include perspectives of all members of the system.

References

Andersen, T. (1987) The reflecting team: dialogue and metadialogue in clinical work. *Family Process, 26*, 415–428.

Andersen, T. (ed.) (1991) *The Reflecting Team: Dialogues and Dialogues About Dialogues.* New York: Norton.

Andersen, T. (1992) Reflections on reflecting with families. In S. McNamee and K.J. Gergen (eds.) *Therapy as Social Construction.* Newbury Park, CA: Sage.

Andersen, T. (1993) See and hear, and be seen and heard. In S. Friedman (ed.) *The New Language of Change: Constructive Collaboration in Psychotherapy.* London: The Guildford Press.

Andersen, T. (1996) Language is not innocent. In F. Kaslow (ed.) *The Handbook of Relational Diagnosis.* New York and Oxford: Wiley.

Cecchin, G., Lane, G. and Ray, W. (1994) *The Cybernetics of Prejudices in the Practice of Psychotherapy.* London: Karnac.

Coles, S., Caird, H. and Rikberg Smyly, S. (2012) Remember my voice. *Clinical Psychology and People with Learning Disabilities, 10* (2), 44–48.

Fredman, G. (2007) Preparing ourselves for the therapeutic relationship: Revisiting 'Hypothesizing Revisited'. *Human Systems: The Journal of Systemic Consultation and Management, 18*, 44–59.

Fredman, G. (2017) Using supervision to prepare our bodies for the therapeutic relationship. In J. Bownas and G. Fredman (eds.) *Working With Embodiment in Supervision: A Systemic Approach.* Oxon and New York: Routledge.

Lang, P. and McAdam, E. (1995) Stories, giving accounts, and systemic descriptions. *Human Systems: The Journal of Systemic Consultation and Management, 6,* 72–103.

Mason, B. (1991) *Handing Over: Developing Consistency Across Shifts in Residential and Health Settings.* London: Karnac.

Reder, P. and Fredman, G. (1996) The relationship to help: Interacting beliefs about the treatment process. *Clinical Psychology and Psychiatry, 1* (3), 457–467.

Rikberg Smyly, S. (2006) Who needs to change? Using systemic ideas when working in a group home. In S. Baum and H. Lynggaard (eds.) *Intellectual Disabilities: A Systemic Approach.* London: Karnac.

Rikberg Smyly, S. (2012) How do we know what to ask? Using pre session hypothesising to develop systemic questions. *Clinical Psychology and People with Learning Disabilities, 10* (2), 4–11.

Rikberg Smyly, S., Elsworth, J., Mann, J. and Coates, E. (2008) Working systemically in a learning disability service: What do colleagues and carers think? *Learning Disability Review, 13* (2), 15–24.

Selvini Palazzoli, M., Boscolo, L., Cecchin, G. and Prata, G. (1980). The problem of the referring person. *Journal of Marital and Family Therapy, 6* (1), 3–9.

Smith, T.E., Yoshioko, M. and Winton, M. (1993) A qualitative understanding of reflecting team: Client perspectives. *Journal of Systemic Therapies, 12* (3), 28–43.

Chapter 9

Playing with perspectives to invite wonder and curiosity

Consultation with staff supporting people with intellectual disabilities

Joel Parker

My journey working with people with intellectual disabilities began at twenty years of age when I was a volunteer on a play scheme with children with profound and multiple disabilities. *Wonder* is the overwhelming sense I recall when I witnessed the children's abilities to deeply engage with the world around them, with each other and with those supporting them, in the face of many challenges and apparent limitations. *Wonder* also sparked my *curiosity*: How were these children perceiving and making sense of the world around them? What was their sense of themselves? How could we provide them with optimal care and stimulation? I learned that my colleagues were also engaged in an ongoing process of trying to create meaning from their experiences of working with these children, through conversation with one another and with the parents at pick-up and drop-off times. From this experience, I learned that people are in an ongoing process of meaning making. Therefore, as a consultant to staff working with people affected by intellectual disabilities, I try to honour and learn from the meanings practitioners have been making and sharing with each other.

Over the subsequent thirteen years, I have worked with children and adults with intellectual disabilities in a wide variety of roles including as a support worker and in my current role as a clinical psychologist. My wonder and curiosity have grown through these experiences, as I have sought to make sense of the interplay between the wants, needs and yearnings of people with intellectual disabilities and the factors that make their realisation extremely challenging. The wonder and curiosity that have inspired my practice have been enhanced by opportunities to reflect upon my experiences and engage with others to make meaning in a variety of reflective spaces within my working life. For example, when I was a support worker, colleagues and I were helped to feel valued, respected and motivated when our staff team worked with a consultant who appreciated our competence and sought first to learn what we were doing that worked. Therefore, as a consultant, I begin with an assumption that systems hold the competence to find solutions to their problems and dilemmas, which enables me to work respectfully and collaboratively with staff teams. I am mindful of the effects I can have on practitioners, and try to ensure that my participation leaves staff feeling appreciated and respected by me and each other. When I appreciate 'local knowledge' (Geertz, 2008), I give value to the skills of those working directly with people with intellectual disabilities. In this way, I hope to contribute to a sense of wonder by opening space for appreciation of new perspectives and for creativity to flourish.

In this chapter, I describe consultation to a supported living service for people affected by intellectual disabilities. I will outline a method I call *Playing with Perspectives* that invites practitioners to view the client and their work from a variety of points of view. This method is informed by the systemic approach, in particular the work of Boscolo et al. (1987), Cecchin (1987), Andersen (1995), Anderson (1997) and Madsen (1996).

Wonder, curiosity and collaborative consultation

Jen, a social worker in our multidisciplinary team, referred Abul, a twenty-four-year-old man affected by mild intellectual disabilities. Abul, the eldest child of a large Bengali family, had spent eighteen months in a forensic secure unit for adults with intellectual disabilities following his arrest for a violent assault against his grandmother. He had recently been discharged to Grange Close, a supported living project in the community. Despite Grange Close being a well-run service with a very stable, experienced and confident staff team, several members of the multidisciplinary team anticipated 'a high likelihood that Abul's placement would break down' since, at the age of seventeen, he had been 'kicked out' of his family home and had 'not managed to settle' in several placements.

Learning that the social worker was concerned about the relationship between the staff at Grange Close and Abul, I initially contacted Elizabeth, the manager of Grange Close, to clarify 'who wanted help for what for whom' (Fredman and Rapaport, 2010; Mattison and Fredman, Chapter 2). Elizabeth told me that staff were 'finding Abul's refusal to cooperate very difficult … he is much more able than the other residents … we have not had contact with the criminal justice or forensic system before … we are worried we might face other problems we are not experienced with …' We agreed that I would offer monthly consultation meetings to the staff team through the first few months of Abul's placement.

The staff team made very good use of the collaborative consultation approach described in Chapter 3, which enabled us to co-create a trusting and productive space to explore their work with Abul. This included co-creating a focus using future questions, tuning in to the consultees' language, bringing forth the team's resources and generating multiple perspectives from the viewpoints of different people in Abul's network as well as sharing my expertise and specialist knowledge.

Approaching 'Refusal' with wonder

Since the staff talked a lot about Abul's 'refusal to cooperate', I became curious about this 'Refusal' and asked them, 'If the 'Refusal' were a character, what name would you call it? What shape or form would it take?' Responding enthusiastically to my invitation to characterise 'Refusal' (White, 2006), the team settled on the name

'Kevin the Teenager',[1] suggested by one of the support workers. Intrigued, I went on to ask a series of questions to further externalise (White, 2006) the 'Refusal', like 'How can you tell when "Kevin the Teenager" is around? How does "Kevin" affect Abul's tone of voice and his body language? What's it like for you when "Kevin the Teenager" is present? Does "Kevin" get in the way of how you can be with and support Abul? What do you think it is like for Abul when "Kevin the Teenager" hangs around him?' Our animated conversation enabled us to shift the focus from Abul as the problem to the effects of 'Kevin the Teenager' on Abul. I learned that 'Kevin the Teenager' drew Abul into difficulties with staff and deprived him and the staff of the opportunities to make the most of what Grange Close wanted to offer Abul.

The staff team gave repeated feedback that they valued our meetings and found them useful. In particular, 'seeing Abul as separate from the problems' helped them feel more 'interested' and 'affectionate' towards Abul. At the end of each consultation, there was generally a move towards a more sympathetic view of Abul and a more positive self-evaluation of their work as a team.

> Towards the end of the third consultation session, the manager reported that the work with Abul continued to be 'stressful' for staff. She described 'disagreements' in the team about how to respond when 'Abul does a bunk ... coming back so late ... and we have no idea where he is or what he is up to'. Don, Abul's key worker, explained, 'Abul can be both strong and absent-minded you know ... But we just don't know which state of mind he is in when he comes back late at night ... So it depends what you do ... what you say ... You don't want to make him worse ...' The staff team settled on the word 'Lateness' to describe this problem, and everyone agreed that 'Lateness' was an issue creating difficulties for the team.

Holding curiosity for 'Lateness'

When I explored the effect of 'Lateness' on the staff team, I learned that 'Lateness' was leaving staff 'pulling in different directions', with some focusing on Abul's needs as a young man from a Bengali culture, others pressing for attention to safety, while others emphasised his rights for freedom and choice. I had noticed that different staff members tended to take *either-or* positions in their attempt to achieve a sense of some ultimate 'truth' with regard to the team's work with Abul. Although they contradicted or interrupted each other amiably when they had a different idea, I was aware that certain members of the team were much more dominant in the conversation, while others were quieter or contributed less.

My sense was that our conversations were becoming rather samey; the material we were generating appeared to be somewhat similar across meetings and the team seemed to be struggling between meetings to hold onto and build upon the new understandings we had generated. By the end of our third consultation, I felt less enthusiasm than I had at the beginning of the work. Realising that I had lost *my* 'curiosity' (Cecchin, 1987), I decided that I needed to do something to breathe some new life into our consultations.

Entertaining multiple perspectives

Noticing that different perspectives were pulling the staff into either-or positions, I contemplated how I might invite the consultees to welcome and entertain multiple perspectives at the next meeting. My intention was to enable a context in which the staff-consultees and I could generate a rich repertoire of ideas about 'Lateness', and hold not only our own perspectives but also the perspectives of the other, thereby 'coordinating a multiplicity of views' (McNamee, 2005:77). This sort of dialogic space where different, even contradictory, beliefs and meanings can co-exist invites reflecting processes (Andersen, 1987; Rikberg Smyly and Coles, Chapter 8). Thus new perspectives can emerge, creating new meanings and possibilities to go on.

Therefore, I went on to develop an approach to '*Playing with Perspectives*' on 'Lateness' whereby staff/consultees could juxtapose their different ideas by moving from an 'either-or' to a 'both-and' position and holding their beliefs lightly. I have drawn inspiration from Harlene Anderson's (1997) '*As If*' consultations and William Madsen's (1996) '*Integrating a Client Voice*'. Both these approaches invite multiple perspectives in consultation and supervision. To make it easier for participants to sit with the 'tensionality of dialogue' (McNamee, 2005:77), they separate talking from listening, which facilitates the process of holding on to our own ideas while letting the other happen to us (Stewart and Zediker, 2000).

Listening 'As If'

Harlene Anderson's (1997) *As If* consultations reflect a view of our social worlds as made up of the interplay of multiple voices. The consultant invites the consultee bringing an issue for consultation to generate a list of important people, or voices, in the system with a question like 'Who is in conversation about this issue?' Noting these people on a flip chart, the consultant positions the other group participants to listen 'as if' they are one of those significant people or voices on the list, explaining that the participants who are listening 'as if' will share their perspectives at the end of the interview.

The consultant goes on to interview the consultee about the issue with questions like 'What do we need to know in order to be useful in this conversation? How have you responded to this so far? Who do you talk to about this? Who sees this differently? What would you be most interested to hear from the listeners?' During this interview, the listeners listen from their different 'as if' positions. After the interview, the consultant invites the 'as if' listeners to share their feedback, speaking in the first person ('I' voice) with each other, thus allowing the consultee to listen without having to respond. Separating talking and listening in this way enables the listeners to tune in and be touched by the consultee's descriptions from their 'as if' position and allows the consultee to listen and have his or her own thoughts while listening.

The consultant/interviewer then asks the consultee about his or her experience of the listeners' feedback: 'What most struck you or interested you? Are there voices that you have got a greater glimpse of? And finally, the consultant invites the 'as if' listeners to step out of their particular listening brief and all consultees return to their professional positions to draw on the resources and knowledges they have generated in the course of the consultation.

Haydon-Laurelut et al. (2012) have used *Listening As If* to support clinical psychologists and systemic psychotherapists navigating complex networks in community services for people affected by intellectual disabilities. Consultees reported that *As If* consultations helped them connect with the voices of the service users and create new possibilities to go on.

Integrating a Client Voice

Madsen (1996) has developed a practice of *Integrating a Client Voice* within practitioners' conversations about clients to invite practitioners' awareness and sensitivity to the possible effects of how they talk about clients. The consultant interviews the practitioner-consultee about a client. One member of the group is invited to sit to the side during the interview and listen from the position of a member of the client-system, thereby representing the 'Client Voice', which is usually that of someone who is marginalised or whose voice is less dominant or silenced. The rest of the group listens to the interview and may ask questions for clarification.

Following the interview, the group talks together in response to what they have heard from the consultee during the interview. The person holding the 'Client Voice' does not join this conversation but continues sitting to the side, listening from the client's position. The consultant then interviews the 'Client Voice' (who speaks in the first person, 'I') about his or her experience of the group's discussion, with questions like 'When during the conversation did you feel respected or empowered? At what points did you feel disempowered or disrespected? What effects did this have?' The consultee responds to the conversations between group members and between interviewer and 'Client Voice'. The whole group go on to discuss their learning from the process.

Playing with perspectives in consultation

As the staff team above was having many different and opposing views about how to manage and respond to the 'Lateness', I invited staff to *Play with Perspectives* in our fourth consultation. Drawing on both *As If consultations* and the practice of *Integrating a Client Voice*, I interviewed one staff member-consultee, inviting the others to take on different listening briefs. In order to maximise the number of ideas they generated, I invited each 'listener' to take a different listening brief. Whereas Harlene Anderson and William Madsen brought forth the perspectives of different *people in* the system, I invited the listeners to listen from different *contexts* since the Grange Close staff seemed to be drawing on different contexts to inform their understandings of Abul.

Identifying contexts: Creating Perspective Cards

Before the meeting, I created *Perspective Cards* on which I wrote different contexts to bring forth perspectives. I took these cards, as well as a few blank cards, to the fourth consultation. On each card I named a context that might generate new meanings in relation to the 'Lateness'. Approaching identity as 'multi-voiced'

(White, 2005), Abul's identity offered many contexts for listening, including his *life stage* (a young adult in his twenties), *gender and sense of masculinity, cultural identity (Bengali), interest in street culture, experiences within his family* and *experiences in the Secure Unit.* I wanted to honour the work of the support workers and tease out the complex and potentially contradictory demands that all Grange Close staff were facing in managing the 'Lateness'. Therefore I drew out key principles from significant policy documents that were guiding the staff team's practice with Abul, namely *'Rights'*, *'Independence'*, *'Choice'* and *'Inclusion'* (informed by the Department of Health white paper 'Valuing People', 2001) and *'Safety'*, which is identified as a key issue in the lives of people with intellectual disabilities in the paper, 'Valuing People Now' (Department of Health, 2009). Since these contexts are pertinent to all the clients we work with, I hoped the new perspectives we generated might transfer to other work.

Contracting and preparing for Playing with Perspectives

The consultation was attended by Elizabeth (manager of Grange Close), Don (Abul's keyworker), Kate, Alfie, Mary and Rosa (support workers). Intending to work in a significantly different way from our previous meetings, I took time at the beginning of this consultation to create a context for this 'different kind of conversation' by carefully explaining the structure as follows:

- 'In this conversation, we will *separate talking from listening*. So I will begin by talking with one of you while the rest of the group listens. In this way you can have your own thoughts while you are listening, without feeling the need to respond straight away.
- So first I will talk for about twenty minutes with one person who knows Abul really well. I will ask you about the team's work with Abul, in particular about the "Lateness". Everyone else will have a chance to contribute after we have talked'.

Don volunteered for the interview because 'I know Abul very well ... as his key worker, I've spent the most time with him'.

- 'As I am talking with Don, the rest of you will listen from different angles'. (Showing and naming the *Perspective Cards*: 'Abul's Stage of Life as a Young Man'; 'Abul's Sense of Masculinity'; 'Abul's Bengali Identity'; 'Abul's Interest in Street Culture'; 'Abul's Family Experiences'; 'Abul's Experiences in the Secure Unit'; 'Independence'; 'Rights'; 'Inclusion'; 'Choice' and 'Safety'.)
- I presented a few blank cards on which participants could add their own contexts, offering, 'I have a few blank cards here. Do you want to add any other angles – other perspectives?'

Alfie noted that Abul 'always says he wants "freedom" when we ask him why he has come back later without letting us know'; the group chose to add another card, 'Abul's Hopes for Freedom'.

- 'Before Don and I start talking, I invite you each to choose a card which shows the angle or perspective that interests you or you think is relevant to "Lateness". After Don and I have finished talking, I will ask each of you in turn for your thoughts about "Lateness" from the angle or perspective that you have been listening from. You might have a few thoughts or lots of different ideas as Don is talking. Either way is fine; it will be really helpful if you can note these down on paper so you can hold on to your ideas to share with the group after Don and I have talked.
- When I ask you to share your ideas, talk with me and each other directly, not to Don. This will leave Don free to listen without feeling he has to reply to you.
- After everyone who has listened to us talking has shared their ideas, I will ask you, Don, for your thoughts about what you have heard so you can let us know what interested you, what our talking has got you thinking, and any new ideas you have for next steps.
- Finally, we will talk as a whole group about where the session has taken us and how you might go on from this point in your work with Abul. It is useful to come together at the end so that we can develop a useful plan together'.

Before continuing, I checked the staff team's agreement to work in this way. I noted that it was a new way of structuring our conversation, 'It is very generous of you to try this out. I hope it will help us to come up with some useful ideas. I would also like to hear your feedback on the process'.

'Listening participants' choose contexts from which to listen

I laid out the *Perspectives Cards*, reading them aloud to the group, and invited the staff to choose their perspectives. I asked them to listen to the conversation between Don and me with their chosen perspective in mind and think about how the issues Don was discussing were linked to the perspective they had selected. I took care not to put consultees 'on the spot', making it clear that they could opt out or change perspectives.

Alfie chose '*Safety*', Mary chose '*Abul's Hopes for Freedom*', Kate chose '*Rights*', Elizabeth selected '*Choice*' and Rosa opted for '*Abul's Experiences in the Secure Unit*'. I invited them to note down anything that they thought might be interesting or relevant while Don and I were talking. I commented that I would be interested in any ideas they came up with, and not to worry if what they wrote seemed obvious or 'off the wall', as every idea could contribute to our understanding.

The interview

I began interviewing Don by asking him some appreciative questions about the team's work with Abul to connect Don and his listening colleagues with a sense of the successes they had achieved with Abul, before exploring the difficulties with 'Lateness' (see Chapter 4 for an appreciative approach to consultation).

Joel: What progress do you see with Abul?

Don: Well, you know at first he came across as quite surly, but I think we see now that is a bit of bravado and he is quite vulnerable and sensitive underneath.

Joel: What ways have you made a difference as a team in your work with Abul?

Don: We are coming to know Abul better ... yes we are ... I think he sees me as someone he can trust now, like a kind of uncle or father figure in a way. You know he's not had a lot of male role models in his life...

Joel: How have you built this trust with Abul? What are the steps you have taken?

Don: Well it takes a lot of patience, listening to him. You know really listen and checking with him if you're not sure what he says. And also pointing out what he does well. At the same time, he responds to clear boundaries and expectations. I think that helps Abul to feel safe.

We went on to explore the issue of 'Lateness', the agreed focus of this consultation:

Joel: Can you say a bit about 'Lateness' in the work you have all been doing with Abul?

Don: When Abul goes out in the evening, we're not sure where he goes, but we think it is with his family. But then he doesn't call to let the staff team know if he's running late. He's been told to do this countless times. And you know this really impacts on everyone here, clients and staff, because if the sleep-in staff member is sleep deprived, ultimately the clients pay the price.

Joel: If Abul was here, what do you think he would say about this?

Don: Oh, he is always apologetic, but he keeps doing the same thing over and over again.

Joel: What do you think influences this repeating pattern with the 'Lateness'?

Don: Well, growing up I think he was left to his own devices and he could do what he wanted. And then, in the Secure Unit, he had very limited freedom and choice. Maybe he is trying to test what the limits are.

Joel: And how have you managed the situation so far?

Don: We always follow up with him the next day. I think we do this in different ways. Some of us really lay down the law about it being unacceptable. Some of us try and talk to him more about what is going on in his life.

Joel: What are the effects of these approaches?

Don: It's tough. If you take a firm line, he can sulk and stop talking to you. But sometimes it is worse if you try to be sympathetic, as he seems to get paranoid – checking with us, 'Who are you going to tell?'

'Listening Participants' generate perspectives
from different contexts

I proceeded to ask each Listening Participant in turn to talk with me and each other from the contexts and perspectives that they had been listening. For instance, I asked, 'Alfie, you were listening from the perspective of *Safety*; what connections did you make between this and *Lateness*? Did you have any other ideas about how *Safety* could help us understand Abul?'

> Alfie reflected, 'When Abul first moved in, he showed hostility. I think this made him feel safe. But this has got better. Abul has responsibility for maintaining his own safety by keeping to the times we agreed for him to come home. At the same time, as a team we are assessing Abul's safety all the time. But maybe we need to find ways to include Abul in this more. For example, we need to explain to him in a way that makes sense to him that we have a duty of care towards him. So far it hasn't been easy. But it will help if we can get Abul's family involved'.
>
> From the perspective of 'Freedom', Mary added, 'Abul's vulnerability limits his freedom. This must be hard for him, as he is aware of the freedom other men his age enjoy. He does not see himself as having intellectual disabilities and might see our rules as stopping him. The irony is, if he came back as agreed for a couple of weeks, we would feel confident to give him more freedom. Mind you I am not sure he understands this. I also think his intellectual disabilities may contribute to the lateness. I'm not sure he has a sense of when he needs to set off to get back here on time'.
>
> From the perspective of 'Rights', Kate added, 'Abul has the right to be respected as an individual, to be heard, to safety, to security, to not be afraid and to have choice. In Abul's past, he has not had his rights respected at times. People have taken Abul's possessions from him and I wonder whether this makes it hard for him to trust. Coming home late might be a way that he can feel in control. I think Abul knows this is a good place to live and he may be testing how secure his rights are, and asking, "Will they still love me if I'm late?" "Will they still let me live here if I'm naughty?"'
>
> From the perspective of 'Choice', Elizabeth proposed, 'Don is giving Abul choices that he responds well to by framing them in ways that are realistic and clear. Abul tends to focus more on how his decisions affect himself, rather than others. But I know he does care about other residents. When he apologises, I think he is like a child being told off. We need to find a way to talk to him so that he knows the limits and the consequences of going outside them – then maybe he can take more responsibility for his choices'.
>
> From the perspective of Abul's 'Experiences in the Secure Unit', Rosa shared, 'I think Abul is asking himself "how will I be perceived or treated?" When he was in the Unit, it was not a very nurturing place and

he probably felt judged and that it was "us versus them". I think Abul has experienced trust and respect, and felt listened to and not judged by Don and the rest of us even when there are challenges. We have seen with other residents who have been in difficult placements that this is a place they can heal and grow. I think that this problem will improve when Abul learns he can get more by working with us than by challenging us'.

The Interviewee (Don) responds

I then invited Don to respond to the staff team's perspectives.

Joel: Don, your colleagues have shared a really wide range of ideas. What caught your interest or resonated with you?

Don: Wow! Well first of all I think we are on the right lines. It really stood out that building on the relationships we have made to date is key.

Don went on enthusiastically to mention a number of ideas that stood out for him such as 'Abul testing the boundaries and security of his placement – I had not thought of that before ... The more he trusts we genuinely care about him, respect him and are not going to reject him the more manageable things will be ... From all these different ideas, I am seeing that coming home late without informing us is very tiring but it also gives us a chance to get to know Abul – because we are making the time to find out what might be influencing this behaviour'.

Whole group discussion

Playing with Perspectives

I invited the whole staff team, including the interviewee (Don), to reflect upon our conversation as a whole, with questions like

- What struck you from our conversations today?
- What ideas stand out for you?
- What new thoughts or ideas are you having or playing with now?

The staff team described having a much richer range of ideas. Kate said, 'It's not that Abul is just being difficult, or that we are failing. It is more a gradual process of us learning to work together'. Mary noted, 'He always comes back ... we must be doing something right ... he clearly does see Grange Close as his home', and Alfie thought that Abul was 'receiving a level of care and respect that has been rare in his life'. Staff members identified the 'Lateness' as 'Abul's way to rebel ... like an adolescent testing boundaries'.

Connecting meaning and action

I went on to invite the group to connect the new meanings emerging in the consultation with a plan for action, with questions like

- Where has our meeting today taken you?
- How might we use these ideas?
- What do you think the next steps are in your work with Abul?
- Who is going to do what?'

> The group began to generate rich ideas quickly so that in only a brief amount of time, they had identified several key actions and a meaningful plan to take forward. There was a shared commitment to highlighting and celebrating Abul's successes. Mary suggested putting candles on his (forthcoming) birthday cake, 'each standing for an achievement or positive quality we have noticed'. Alfie thought this could be an opportunity to invite family members with whom Abul was close, 'where they can also see that we are trying hard to really genuinely value Abul'. Don planned to revisit with Abul his rights under his tenancy agreement and to explain that 'Lateness' was an 'issue of respect' rather than something that had any consequence for his tenancy. Alfie and Mary offered to explore with Abul whether setting an alarm on his mobile phone before he went out in the evening could help to remind him it was 'time to come home', and Don and Elizabeth offered to organise a Person Centred Planning meeting to involve Abul in managing his own safety and 'Lateness', inviting his family to contribute suggestions and ideas.

Reflecting on the process of consultation with the group

When I asked for feedback on this consultation, the Grange Close staff members said that they had found it interesting to listen from different perspectives and that it had opened up new ways of understanding Abul's behaviour. Although it had seemed 'a bit of a strange idea ... a little wacky at first', they were 'pleasantly surprised by how well it had worked in practice' and 'it was very interesting what came up'. Elizabeth commented, 'The team always enjoys these meetings, but today I think the way we worked helped us to take it to another level. I am really proud of how much the team has achieved in coming up with all these ideas'. Don had the last word, stating, 'I think we were getting a bit stuck with Abul. So it's a relief to have a plan and even if that doesn't work out, I know we will always be able to come up with new ideas'.

Nourishing wonder and curiosity

At the time of writing, Abul remains living at Grange Close where he has been a tenant for three years. The 'Lateness' improved steadily and has now largely been resolved. Recently, Don described Abul as consistently 'positive and caring in his interactions with both staff and other residents'. Last month I was honoured with an invitation to Abul's birthday party at Grange Close. I looked on in wonder as he defused potential arguments between his housemates and then gave a speech, naming specific contributions each person present had made to enrich his life.

The staff team at Grange Close engaged fully with the different perspectives they had chosen to orient their listening in the consultation since they were relevant to them and the clients they work with. Positioning consultees to listen from different contexts and then share their ideas with each other from different perspectives created the opportunity for the staff to hold all the contexts in view together in the conversation. This opened space for them to play with the multiple perspectives rather than see the different ideas as contradicting each other. By playing with multiple perspectives in consultation, the staff team were able to hold and 'unpack' the complexity and tension that are inherent within complex concepts such as 'choice' and 'inclusion' (Burton and Kagan, 2006) and navigate the complex relationship between these contexts, thereby opening space for new meanings to emerge. For instance, juxtaposing their different ideas on 'Lateness' from the perspectives of *'Safety'*, *'Abul's Hopes for Freedom'* *'Rights'*, *'Choice'* and *'Abul's Experiences in the Secure Unit'* enabled the staff to move away from taking either-or positions such as either Abul 'just being difficult' or staff 'failing' to seeing the situation as 'more a gradual process of us learning to work together', and Abul's coming home late without informing the staff as 'a chance to get to know Abul – because we are making the time to find out'.

Wonder and curiosity generated through playing with perspectives in this consultation reinvigorated the staff team's approach to the work with Abul. I too was left with a sense of wonder and curiosity at what enabled Abul's resilience and what sustained the dedication and painstaking work of the team supporting him. Thus, *Playing with Perspectives* nourishes and sustains my own practice and confidence in the capacity of staff teams to find creative solutions to the complex challenges they face in their work and for individual clients to make use of the opportunities offered them to grow and develop.

Guide 9.1 Steps to guide the consultant wanting to 'Play with Perspectives'

- Before the consultation, the consultant uses information gleaned about the client and comments from prior communication with consultees to identify a range of contexts that may be informing the issue the consultee is bringing for consultation.
- The consultant creates Perspective Cards, naming these different contexts, and takes these cards, including some blank cards, to the consultation meeting.

- The consultant takes time at the beginning of the consultation to explain in detail how we will work and gain agreement for *Playing with Perspectives*, offering opportunities for consultees to ask questions.
- The consultant invites one consultee to volunteer to be interviewed.
- The consultant invites the other group participants to select their Perspectives (Cards) from which to listen to the interview and to note (in writing) their perspectives during the interview.
- The consultant invites the listening group participants to provide feedback from their different perspectives. (The consultant can facilitate their feedback with questions.)
- The interviewee-consultee responds to the different perspectives.
- The consultant facilitates a discussion with the whole group, inviting the consultees to use the new meanings and ideas they have generated to create an action plan.

Note

1 A character amusingly and affectionately caricatured by comedian Harry Enfield as a recalcitrant teenager.

References

Andersen, T. (1987) The reflecting team: dialogue and meta dialogue in clinical work. *Family Process*, *26*, 415–428.

Andersen, T. (1995) Reflecting processes; acts of informing and forming: You can borrow my eyes but you must not take them away from me! In Friedman, S. (ed.) *The Reflecting Team in Action: Collaborative Practice in Family Therapy*. New York: Guilford.

Anderson, H. (1997) *Conversation, Language and Possibilities: A Postmodern Approach to Therapy*. New York: Basic Books.

Boscolo, L., Cecchin, G., Hoffman, L. and Penn, P. (1987) *Milan Systemic Family Therapy: Conversations in Theory and Practice*. New York: Basic Books.

Burton, M. and Kagan, C. (2006) Decoding valuing people. *Disability and Society*, *21* (4), 299–313.

Cecchin, G. (1987) Hypothesizing, circularity, and neutrality revisited: An invitation to curiosity. *Family Process*, *26* (4), 405–413.

Department of Health (2001) *Valuing People: A New Strategy For Learning Disability For the 21ˢᵗ Century*. London: HMSO.

Department of Health (2009) *Valuing People Now: A Three Year Strategy For People With Learning Disabilities*. London: HMSO.

Fredman, G. and Rapaport, P. (2010) How do we begin? Working with older adults and their significant systems. In G. Fredman, E. Andersen and J. Stott (eds.) *Being With Older People: A Systemic Approach*. London: Karnac.

Geertz, C. (2008) *Local Knowledge: Further Essays in Interpretive Anthropology.* New York: Basic Books.

Haydon-Laurelut, M., Millett, E., Bissmire, D., Doswell, S. and Heneage, C. (2012) It helps to untangle really complicated situations: 'AS IF' supervision for working with complexity. *Clinical Psychology and People with Learning Disabilities, 10* (2), 26–32.

Madsen, W. C. (1996) Integrating a 'client voice' in clinical training. *American Family Therapy Academy Newsletter, 64,* 24–26.

McNamee, S. (2005) Curiosity and irreverence. Constructing therapeutic possibilities. *Human Systems: The Journal of Systemic Consultation and Management, 16,* 75–84.

Stewart, J. and Zediker, K. (2000) Dialogue as tensional, ethical practice. *Southern Communication Journal, 65,* 224–242.

White, M. (2005) *Workshop notes* (updated 21st September 2005) retrieved on 28th May 2015: www.dulwichcentre.com.au.

White, M. (2006) Narrative practice with families and children: Externalising conversations revisited. In M. White and A. Morgan (eds.) *Narrative Therapy with Children and Their Families.* Adelaide: Dulwich Centre Publications.

Chapter 10

Working at different levels of context in consultation

A framework informing our practice with staff teams

Eleanor Martin, Alison Milton and Glenda Fredman

In this chapter, we describe a framework we have developed to inform and guide our consultation practice with staff teams working with older people showing challenging behaviour. This framework, which is useful for any client group, draws on communication theory, in particular *Coordinated Management of Meaning* (CMM) (Cronen and Pearce, 1982), which pays attention to different levels of context that inform meaning and action. We identify different levels of context that inform requests for and expectations of consultation, as well as the practice or activity involved in consultation. These levels include inter-action, relationship, meaning, professional identity and organisation. There is a recursive relationship between the levels of contexts so that inviting change at one level of context creates opportunities for change at other levels of context.

When working with staff teams in collaborative consultation, we consider 'at which level of context are we being asked to intervene?' As consultants, we are most commonly requested to intervene with staff teams at the level of inter-action, where problems are generally framed in terms of what the older person does that is experienced as challenging, and how the practitioner-consultees respond to the (problem) behaviour. Intervening at the level of inter-action often creates opportunities for change between consultees (the staff team) and clients (older persons), opening space for new ways to go on. However, when consultees give us feedback (both verbal and non-verbal) that the consultation is not proving useful, when their accounts are repetitive and stories seem immovable and unproductive or when consultees are disengaging from the process of consultation, we move our enquiry to other levels of context with the intention that inviting new perspectives and new meanings at another (different) level of context might open space for shifts at the level of relationship and action.

> I (Eleanor) came into the office to a phone message from John, a community psychiatric nurse, in our team. While listening to the message, an email popped up from him, and before I had replied, I heard him dashing down the corridor. He enthusiastically asked, 'Could you do one of those staff consultation meetings that you do with the first floor at Moorcroft nursing home?' Without taking a breath, he described how the staff were 'at their wits end ... things are escalating' with Antonio, a very mobile and active Italian man with dementia, who was causing

'havoc' as he had 'threatened staff with cutlery' and was 'stealing from other residents'. John explained that the staff team 'were crying out for some strategies to help manage Antonio's behaviour'. When I asked if the team knew about his idea for us to meet with them and what they made of it, John said, 'They all know about it ... seem completely up for it ... are really struggling ... want everyone to feel safer'.

When we approach a new request for consultation, we start by considering 'who is asking for what, for whom?' (Mattison and Fredman, Chapter 2; Fredman and Rapaport, 2010). We understood that John, the referrer, was commissioning the work; he was asking for 'strategies' to help the staff manage Antonio's behaviour. This request was not uncommon to us; we are often invited to help staff 'manage behaviour' of clients which is experienced as 'challenging'. We understood that John was not expecting us to work directly with Antonio but with the staff team, to develop these 'strategies' so they could 'manage' Antonio. We therefore went into our meeting with the staff team with the assumption that the conversation would be about Antonio's behaviour and the staff's responses.

When offering consultation to larger systems or teams, we try to work as a consulting pair, a team of two, where one consultant interviews the consultees and the other takes the position of a reflecting person, or team member, listening for the strengths and abilities of the consultees and tentatively sharing different ideas or connections. (For a detailed description of how we set this up with consultees, organise the seating and share responsibilities between the two consultants, see Selma Rikberg Smyly and Sarah Coles' Chapter 8.) While it is not always possible to work as a team, we find it allows us to notice the subtleties of communication that can be difficult to spot when working alone. For example, the reflecting person can notice who is speaking most, who speaks least, the gestures of those who speak and do not speak and, importantly, the emotional energy in the room.

Levels of context in consultation

As well as considering 'who is asking for what for whom', we take into account at which level of context we are being invited to intervene. We find it helpful to visualise the different levels of context within which we are called to offer consultation, as we present in Figure 10.1.

Requests for consultation are often framed by referrers and consultees in terms of difficulties 'managing behaviour' or problems dealing with what the older person is 'doing', that is, at the level of *action* or what we refer to as *inter-action*, since included or implicit in the request is how people respond to the behaviour, relate to and affect each other, the interactions between people. With requests at the level of inter-action often come expectations that we will offer strategies for behaviour management or training in techniques to change the client's behaviour. For example, John, the community psychiatric nurse, located the problem at the level of inter-action: the effects of Antonio's behaviour ('stealing' and 'threatening') on staff and residents, which was causing 'havoc' and left them feeling

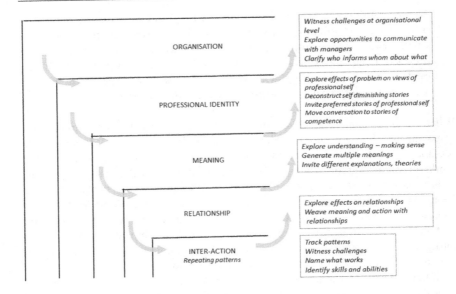

Figure 10.1   Levels of context in consultation

unsafe. This was not simply a request for us to work directly with Antonio to help change or 'modify' his behaviour but a request to work with the staff team on 'strategies' to help them better manage this 'havoc'. Therefore, as we were being asked to address the interactions between the staff, Antonio and other residents, we understood that we were being asked to intervene at the level of inter-action (behaviour and interaction).

Having established that we were meeting with the staff team who work with Antonio, we arrived at the nursing home the following week. Eleanor took the position of interviewing consultant and Alison elected to be the reflecting person, to observe the process and offer reflections. When we meet with a staff team, we usually begin by following the collaborative consultation process we have described elsewhere (Martin and Milton, 2005), and which Andia Papadopoulou and Glenda Fredman have elaborated in Chapter 3, including co-creating a focus for the conversation, exploring what the consultees have already tried and other ideas they have, as well as inviting perspectives of the wider system involved (including people who are not present, for example, the referred person and the client's family, other staff members and managers).

> The room was crammed full with staff, sitting ready for 'the meeting'. They were very welcoming and engaged, quickly telling us that the idea for this meeting had come from John, the community psychiatric nurse. When I (Eleanor) asked what they wanted from the meeting, the staff described with passion that Antonio was 'impossible … he hits us, scratches us, steals from us and other residents … he always seems to pick on new staff'.

They said that they were often 'afraid of him … because he is so strong'. I summarised and checked that I had understood what they wanted (the focus) from this meeting: to 'think together about how to improve the situation with the "hitting" and "threatening" so everyone could feel safer'. No one in the group said they wanted something different.

Working at the level of inter-action

We understood that John and the staff team were inviting us to intervene at the level of inter-action. When called to intervene at the level of inter-action, we often begin by *tracking the sequence of interaction* to get a picture of the *pattern* of interaction. Therefore, I asked the consultees for a recent example of an episode (of 'hitting' or 'threatening') to 'help me get a picture of what is happening', and went on to explore:

- And then what happened?
- What did [you/others] do? How did [Antonio/others] respond?
- What effect did that have on [you/Antonio/the residents]?

We also draw on a solution-focused approach (de Shazer, 1985) where we assume that change is always happening; whatever the problem, there are always exceptions; if something works, encourage or affirm it, if not, do something different; and using consultees' existing solutions is empowering as well as economical. Therefore I listened for skills, abilities and resources in the team. To bring forth what consultees were already doing that was working, I asked questions like

- When was the last time you were expecting Antonio to hit or scratch and it didn't turn out that way? What was different about that situation? What did you do differently?
- How have you managed [this difficult situation]?
- What has worked? How did you do it?
- What have you done to stop things getting worse?

> We were struck by the sophisticated range of strategies the staff were using, for example: 'There are often signs that Antonio is about to lash out … we can spot that now, like his voice starts to get louder and he wrings his hands … we can sometimes predict it if we have time' (Anna, carer); 'yes and we have tried to make the lounge and dining room safer by clearing away cutlery as soon as lunch is finished …' (Jamila, carer); 'and if we distract Antonio we can sometimes stop him from stealing from other residents' (Colin, support worker); 'when he is having a really bad day, we make a decision to manage him in pairs … the manager has said that is okay' (Anna).

We have found that inviting consultees to notice and collectively give an account of what they are already doing that works can enhance consultees' confidence, improve their morale and develop their competence through a process of mutual skills shar-ing. When the consultant 'captures, names and gives back' the effective strategies, skills and abilities they have been using, consultees are able to go on to use their named skills and abilities with intention in future similar situations (Papadopoulou and Fredman, Chapter 3). Thus, intervening at the level of inter-action can produce a change in consultees' skills with and responses towards the client, thereby creating a shift in how the staff-consultees relate to the older person. These changes can also open space for change at other levels of context, for example, how staff feel towards or about the client (relationship) and what sense they make of the problem (meaning).

However, witnessing the challenges, reflecting back consultees' solutions that were working well and identifying their many skills and abilities did not prove use-ful in this consultation with Antonio's team. Christine, a support worker, sighed, 'We do this but it's still hard … it takes every effort and stops me wanting to come to work … he definitely knows when you're having a bad day'. And Jamila added, 'And he can prey on that'. Our approach seemed to invite more vigorous complaints that Antonio was 'singling out some staff deliberately', 'doing it on purpose', and critical labelling of Antonio as 'just an aggressive man'. Noticing that the staff were construing Antonio's actions as deliberate and were attributing conscious intentions to his 'picking on new staff', I (Alison) considered moving the conversation from the level of inter-action to the level of meaning with the intention that inviting consultees to explore new meanings might open space for shifts at the level of relationship and action.

Exploring at the level of meaning

To bring forth new meanings with consultees, we ask questions like

- What sense do you make of [the behaviour]?
- How do you understand [what is happening here]?
- What theories or explanations do you have for [the problem]?
- How do you explain [the situation]?

The intention is not to find the correct explanation for the problem situation, but rather to generate multiple meanings. I (Alison) hoped that change at the level of meaning (understanding) might have an effect on the quality of the staff's rela-tionship with Antonio and thereby open space for new ways to go on with him.

Therefore I (Alison), as reflecting person, invited Eleanor to explore with the staff-consultees alternative understandings of what Antonio was doing and what was happening between them. I asked, 'Eleanor, I wonder whether you could ask the team how they make sense of, or understand, why Antonio hits out at them? What explanations do they have for why he likes to take things from others and put them in his room?' There was a pause while the staff thought about this. Then Anna said that Antonio had worked as a chef and she wondered whether taking cutlery might be 'an old habit' from his working days. Christine shared an idea that 'maybe he misses his wife, as I think he is a traditional Italian man, so he doesn't like other women helping with cleaning and washing him, so maybe he kicks at us when we do this'. Jamila said that idea made sense to her, since in a recent training she had been reminded that people's behaviour can be more impulsive when they have dementia because a certain part of the brain is damaged. Colin said that he recalled Antonio's son saying that his father had always taken a while to 'feel at ease with new people, which might explain why he goes for new staff'.

In an agreed one-month telephone follow-up of this consultation with the team leader, Julia, my heart sank when she told me (Eleanor), 'Nothing has changed, Antonio is exactly the same … shouting and taking things that are not his'. When I asked, 'How has this been for the staff?' she replied, 'Oh the staff are fine … I have not heard any complaints from them about Antonio'. Julia acknowledged that this was very different from how things were before, when staff were 'upset … stressed … constantly coming to me with complaints and worries about Antonio so that I had to keep calling John (community psychiatric nurse)'. Julia said that they did not need to meet again as they were 'managing well'.

Working at the level of meaning allowed staff to develop a different understanding of Antonio's behaviour, which in turn enabled them to shift how they related to him, even though the behaviour itself did not change. No longer construing what Antonio was doing as 'on purpose' or 'because he is just an aggressive man', or 'picking on new people', but attributing meanings of 'because he takes a while to get to know new people' and 'misses his wife' not only seemed to change staff's perceptions of Antonio but also affected how they spoke about him. They used softer, more compassionate tones and less critical language such as 'taking things' rather than 'stealing', 'shouting' and 'threatening'. As their communication softened with Antonio, we saw a shift in their relationships with him.

Addressing one particular level of context can have an effect at another level; therefore, intervening at one level of context can facilitate helpful change at another. Thus change at the level of meaning (from seeing Antonio as 'deliberately aggressive' to understanding his taking cutlery as an 'old habit' or his 'going for new staff' because of his tendency to take a while to get to know new people) had an influencing effect on (contexts of) relationship (how staff felt about and communicated with Antonio) and interaction (their responses to his actions). Julia's conclusion that 'because of who he is and his dementia, we have realised that Antonio isn't going to change. So we just try to not feel that what he does is on purpose … we don't take it personally', illustrates the recursive relationship between these levels of context.

Connecting with the level of professional identity

I (Alison) was leading a consultation at an extra care sheltered facility. The heating was on full blast and we were all squashed into a small lounge on plastic chairs. There were five members of staff who wanted help with Phyllis, who was 'refusing absolutely all personal care'. Staff said Phyllis would insist she had already had a shower that day and on the rare occasions she did shower she would refuse to change into clean clothes, 'putting her dirty, smelly clothes back on'. Denise, a nurse, said she 'smells to high heaven … It's worse than ever at the moment'.

As with Antonio, it seemed that we were being invited to intervene at the level of inter-action. The staff team were asking for help to 'get Phyllis to agree to shower and wear clean clothes'. Having clarified this focus with the consultees, we explored what they had tried to engage Phyllis and to encourage her to accept personal care, and what other ideas they had considered. We also invited ideas and perspectives from others involved ('Who else has a view on this?' 'What might they say about …?' 'What would they like you to do?').

We learned that the staff-consultees had been thoughtful, persistent and creative in their approach. For example, they used old photographs of Phyllis captured as immaculately dressed with perfectly styled hair, looking proud of her appearance, as a basis for conversation about which clothes she was choosing that day. However, they felt their creative efforts had varying or little effect on their ability to shower Phyllis. I (Alison) experienced a rising sense of panic that we would have nothing to offer this committed team, who were already doing so much. I began to notice the initial energy and enthusiasm they had had for talking with us wearing off. Taking this as a sign that I was missing something, and wondering if we should move our enquiry to another level of context, I turned to Eleanor, in her reflecting person position, and talked so that the staff could hear our comments.

> Alison: Eleanor, I'm wondering whether I should continue to hear about the skilled attempts of the staff team to provide care for Phyllis, or is there something else you think I should be asking?

Like Alison, I (Eleanor) had noticed a change in atmosphere in the room, a dip in the energy and engagement. I was also aware that I kept thinking about a comment made earlier by Barbara, Phyllis's key worker, that Phyllis's refusing her care left Barbara feeling 'useless'. I began to develop a hypothesis that Phyllis's refusing to shower was challenging the professional identity of all the carers. Therefore, I invited Alison to move to another level of context, the level of *professional identity*, to guide our conversation.

> Eleanor: Well, Alison, I keep going back in my mind to something Barbara said earlier – that caring for Phyllis can make the staff feel 'useless'. I am wondering who is most concerned by Phyllis refusing the staff's care? What effect is Phyllis's refusing to shower and change her clothes having on the staff? And how does this make them feel about themselves as carers?

I (Alison) recognised Eleanor's questions as an invitation to move to the level of *professional identity*. Therefore, I explored the link between Phyllis's refusing the care the staff were offering (inter-action) and the teams' view of their professional selves (professional identity) with questions like

- What troubles you the most about Phyllis's refusing to shower?
- What effect is Phyllis's refusing your care having on you?
- How does this affect how you view yourself as a care worker?
- Who is most concerned by her refusing to shower and wear clean clothes?

> The sudden change of atmosphere in the room was palpable. The staff team were immediately more animated and talkative. They all shared the feeling of 'uselessness' Barbara had described. Padraig, a support worker, added that he felt 'frustrated', and Angela, another support worker, 'worried' that Phyllis would become ill if she remained 'dirty'. They said that they were concerned what visitors to the home would think – 'that we are lazy ... neglectful ... don't care about Phyllis'. They worried what the doctors would think if Phyllis were admitted to hospital. All the consultees were nodding and joining in as they shared, 'We are not doing our job properly'; 'You leave after a shift thinking you haven't done a good job at caring for her, and none of us like that'.

Professional identity in contexts of stories and theories

As practitioners, we act out of multiple contexts, for example, our personal experience, our family, our gender and our ethnicity, that inform and influence our professional practice. There are stories and theories connected to these multiple contexts. These stories and theories guide and give meaning to our actions, influence our relationships and inform how we value ourselves as people and practitioners (our identities). Thus our professional identity as practitioners is created in the contexts of stories and theories that 'talk to us of our abilities, of who we were, who we are and who we can become' (Fredman, 2004:53). These stories can therefore enhance or diminish our experiences of ourselves as professionals. We are mindful that there will not be one preferred professional identity story common to all practitioners. Therefore, each staff member's ideas about what makes a 'good carer' will be informed by many stories and values from multiple contexts of their lives, including the carer's personal experience, their family, gender, culture and professional training, as well as the culture of the organisation, to name a few. Therefore, Alison went on to explore what it meant to be 'a good carer' for each staff member working with Phyllis.

> When I (Alison) asked, 'What do you have to be doing to be a good carer to Phyllis?', Angela responded with certainty, 'Showering her and changing her clothes every morning, as soon as she gets up, and making sure she is taking medication'. There was a lot of nodding and agreeing. When I enquired whether anyone had a different view, I was met with silence.

The staff seemed to hold a dominant value that 'good care' involved personal care of the older person, which informed their shared moral obligation that they 'should' shower Phyllis every day. Recognising that they had not met this 'standard', they shared a sense of themselves as 'useless' or having failed in their care of Phyllis. We got the sense that this dominant belief was affecting the staff's confidence in their competence that they could take care of Phyllis, undermining their view of their professional selves.

When we notice consultees presenting self-diminishing descriptions that undermine their professional identity such as 'feeling bad about our work' or 'not doing our job properly', we try to encourage them to talk from a position of competence and ability, rather than from a position of not doing a good job, so they can begin to tell a different story about themselves, for example as 'good carers'. Our intention is that changing the story that they tell about their professional selves might exert an impact on other levels, such as the relationship between the staff and Phyllis. We also hoped and hypothesised that, if the staff's view of themselves as good carers changed and, in turn, the relationship between Phyllis and the staff shifted, that over time, the staff might find new ways to engage in the challenging task of providing personal care to Phyllis (change at the level of inter-action).

Locating identity stories in contexts

In situations like this, we do not challenge consultees' beliefs or values; we do not intend to prove wrong or contest the theories or stories they hold. Instead we try to deconstruct self-diminishing stories of identity by exploring how the dominant story came about and to consider what keeps it going. If it is not enabling or if it is undermining, we try to bring forth alternative stories that open space for the creation of new meanings and hence new and preferred views of self as well as new possibilities for action.

We usually begin by inviting consultees to reflect on contexts informing their beliefs. Therefore I (Alison) invited the consultees to locate in context their shared belief that 'good care requires keeping Phyllis clean and medicated' by asking each member of the team

- Where do your ideas about what it means to be a good carer come from?
- When were you first aware of holding that belief?

The conversation opened up as staff members shared: 'I learned this in my nurse training' (Denise); 'When I first started working at this home, my manager told me we are expected to prioritise that residents are clean and don't smell – it is the first thing the inspectors look for when they walk through the door' (Angela); 'It's what I would want for myself if I need care in a home like this' (Barbara), and 'My grandfather lived with us to a ripe old age – my mother took such good care of him and he really enjoyed being so dapper' (Padraig).

Generating alternative stories from multiple contexts

We continued to invite alternative stories and theories from different contexts of consultees' professional as well as personal lives to elaborate on the story of what makes for good care, with questions like

- How might others (family, client, other staff/manager) see this?
- What does being a man/woman tell you about what constitutes being a good carer?
- What would your profession/supervisor say about her refusing to shower?
- What does your organisation say about what constitutes 'good care'?

Our intention is to invite consultees to identify a range of stories and theories, perhaps previously untold, from the different contexts of their lives, with a view to opening space for new meanings and new ways to go on. For example, addressing the context of *family*, Alison asked, 'What would your family say about what else we need to be doing to be a good carer, as well as giving personal care?' And connecting with the context of *gender*, she enquired 'Do you think there are different ideas or even rules for men and women about what good caring involves?'

Initially the staff team's privileged story that 'good care requires the older person to be showered and medicated every day' informed their belief that they were doing a bad job and brought forth a negative view of their selves as 'useless'. When Alison brought forth different beliefs and values from other personal and professional contexts of their lives, the consultees spoke passionately of how good care meant 'treating Phyllis with dignity and respect', 'trying to give her some good quality of life', 'getting to know her as a person', 'keeping her safe' and 'communicating well with others' involved in her care, such as her family and her GP.

Juxtaposing different beliefs, values and stories

We have found that juxtaposing different beliefs, values and stories in this way can be especially useful when the narratives of people, like the staff in this team, bring forth disapproving views of self. Inviting alternatives, exceptions, opposites or even contradictions can make it possible for people to make new connections and associations between their story and the alternative story, thereby 'creating opportunities for syntheses that might offer new meanings and alternative options for action' (Fredman, 1997:73).

Thus the consultees generated a rich collection of stories from 'multiple contexts of their lives' (Fredman, 2004:60). The juxtaposing of these different stories created opportunities for staff to talk about 'finding a balance' between what Phyllis would agree to and what they wanted for her. They began to recognise that 'we are doing the best we can for Phyllis, even if this isn't perfect'.

Navigating the pull between contradictory commitments

Towards the end of our previously agreed three-week follow-up telephone conversation with the staff team's manager, Comfort, she concluded that 'Everything with Phyllis is going quite well now – but there are a few who are not best pleased ... so I think another meeting with you to review might be a good idea'. At the start of the follow-up consultation with the staff team six weeks after the initial meeting, we learned of many positive developments with Phyllis. During a reflecting conversation, we started to name the strategies the team had been using and the qualities, abilities and resources they were drawing on. As we spoke, I (Eleanor) sensed a change in the atmosphere in the room; while some staff appeared deflated, others were fidgeting, as if agitated.

Recognising that our witnessing the abilities and resources of the consultees was not having our intended outcome of enabling them to view themselves in a positive light, I (Eleanor) took this as information that we were probably not working at the most useful level. Therefore, I tentatively wondered aloud, 'The staff team seem to be doing a really impressive job, showing respect and good care to Phyllis despite it being a very challenging situation, and to me there seem to be many positive developments since we first met. But I am wondering whether these seem like positive developments to the staff or whether we have missed something about the situation? I don't know – maybe there are other issues, such as personal experiences or organisational issues – or something else that we have not asked about or picked up on?' Following these reflections, Alison asked the team what had struck them from our conversation.

> After a long silence, Angela replied, 'To be honest, I can't feel that respect for a woman who abuses us'. We learned that Phyllis had recently been 'making racist comments', telling Black workers, 'Go back to your country ... you're not welcome here'. The team had found ways to support each other, like using humour and texting each other to check they were okay after a particularly difficult day. However Angela, a White Irish woman, continued, 'I can't stop myself talking to Phyllis in a harsh voice when she says something like that – even though I know she doesn't really understand what I am actually saying ... I find myself avoiding eye contact with her ... not talking to her if I do not have to ... avoiding working with her when possible ... I don't like being like this ... but this is so important to me'.

Angela seemed to experience a pull between her professional moral obligation to respond compassionately and respectfully to older vulnerable people on the one hand and her personal responsibility and commitments (informed by her ethnicity, culture and family contexts) to take a stance against 'racial abuse'. She expressed her dilemma as 'I don't like being like this ... but this is so important to me'. When we notice consultees being pulled between competing or contradictory principles and commitments informed by different levels of context like this, we tentatively pick up on this possible dilemma during a further reflecting conversation.

Therefore I (Eleanor) reflected, 'Listening to Angela's dilemma made me think of my own commitment to be the best kind of carer or practitioner according to what I stand for. There have been times when it has been more difficult for me to do my job well – when I want to give good care, but strong personal or even political values take over and make it hard for me to let them go and focus on my professional responsibility without feeling I am compromising my values – what is really important to me. I'm not sure if the staff team recognise this dilemma at all, but what I was hearing made me think about it'.

Our intention in very tentatively naming the dilemma is that if it connects with the consultees, they may begin to reflect on the possible competing contexts informing them and how these can influence their interactions and relationships with the people they care for. After the reflections, Lena, a Black support worker who, according to Angela, had been the 'butt of a lot of Phyllis's racism', said that 'it is harder to like some patients, but there is always something that you can find to like'. This provided an opportunity for Alison to respond by asking the consultees, 'What have you found to like in Phyllis?', followed by 'What have you appreciated about working with Phyllis?' and 'What has kept you going with looking after Phyllis, when it's been at its toughest and the abuse has been at its worst?' Lena told us that Phyllis 'always has a story to tell'. We learned that Phyllis had 'been very wealthy and well-connected' as a young woman. Denise said 'she met all sorts of famous people like Greta Garbo and Winston Churchill; if you can get her on that topic it's wonderful, you could listen to her all day long'. Padraig commented in a reflective tone, 'Maybe it is a bit of a come-down ending up in a nursing home. She is probably used to having things her own way and now she has us forcing her to shower and change her clothes, maybe we need to let her take the lead more'.

Angela sat quietly with a fixed frown on her face throughout this part of the conversation. When I (Alison) wondered if anyone else wanted to add something, she spoke with a tight voice and clenched jaw, 'Yes you are missing something. This isn't just about us dealing with racial abuse, someone who smells of urine because you can't get them to shower or even having to take time off work like Jill (a member of staff not present) did when another resident hit her. It is about us continually filling in incident forms, sending them off and not hearing a thing back. Where do these forms go anyway? Who reads them? No one ever calls us to check we are ok when our skin has been pierced from scratching'. Padraig interjected, 'Or when we are feeling humiliated', and Angela went on, 'So yes, this is about management, about management not caring'.

Engaging with the level of the organisation

Although initially taken aback by the force of Angela's response, we were quickly able to see this as useful feedback. Angela's voice communicated strong emotion and others quickly joined in connecting and sharing their views. Responding from the organisation context, Angela had shared new and different information that we had not yet heard.

When we contract for consultee-centred consultation, where the focus is on facilitating the consultee's work with the client, we clarify that we will not be working directly with the whole service, team or organisation (as in system-centred consultation). When consultees, like Angela, call forth a response at the level of the organisation, however, we do talk with consultees about what issues they want addressed, what they want to say and what they want heard and witnessed, as well as who will talk and liaise with whom about what within the organisation. Therefore, I (Alison) asked, 'What would you like to happen differently at a management or organisational level?', 'Who might you let know about this?' and 'How will you do this?' The staff team requested we give feedback to their manager, Comfort, that 'what gets to us' is not the actual challenge of delivering care 'but the fact that all the problems get recorded and no one ever follows this up with us'.

Since Comfort had requested this follow-up consultation to 'support' her staff, we felt confident that, shared sensitively, she would be genuinely interested to hear the views of the staff team. When we met to give feedback from this second consultation, Comfort wondered with us whether 'closing the loop' on the staff's feedback would be welcome by 'routinely checking in with them following every incident report they submit'. Appreciating Comfort's idea, and mindful to link the new ideas and meanings with action and relationships, I (Alison) explored, 'What could this communicate to the staff?' and 'How do you think the staff would experience this?' Comfort explained that she hoped 'to show that I am supporting them … It is important that they really know I take what they endure seriously'.

Moving between levels

In this chapter, we have identified different levels of context that inform requests for consultation: inter-action, relationship, meaning, professional identity and organisation. We recognise that consultees act out of multiple professional and personal levels of context that will shape their practice and inform their perspectives.

We pay attention to the level at which we are invited to work in consultation and we try to respond first at this level to coordinate and find a fit with what consultees are wanting from the consultation.

Certain signs point us towards which level might be useful to explore. For example:

- We construe requests for strategies or advice about how to 'manage behaviour' as invitations to work at the level of inter-action.
- When asked for help with understanding or making sense, we explore at the level of meaning.
- Concerns about how to 'be with' clients invite us to attend to the level of relationship.

- When consultees express a loss of confidence or morale, or struggle between competing or contradictory principles, we tune into the level of professional identity.
- Difficulties in staff relationships or complaints about policies within services draw our attention to the level of the organisation.

There is a recursive relationship between these levels of context whereby change at one level will inform and influence change at another level. For example, we have shown how inviting new meanings of a problem among consultees has enabled a shift in their relationships with the client and opened space for new possibilities for action, and how bringing forth consultees' preferred stories of their selves (professional identity) softened their self-criticism, invited more appreciative perspectives on their own competence, brought forth more appreciative stories of the client and enabled more compassionate relationships with clients.

Therefore we move or weave our enquiry between levels of context with the intention to create opportunity for change at one level of context to facilitate change at other levels. For example, Alison moved from the level of professional identity to the level of inter-action, asking consultees for examples of how they had put their values into practice with Phyllis, with questions like, 'Can you describe how you have treated Phyllis with respect/tried to give her some good quality of life/ got to know her as a person while keeping her safe?' As the emotional temperature in the room changed, the consultees became animated and shared numerous examples of how they had engaged Phyllis in 'activities she enjoyed', managed to 'encourage her to eat well' and were able to 'support her to go to the hairdresser'.

Moving from meaning to (inter)action can create opportunity to ground new ideas in practice and thereby open space for practical discussion about who will do what. To facilitate this sort of discussion, we ask questions like

- Now you know this/have these ideas, what will you do?
- Who needs to be involved in a decision about [what is 'good care']?
- How and to whom should this [change in the care plan] be communicated?

Weaving between meaning and action with Phyllis's staff team invited suggestions that Phyllis's care plan could be modified. Denise agreed to discuss this with the team manager, Comfort. We later learned that Phyllis's sister, nephew and GP attended a meeting where Denise represented the care staff's commitment to 'do the best they can for Phyllis' and 'find a balance' between ensuring she is well and safe and feels respected and has a good quality of life'. They had all agreed a new care plan where Phyllis would have a shower and clean clothes at least once a week, which everyone concurred was in Phyllis's 'best interests'. Comfort reported that the situation 'has improved a lot … Phyllis is settled with most of the staff'.

In this chapter, we show how our decision about whether and when to move our enquiry to a different level of context is usually guided by the usefulness and effectiveness of the consultation. When critical or blaming stories of clients continue to dominate and when consultees judge themselves negatively, we move levels with intention to invite different stories. Feedback from consultees, their verbal and non-verbal communication and the emotional atmosphere and energy level in the room, as well as moments within the consultation when a particular word or response touches or moves us, gives us a sense of whether we are engaging or losing connection with consultees. We try to be as transparent as possible with consultees, checking when we can, 'Are we talking about what you want to address?' or 'Is there something we are missing?'

Guide 10.1 Working at different levels of context in consultation: A practice guide

Working at the level of inter-action

- Track the sequence of interactions. Identify patterns of interaction. Witness challenges.
- Draw out what consultees' are already doing, what they have tried and what is working.
- Name skills, abilities and resources.

Exploring effects on relationships

- Weave meaning and action with relationships.

Exploring at the level of meaning

- Explore understanding and explanations of the problem.
- Ask questions to generate multiple ideas, meanings and theories from consultees and from the perspectives of others, such as family members and managers.

Connecting with the level of professional identity

- Notice descriptions that undermine consultees' preferred view of their professional selves, as in, 'I'm not doing my job well'.
- Ask questions that explore consultees' experiences of themselves as professionals.
- Locate the stories and theories of professional identity within multiple contexts, by asking where the ideas come from and how long they have had these ideas.
- Listen out for alternative stories, exceptions, opposites or contradictions about professional identity.

- Ask questions to generate alternative stories from multiple contexts (for example, personal, family, age, culture, professional training or the organisational contexts).
- Always look for openings to move the conversations to stories of competence and ability.

Engaging with the level of the organisation

- Notice when consultees are being pulled between competing or contradictory stories/values informed by different levels of context. Tentatively name this dilemma.
- Consider who else needs to hear about the consultation conversation and who will take responsibility for doing this.

Moving between levels of contexts

- Move to another level of context when the emotional energy in the room and engagement with consultees is dipping, when critical or blaming stories are not changing or when self-diminishing stories of professional self are dominating.
- Weave the conversation between meaning and action; so, for example, when new ideas about preferred professional identity come forth, ask how this affects what consultees will do differently.

References

Cronen, V.E. and Pearce, W.B. (1982) The coordinated management of meaning: a theory of communication. In F.E.X. Dance (ed.) *Human Communication Theory*. New York: Harper and Row.

de Shazer, S. (1985) *Keys to Solution in Brief Therapy*. London: W.W. Norton.

Fredman, G. (1997) *Death Talk: Conversations With Children and Families*. London: Karnac.

Fredman, G. (2004) *Transforming Emotion: Conversations in Counselling and Psychotherapy*. London: John Wiley and Sons.

Fredman, G. and Rapaport, P. (2010) How do we begin? Working with older people and their significant systems. In G. Fredman, E. Anderson and J. Stott (eds.) *Being With Older People: A Systemic Approach*. London: Karnac.

Martin, E. and Milton, A. (2005) Working systemically with staff working in residential homes. *Context: The Magazine for Family Therapy and Systemic Practice. Grey Matters: Ageing in the Family*, 77, 37–39.

After words

Collaboration: Bridging possibilities in mental health consultation

Sheila McNamee

In his book, *Together: The Rituals, Pleasures and Politics of Cooperation*, Richard Sennett (2012) associates collaboration with cooperation. And of cooperation, he says, 'It requires of people the skill of understanding and responding to one another in order to act together' (p. x). Further, he claims, 'My focus in *Together* is on responsiveness to others, such as listening skills in conversation, and on the practical application of responsiveness at work or in the community' (p. ix). I believe that Sennett's words capture what Fredman, Papadopoulou and Worwood have offered in this volume. They have guided us through our unfortunate stand-ard professional quicksand, where one's survival depends upon locating solid ground or a low-hanging branch upon which to climb. Let's imagine that this solid ground or branch, sturdy enough to accept our weight and somehow carry us to security, represents 'correct' professional practices, expert opinions and certainty of knowledge and action. This is the standard narrative many professionals carry. Culturally, it is precisely what it means to be a professional – to stand on solid ground with the right answers, the right techniques and with the right models and theories as guidance.

And, while this remains an enduring assumption about professional practice, we have also developed over the past decades an appreciation for a relational stance to professional practice (McNamee and Gergen, 1999; Gergen, 2009; McNamee, 2016). This relational stance begins with the assumption that meaning emerges in what people *do together*. Thus, expertise and knowledge are not qualities of a person (e.g. consultant) but rather are by-products of coordinated actions among, for example, consultant, consultee, commissioner and other involved participants. Our focus shifts from individuals and their individual actions or thoughts to what people do together and what their 'doing' makes.

But we must note that there is nothing inherent in this relational stance that is necessarily collaborative. Participants – let's say consultant and consultee – can and do, together, create possibilities and constraints in their joint actions. But to identify all of their co-actions as collaborative would be misleading. This is where the present volume assists us in our understanding of collaborative practice, in general, and collaborative consultation, in particular.

In their introductory chapter, the editors specify collaborative consultation as guided by several principles that might be summarised as the forming of partnerships that are (1) attentive to power and difference, (2) appreciative in focus, (3) centred on participants' competencies and abilities, (4) always attentive to multiple contexts, (5) focused on language and communication, (6) valuing multiple perspectives and (7) attentive to self-reflection in the process of consulting. These principles provide a very specific understanding of interactions that are collaborative and that distinguish collaboration from the ordinary coordination of actions. It is useful to note that an interaction where expert advice is given and accepted is a well-coordinated interaction. But it might not be collaborative.

Collaboration and relational practice

When we think about consultation in mental health, like any other field, we are confronted with a vast array of assumptions, models and techniques. It is likely that a consultant and those to whom she consults hold very different assumptions about mental health care. We have available not only psychoanalytic orientations, but behavioural, cognitive, expressive and systemic, to name a few. The consultant who enters into the consultation process already equipped with her theory and method is less likely to give space to others' theories and methods – to others' ideas about the situation. As well, others are not necessarily expected to share their views about mental health, human interaction, what 'good' consultation looks like, etc. Or perhaps we should say their views are often not welcomed with enthusiasm. In contrast, the collaborative consultant presumes difference of opinion, orientation, assumptions, techniques, etc. and appreciates difference without attempting to minimise or transform those differences.

Collaborative consultation means embracing differences and learning how we might become curious about alternative views. Can we approach the other or the consultation process from the stance of *interested inquiry*? If we adopt a stance of interested inquiry, we explore how various and often competing worldviews enable possibilities, open us to alternatives and give way to creative, collaborative problem solving. To do this requires a major shift in our thinking about consultation; it is a shift from a goal of agreeing on the 'right' solution to an attempt at the coordination of incompatible but potentially comparable discourses. Our question becomes: How might we coordinate multiple worldviews rather than obliterate differences through agreement on 'one right solution?'

Daily, we are faced with complex issues, many of which are addressed in the present volume: working with challenging cases, with diverse colleagues, with politically initiated constraints, with budget cuts and, most importantly, with multiple values and beliefs. Every time we are confronted with a problem, we are confronted with a different worldview. And each worldview is taken for granted as 'right' by those who unquestioningly embrace it.

We can recognise our own and others' worldviews when we hear comments such as 'This is the best solution because this is the way we've always done it,' or 'This is the right solution because the majority agree'. But we must remember that these common beliefs and values each represent their own orientation to the world – the taken-for-granted expectations we have for 'how things should be'. And each is no more permanent or solid than the patterns of interaction that create them. Worldviews arise out of our interaction with others. They are *made*, not *found*.

When we step into a collaborative form of consultation, we entertain the possibility that each different stance is actually coherent within a particular group or community. Rather than combat the logic of that orientation, can we become curious about how it has become sensible, meaningful and important to its advocates or, as Webb and Fredman argue in Chapter 4, can we take an appreciative stance toward difference? What if our goal of having the 'right' answer was replaced by the opportunity to be in extended conversation with the other where new understanding – not agreement or validation – could be constructed? Can we value connection over certainty, relationships over answers? This is the difference of engaging with others to *understand and build relationships*. Engagement of this sort opens space for the exploration of diverse worldviews. This is collaboration.

In most aspects of our lives (and particularly in the professional domain), it is rare that we enter into interaction with others curious about their *local* coherence – if they disagree with us, we are apt to proclaim that they are misled or mistaken. We rarely ask for detailed descriptions of how and why this very different view has emerged as viable and logical, and for whom. Instead, we typically enter into these interactions with the idea of persuading others to accept our view as the 'right' view. And yet, if we enter into consultation with the hope of understanding differences rather than attempting to reach agreement (i.e. to persuade), we are more likely to forge new relational and interactional possibilities. We are much more likely to stay in conversation with someone who genuinely wants to understand our position than with one who simply attacks us, claims we are wrong or ignores our contributions. Note how collaboration opens us to the possibility of creating new forms of understanding with others. We are no longer talking about universal good or bad but good and bad that are worked out at a very local level. This is the shift from expert knowledge to processes of engagement that build understanding and community.

Is it possible to create opportunities where we can engage in *interested inquiry* and *curiosity* with others? And, in dissolving the good/bad, right/wrong dichotomies we encounter in social problems, how might we achieve some form of coordinated social action where diversity is more than simply tolerated and respected but anticipated and welcomed? How might we imagine – and more important, create – a social order that is not *ordered* by similarity but is ordered by coordination of diversity? The present volume offers a wealth of resources to achieve the coordination of diversity through collaborative practices.

Coordinating difference through collaboration

Our professional urge to follow strict methods that emerge from well-honed theoretical orientations has created a mechanised approach to mental health consultation. While there may be varying theories and methods to employ, the taken-for-granted stance is one of correct usage as opposed to a stance of curiosity concerning differing stances. The latter – curiosity for difference – humanises mental health consultation to the extent that it invites all voices, appreciates the local coherence of each voice and centres on competencies as well as self-reflection and attentiveness to what one's own actions invite in response.

When consultation is approached as an outside expert giving advice to mental health workers, teams or organisations, the risk is a diminishing of the consultee's competence and engagement in the consulting process itself. Several of the stories included in this volume make this particularly clear. Yet when a consultant – no matter what theoretical approach she or he adopts – genuinely invites the voices of those being consulted, when a consultant opens space for different points of view to be offered but not judged, the terrain shifts from a problem-solving mission to a moment of co-construction. It is a co-construction of the possible future, a way forward that unites participants, stakeholders and consultants alike.

Instead of issuing specific strategies or techniques for consultation, we can draw upon many fluid and flexible conversational resources. These resources are overlapping possibilities one might use to engage in collaborative consultation and each may foster new possibilities for action. They are resources embedded in each of the chapters in this volume.

- **Engage in self reflexive inquiry**. In other words, question your assumptions, your understandings. Ask yourself how else things might be described and understood. Don't be too quick to 'know'.
- **Try to avoid abstraction**. Try to avoid global statements about good/bad, right/wrong, etc. and invite people to speak from their lived stories, culture and values.
- **Try to suspend the tendency to judge**. We often want to judge, evaluate and problem solve. Speak instead from a desire to understand and from a position of curiosity about differences.
- **Engage in relational reflexivity** (Burnham, 1993). Check in with those you are in conversation with concerning how the interaction is going for them. Are there other topics all of you should be discussing? Are there questions they were hoping you would ask or details you would provide? Are there other issues to be addressed?
- **Coordinate multiplicity**. Let's not try to force everyone into the same understanding or the same 'position'. And let's also not move towards consensus (a small overlap in agreement). Can we open a space where we can talk about our differences without trying to persuade or prove that one position is superior to another? Our focus should not be on agreement but on creating new forms of understanding.
- **Use the familiar in unfamiliar contexts**. In other words, invite yourself and others to draw on conversational/action resources that you use in other contexts, in other relationships. We spend too much time trying to teach people

how to do things in a different way. What if we invite them, instead, to draw upon their familiar ways of interacting in contexts that seem to call for something else? For example, might it be useful to use the voice you harbour as a caring friend when you are confronted with a differing opinion.

- **Imagine the future**. We spend too much of our time trying to figure out what in the past has caused the present challenge. What if we focused, instead, on what we might construct together in the future? How would we like to see ourselves four months from now? A year from now? In ten years? Once we engage in this conversation, we have already initiated the possibility of co-creating that future together.
- **Create the conversational space**. It is not always possible but, if we can invite conversations about difficult topics in contexts, spaces and atmospheres that are more conducive to human care and consideration, we might be surprised at what might unfold. Living rooms and lounges invite human contact and food also helps bring people together.
- **Search for local coherence**. Rather than judge a person's stance on an issue, can we try to understand how that stance has evolved from that person's history of interactions? No ideas, beliefs or values emerge in a vacuum. Similarly, no one is born with a belief or value; they emerge within communities where participants negotiate together what counts as truth, right and wrong.
- **Suspend the desire for agreement and instead seek new forms of understanding**. If we maintain our disagreement on an issue but we come to understand the rationale for the other's position, we have already moved away from framing an issue as true or false, black or white to grey (that is, complex and diverse).

These resources, along with the creative illustrations offered by Fredman, Papadopoulou and Worwood, invite those with whom we are working into a collaborative relationship. Together we craft the consultation process; together we open possibilities. In collaborative consultation, we listen generously, ask questions marked by genuine curiosity, practice self and relational reflexivity and attempt to coordinate difference rather than adjudicate. When we place our emphasis on collaboration, we stand curious about how (not why) particular forms of action become viable and sustainable at a given moment and not others. Attempting to understand such coherence opens possibilities for new forms of coordinated action.

References

Burnham, J. (1993) Systemic supervision: The evolution of reflexivity in the context of the supervisory relationship. *Human Systems: The Journal of Systemic Consultation and Management, 4,* 349–381.

Gergen, K.J. (2009) *Relational Being: Beyond Self and Community.* Oxford: Oxford University Press.

McNamee, S. (2016) The ethics of relational process: John Shotter's radical presence. In T. Corcoran and J. Cromby (eds.) *Joint Action: Essays in Honour of John Shotter.* London: Routledge.

McNamee, S. and Gergen, K.J. (1999) *Relational Responsibility: Resources For Sustainable Dialogue.* Thousand Oaks, CA: Sage.

Sennett, R. (2012) *Together: The Rituals, Pleasures and Politics of Cooperation.* New Haven: Yale University Press.

Index